THE BOOK OF
KESSINGLAND

The Most Easterly Village in England

MAUREEN AND ERIC LONG

HALSGROVE

First published in Great Britain in 2006
Reprinted 2008

British Library Cataloguing-in-Publication Data.
A CIP record for this title is available from the British Library.

ISBN 978 1 84114 505 1

HALSGROVE

Halsgrove House
Ryelands Industrial Estate,
Bagley Road, Wellington
Somerset TA21 9PZ
T: 01823 653777
F: 01823 216796
email: sales@halsgrove.com
website: www.halsgrove.com

Frontispiece photograph: *Kessingland church tower.*

Printed and bound in Great Britain by CPI Antony Rowe, Wiltshire.

Preface

The story of Kessingland is a long and varied one, going back well into prehistoric times. Ancient man settled along the banks of the River Hundred, then the Romans were here, then the Saxons came. The Normans divided the land into four sections at the time of the Domesday Book. In medieval times, the church was built and the estuary of the Hundred was alive with fishing boats. With the silting up of the harbour after the Reformation, Kessingland sank into obscurity, only to revive with the opening of the new Lowestoft Harbour in the 1830s. For the next 120 years the village thrived, as men from Kessingland crewed and owned many of the Lowestoft vessels. With the decline of the fishing industry, the village became better known as a place where visitors could come for a peaceful holiday. At the present time, Kessingland is the largest village in Suffolk, with a population of over 4,000, doubled in the summertime with the holiday visitors.

Eric and Maureen Long are to be congratulated on producing this new book of various aspects of the history of Kessingland. As a member of an old Kessingland family, I commend it to all residents and friends of the village, old or new. So sit back and enjoy!

Gerald Brown, Village Recorder, February 2006

Gerald has researched and catalogued the parish registers, births, baptisms, marriages and deaths for Kessingland and Black Street, Gisleham. He is co-author of two books on Kessingland's war memorial and those whose names appear thereon.

Village sign designed by Thomas Downs, 1970s.

Postcards from Kessingland, thought to date from the 1920s.

CONTENTS

Acknowledgements

It has been both a pleasure and a lot of hard work to document a history of Kessingland that has not already appeared in previous publications. However, we are indebted to Halsgrove Publishing for producing such a beautiful and all-encompassing book on our village. It will be truly a book to treasure for those born and bred in Kessingland and those who enjoy their holidays or residing here.

We acknowledge a great debt of gratitude to all who have told us stories and memories, loaned photographs, or helped in any way with the production of this book. Thanks must go to:

Peter Jenkins, photographer, who made available old glass plates of Kessingland photographs and turned them into photographs for sale in the village and beyond; Alan Studd, for the use of loaned photographs; the late Barbara Todd for information and photographs; Mrs Margaret Davies for the use of her photographs; Mrs Barbara Eyre for the old Beach Post Office photographs; Mrs Christine Satchell for information on the High Street Post Office; the Cheyne family of Ditchingham for permission to use photographs of Sir Henry Rider Haggard and family; Richard Catchpole for photographs and reports; Betty Cherry for permission to use postcards and information from her late husband, historian Peter Cherry; the members of the Methodist Church for excerpts from the centenary booklet; Mrs G. Harvey's family for the photographs of 'Pifco's'; Mike Lynes for the photographs from the Denes Holiday Village; Iris Morphew for her father's story; Tony Hart for family photograph; the Revd Tim and Mrs Marion Hollis; Gillian and Michael Knights for photographs from *The Kessingland Guide*; Ivan Clarke for the photographs of Clarke's early Garage and Cyclemakers shop; all those who were profiled in the local magazine, whose interviews we have reproduced; George Swan, John Blowers, Henry Bennett and S.J. Partridge for their memories and articles; John Catchpole ('Bubbles') for the photograph of the Bethel Group; Roy and Gerald Brown for the Beach School and other photographs; Mick Long for Graphics and IT advice and practical help; Evelyn Mathias for sketches reproduced from those done for *The Kessingland and Broadland Times* (usually referred to in this publication as simply *The Kessingland Times)*, and for practical assistance.

Finally we also extend our thanks to family, friends and church members, who put up with our involvement with the book for so long and helped in many ways, and our apologies to anyone we have inadvertently missed out. Please put it down to age and forgetfulness. Everybody's help and encouragement has been greatly appreciated.

Maureen and Eric Long, February 2006

Swingboats on the beach, prior to the First World War.

Chapter 1

Earliest History

Kessingland's Rich Heritage

The Domesday Book records Kessingland as an important town in 1086, with a November annual fair and a Tuesday market. We can, however, trace its origins back much further, as modern research has shown. At the time of the Norman Conquest there were 8,000 inhabitants, twice the present population, although in the summer months, with the holiday camps and chalets all full, the population increases.

Situated four miles south of Lowestoft and seven miles from Southwold, Kessingland is a former fishing village with a surprising collection of historic treasure. Its quiet and peaceful atmosphere, rich in wildlife, attracts many visitors, including artists and bird-watchers, to the holiday chalets, caravan camps, holiday village and lovely beach.

The village retains an interesting mixture of old and new. A visit to the 'Boatshed' can result in a rich conversation with retired fishermen, who love to tell of the days when Kessingland revolved around farming and fishing. The village has grown to small town status, but retains its rich community spirit.

A century ago the village fell naturally into two parts: 'the Street' and 'the Beach', with a mile of farm land between. They were almost like two villages, each having its own butcher, baker, food shops, school, places of worship, Post Office, shoemaker, and the like and considerable rivalry was experienced between the two areas.

In the 1970s, the Lloyds estate, built on farm land when Mr McLean's farm was sold, joined the two geographically if not culturally, since it seemed for a time to create a third 'village' which the residents soon dubbed 'Little London', due to the fact that the properties had been offered for sale in the London newspapers. With property being so much cheaper here (two-bedroomed bungalows were sold for £2,400 and three-bedroomed for just over £3,000) Londoners were able to retire to the country and seaside with a tidy bit in the bank to keep them comfortably. The Over 60s Club soon grew too large for the fire restrictions in the Church Hall and a second club, the Friendship Club was formed by Bob and Phyllis Grice, who had themselves moved into the village some years before and were dedicated workers at the Methodist Church. Over the years, the London influx has been absorbed and the village now shows a more integrated front; there are no longer two parts to the village.

The coastline of Suffolk has long been wreathed in mists, myths and mystery, and Kessingland is the most easterly village in Britain. However, research as recent as autumn 2005 has confirmed that man has lived here for at least 200,000 years more than at first estimated. It would seem to rate this area as the cradle of civilisation in Britain.

Before the great sea surge that formed the North Sea (formerly the German Ocean), we were joined to Europe, and our River Hundred, along with the Thames, Trent and other rivers, was a tributary of the Rhine.

Fields bordering the River Hundred have thrown up stone axes, choppers, knives, arrows and spear-heads. Flakes of flints are still being found, used in the preparation of animal skins for clothing and rough tents. In 1931 a 9,000-year-old bone harpoon was trawled up by the fishing smack *Colinda*. It is now in Norwich Museum.

As temperatures rose and the glaciers retreated north, conditions changed and life became easier. England was cut off from Europe and the huge herds of mammoths, bison, rhinoceros and sabre-toothed tigers. Pine and alder forests changed very gradually to oak, elm and hazel. Elk, cattle and pigs became prominent in the food chain, along with acorns, hazelnuts, berries and mushrooms. Dogs were tamed and trained for hunting.

A legacy of the Ice Age was a natural harbour at Kessingland and the village became an important port. Ships sailed up as far as Latymere Dam, where the River Hundred now crosses the A12. Later, when the Vikings and Romans came, they over-wintered at Frostenden.

Before the new research, Kessingland historian Peter Cherry wrote during the 1990s:

Man lived here and fished the estuary ten thousand years ago. A tongue of land jutting out into what was once the estuary and fields on the Suffolk Wildlife Park, have been identified as considerable settlements of Stone Age Man and archaeologists believe that an aerial survey would reveal signs of earthworks and habitation of that period.

From the flint implements which have been found – arrow heads, scrapers, knives, etc,. and the thousands of flint flakes, it is clear that this was a prolific Neolithic workshop. Certainly there is no lack of flints in the locality and there is a suggestion that the name of Kessingland is derived from the Scandinavian meaning 'land of flints'. [Dutch invaders were defeated at Bloodmoor Field, c.869AD, by King Edmund of East

Anglia, to whom the church is dedicated.] The more generally accepted explanation, however, is that it means 'Carson's Land' [Carson was a principle landowner on the 1787 map].

The Kessingland estuary, which was certainly much wider and deeper than the present shallow valley suggests, must have been known and used by all the invaders, who, throughout history, came ashore to plunder this most easterly part of our island. The Romans were here, though apart from a few bits of pottery and a few coins little trace of them has been found.

Bloodmoor Hill, between Pakefield and Kessingland, is the legendary site of a great and bloody battle between the Christian-Romano British and the Heathen Angles. The Angles won... This Hill is also claimed as a Neolithic settlement, a great many flint implements having been found there. Other remarkable finds have also been made on Bloodmoor. In 1758 a barrow on the site was found to contain the skeleton of a Romano-British soldier. Around his neck was a gold coin dating back to AD455 and an onyx medallion showing a warrior, spear in hand, standing by his horse. The Romans, of course, had their great fortress at Burgh Castle and must have known this area well, using the Kessingland estuary in war and peace. In the dark ages which followed the withdrawal of the Roman legions, successive bands of invaders ravaged the coast. The Viking long ships would have found Kessingland estuary a snug anchorage and they left evidence of their occupation in the neighbouring estuary of Frostenden.

Frostenden harbour is striking evidence of the way in which estuaries on this part of the coast have silted up... no one looking at Frostenden today would dream that it had once been a Port. Domesday Book provides ample evidence not only that Kessingland was a port, but an important one. Probably decimated by the Black Death, its harbour silted up, Kessingland slid into obscurity. For over 400 years it never recovered and only the Turnpike Road in the late eighteenth century saved it from total disappearance.

By 1547 the parish was selling off the treasures from its church. Little over a century later, in 1668, the Church itself fell in ruins and divine service was discontinued. Eventually the main body of the church was rebuilt on a smaller scale, amid the ruins of the old, portions of which still survive...

Looking out over the sea of grain, grass and reeds, one can try to picture the sight of the old harbour. A tongue of breed land running deep into the heart of the Beach village is the obvious spot for the medieval harbour, but probably we shall never know the exact site of Portu de Kesynglande.

The newly-formed North Sea was eventually colonised by shoals of saltwater fish, including the herring on which the prosperity of Kessingland was founded.

Prehistoric man, it would seem, was Kessingland's first fisherman, the first to sail, or rather paddle, his dug-out canoe out of Kessingland harbour. He was the first of a long line of fishermen.

Roman Pot Found at Century House
By Chris Barker

The Pot (it is 10 inches across the top) was found 18 inches below ground when digging a trench next to the back of the garage, at Century House in 1980. It was reconstructed at Oulton Broad Museum, then put on display for a year afterwards and dates from the 1st century AD. It has a small, unexplained drain hole pierced in the base.

Ten years later, when a garden water tap was being installed a pit containing large amounts of bone from domestic cattle, sheep and pigs, with some bird and rodent bones and large numbers of oyster shells were found. Mixed in with these were pottery, heavy roof and floor tiles, a loom weight, part of a cheese press and a complete bronze pin about four inches long. All these finds were recorded by local archaeologist, Paul Durbridge and detailed in the Lowestoft Archaeologist and Local History Society's annual report, 1999/2000. The only coin found was a bronze dating from between 161–181 AD which had the head of Marcus Aurelius on it.

The Early Village

The Knoll, now a bed-and-breakfast establishment, is one of the oldest residential sites in Kessingland. The village was once a prosperous town port, larger than Lowestoft or Yarmouth, with a harbour and an estuary stretching as far as what is now Frostenden. Bearing in mind the different geography of the village, we know from an Enclosure Award and its old map of 1787, that there were only two buildings in the harbour area. One was the Old Vicarage, not to be confused with the present building of that name. This one was a clay lump building standing on the corner of what is now Wash Lane and Church Road to the beach side, opposite the present rectory. There was also an old tithe barn there. The rest of the Beach village was built in the fishing boom with the opening of Lowestoft Harbour in 1831. Our harbour and estuary had long since been silted up and turned into marshland.

Yet even before this, a house was on the site of The Knoll, 'sometimes called Berdys', as long ago as 1534, as mentioned in the will of Thomas Wardale.

It is also interesting to note that in 1502 John Cok left to his wife Margery, 'my housing mansion and dwelling place syting and leying in Kessingland seerowe.' This house was called Elys, in Sea Row, which has since been taken by the sea in past storms. There was a promontory jutting out into the common marshland after the estuary silted up, shown in the enclosure map of 1787 as 'Ellis Hole'.

A winter of traffic delays, 1997.

One-way traffic disruption on the A12, October 1997 to March 1998.

This bridge carries a lot of weight today.

Mending the east side of Latymere Dam, 1997–98.

Breheney's workforce on the marathon task of strengthening the bridge, 1997–98.

Working on the west side of the bridge, 1997–98.

Dorothy Clarke outside Storm Cottage.

Donkeys, the snow and the field were around when Storm Cottage was built.

It is much higher than the adjoining marshes and is still known by that name. He also left 'my lands which I purchased in ye field of ye said town', some agricultural land, and his house there was occupied by his eldest son. Is this town field the same as the Village Green, where the Village Cross stood? Is this another owner of The Knoll? Could be!

It is fascinating to see that rich men of the day had both farming and fishing interests, as Cok also left boats and nets as well as money for 'the Plough gooyng in Ploughland Monday'. Ploughland Monday was celebrated on the first Monday after Epiphany and was probably a New Year 'Blessing of the Land' ceremony.

Through this history, customs, joys and sorrows, some things still remain; countless generations of Kessingland folk have dwelt on the site of The Berdys or The Knoll.

Research on Kessingland by Revd Chitty, 1950:

By the Norman Conquest in 1066 there were four manors here, given, according to the Domesday Book, to Hugo de Montford, High Constable of William of Normandy's army at Hastings who increased the rents to a combined 22,000 herrings a year, showing how important the village was, since this is the highest rent locally apart from Ipswich...

The early and medieval period of Kessingland history has been well documented in Peter Cherry's *From Stone Age to Stagecoach*, but one building is of special interest, which Peter calls the Town House. Situated in the old Market Place, it fell into ruins but has more recently been renovated as a private residence. Peter recognised the large roof tiles as being extremely old and with his research of the original buildings, discovered that this would have been the town bathhouse, and the tiles would have been part of the refurbishing after the original thatch was burned out.

The Town House in Flames
By Peter Cherry, 1990

There must have been little in the way of excitement in our village of Kessingland some 300 years ago – apart from the annual Fair, the Tuesday Market and the occasional wreck on the seashore. So there would have been a good turnout when the Town House burned down in 1728. The burning of the thatched house must have been a welcome diversion for the crowd although a sad blow for the Overseers and the ratepayers who for several years had watched – and paid for – the renovation of the building.

... Old maps show that it stood on a plot of land with a frontage on Whites Lane – now the approximate site of the bungalow of [the late] Mrs Freda Nathan – and ran through to the Market Place... it appears to have

been a local poorhouse for orphaned children and for those unable to maintain themselves... Possibly our Town House had its origins in 1597 and the renewed pressure led to it being enlarged. At any rate renovation was started in 1714 – the earliest mention of the building in the Overseers' accounts. They detail the buying of large quantities of bricks, sand, lime, tiles and timber as well as 'beer for the carters'.

The carters must have earned their beer since much of the material was shipped by water to Mutford Bridge and was then hauled by horse and cart to the village. It is apparent that poor villagers were already being accommodated there before the fire since alternative housing had to be found for them.

After the fire, work resumed on the Town House and finally, towards the end of 1729, came a welcome celebration: 'Beer at the raising of the House 2s.6d'. The work of the Overseers was to continue for just over another century till changes in the Poor Law were enacted.

Fire was a constant hazard in the days of timber buildings and thatch. Many large towns had their own fire pumps, but Kessingland probably had to rely on long rakes to pull down the blazing thatch, and a chain of buckets from the well to douse the flames. By this time the Town House must have been reaching the end of its useful life and presumably, when it was no longer needed as a local workhouse, it was rented out. The Ordnance Survey map of 1881 shows that it has disappeared. But at the same time the map marks the appearance of a quaint old cottage, now standing empty in the Market Place. Built of old red bricks in rather a random style with a tiled roof supported by ancient timbers, it seems to me the sort of cottage which might well have been contrived from materials salvaged when the old Town House was pulled down. Mrs Nathan told me that when she was getting her garden in order she came across many of these old bricks. It is significant that the back garden of the cottage contains the old Town House well in the same position as recorded on old maps. Now, well over a century old, it is, in its own way, one of our historic buildings...

The old cottage was auctioned by Messrs Durrants of Beccles and sold on Monday 28 October 1996. Restoration was completed by the new owners.

The Overseers' accounts list makes mention of 'Mendyge a bridge called Ladymore Dunma (Latymere Dam) at a cost of 20s.' In the 1990s the bridge was mended again. Photographer Tony Ackers made a pictorial record of the work, which this time involved a £312,000 contract with the contractors, Breheny. The relatively small bridge had to be practically rebuilt and strengthened. It took over four months and caused quite a bit of traffic disruption. Tons of concrete were poured in to keep the bridge safe for the tons of modern traffic piling over it every hour.

Chapter 2

Worship in Kessingland

St Edmund's Parish Church
The late Revd Chitty's research helped considerably with the section on St Edmund's.

The original larger church, of which some of the outer wall remains in the churchyard, was built in the mid-1300s by the Nuns of St Clare. They were granted the right to appoint an incumbent to the parish by Queen Isabella, wife of Edward II, but after Henry VIII's Dissolution of the Monasteries the nuns were driven out. Supported by wealthy villagers, however, they built an imposing church, with a tower added in 1437 which was 98 feet high. Today the smaller church, rebuilt in the seventeenth century, but retaining its landmark tower, continues to serve the parishioners as the backbone of the faith and the community. New seating was installed in 1871 and the bells still ring out in triumph from the tower for worship, national disasters or celebrations. (More detailed information can be found in *From Stone Age to Stagecoach* by Peter Cherry.)

Early Kessingland Rectors
(Taken from a 1936 newspaper article)

There have been 51 rectors of the parish, starting with Adam de Doncastre in 1307 and ending up with Stephen Collier, who retired in 2005 (there is no rector at the time of writing). A key name in this period was Robert Potter, who translated Aeschylus (described as the 'best translation' that ever appeared in English of any Greek poet) as well as Sophocles, Euripides and others. He held his living for 50 years until 1804 and was buried in St Margaret's Church in Lowestoft.

In 1698 William Whiston was installed as rector. A writer, mathematician and the translator/editor of the works of Josephus, Whiston counted among his friends the Pope and Sir Robert Walpole, the first Prime Minister of England. Whiston succeeded Sir Isaac Newton in his Professorship of Mathematics at Cambridge University.

Whiston appears to have been something of an autocrat and apparently did not get on too well with his curates (he held the living at Lowestoft as well) or with local Kessinglanders. No wonder; they probably did not have a clue what the other was talking about! It must have been 'all Greek' to them – and he probably did not understand their Suffolk dialect or accent either!

Another famous rector is John Tanner, who also held the Vicarage of Lowestoft. He was inducted in 1708 and held the Kessingland living for 52 years (1708–60). One of his favourite occupations was to 'beat the bounds' of the parish, though there seemed little reason for keeping up the old custom. Between 1709 and 1753 he went over the ground at least eight times, about once every five years.

Tanner was the donor of much of the church plate, including a cup, paten and flagon dated 1750. Just 200 years earlier, in 1547, the silver of Kessingland church had been sold, raising £43.10s. The proceeds were spent on mending the highway, repairing a

Ancient line drawing of St Edmund's Church.

St Edmund's Church, early 1900s.

The Revd John Hunt with a fishing exhibition at the Flower Festival, 1993.

John Hunt in the Prayer Room at the Rectory, 1993.

bridge, training soldiers, supplying a fire beacon, painting scripture on the walls and 'pullynge downe of ymags' (images).

Besides being a literary man, Tanner appears to have been rather shrewd in business, as he purchased in 1709 from his predecessor Whiston, the impropriation of the rectory for £50 and granted it to the rectory of Kessingland for ever.

John Arrow, who succeeded Tanner in 1760 as rector, remained in possession for 29 years, until the outbreak of the French Revolution. Although Arrow does not appear to have made any pretensions of a literary nature, he planned to write a history of Kessingland and undertook much research.

The Tower
(From a leaflet by ringing master Michael Parker)

The tower was designed by master mason Richard Russell and begun c.1437 when the church was under the patronage of the Nuns of St Clare. Richard oversaw the building of the first 35 feet of the tower before he died. He had also designed the church's splendid font. The tower was completed by an unknown master mason, who changed the decoration on the building. The tower never received its parapet and corner pinnacles but remained unfinished until the present brick parapet was added in the eighteenth century.

The Bells

A record of 1552 records Kessingland as having 'Great Bells'. Nothing is known of these bells or what became of them. It is most probable that they were sold along with the other church plate after the Dissolution of the Monasteries when patronage from the Nuns of St Clare ceased.

There are now six bells, high in the tower in an oak frame. The oldest bell is the second bell, cast in 1615 by the Norwich bellfounder, William Brend. The third bell was cast by another local, Thomas Newman, in 1711.

In 1960 the original five bells were removed from the tower for repairs and retuning. In 1961 a new treble bell (named Andrew) was added to make the ring up to six. The bell was to commemorate the birth of His Royal Highness Prince Andrew in 1961.

The bells of St Edmund's are rung each week for services, weddings and other special occasions. These bells are very much part of village life, and heritage. Bellringing is an ancient art which should be preserved.

Recent Kessingland Rectors
(Taken from the *Kessingland Times*, as provided by Roy G. Brown MBE)

In 1905 Kessingland was a fishing village of about 1,500 inhabitants, a large number of whom were engaged in the fishing trade. The rector at the time was Revd John Cossham Vawdrey, M.A. He commented in the January 1905 church magazine:

The main industry of previous years, fishing, has been fairly productive during the past twelve months. Again we have to say Thank God for his great mercy and the wonderful preservation of the lives of our men. Only one life has been lost.

In those days the Harvest Thanksgiving was held in January, not in November as now. The Vestry meeting was held on Easter Monday at 10.30a.m. and the themes discussed included: the retention of the churchwardens and sidesmen for the coming year and contributions required for repairs to the church roof. For the first six months of the year the number of communicants was 518, there were 30 baptisms, three marriages and ten burials. Offerings totalled £34.4s.10d.

Revd Leslie Harris
(Taken from the *Kessingland Times* interview, 1990)

Trained in counselling for marriage break-up, drug addiction, debt, unemployment, homelessness, family problems and all the usual concerns of Christian ministers, Leslie found plenty to exercise his skills. Leslie came to Kessingland and Gisleham in 1983 and soon felt at home across the denominations with the strong United Christian Fellowship here. In 1986 he was made Rural Dean of Lothingland. He had great plans for the future but his sudden death in May 1992 brought all this to an end.

Many tributes were paid to him as friend and counsellor, so deeply had he touched the lives of many in the parish. Stories were told of Leslie's quiet encouragement and promise to 'pray for you' and some 400 people attended his funeral service.

Revd Joan Oddy
(Taken from the *Kessingland Times* interview, 1998)

You can't be long in Joan Oddy's company without having a laugh and she is the first to laugh at herself, always a sign of true humility. When she first came to the area she acquired a job in Carol's Newsagents at Kessingland Beach:

It was in the shop that I got to know and understand the local people. Many were from Essex, or the

The Palm Sunday procession leaving the Rectory in 1984.

Arriving at the church, Palm Sunday 1984.

London area, then there were the original village folk, all different but all with the same problems and joys. I made many friends...

I never volunteered for anything or asked to do anything when I began to attend St Edmund's regularly. I just seemed to get absorbed into the church life, finding myself in the choir, helping with the Sunday school, and then I was asked to train as a Lay Reader. Studying, writing essays and working on projects for assessment is hard in the midst of family and village life, but if you want to do it you make time for it somehow and everyone is very understanding...

Not only did Joan become a lay reader, but she was recommended to study for the LNSM (Local Non-Stipendiary Ministry). She has now been ordained, with lots of responsibility now that the church is in the throes of an interregnum.

Church Activities

There is always something going on at St Edmund's, such as the annual flower festival, or the Tower Open Days, as well as various fund-raisers with their ever-popular refreshments. Special events are always commemorated and Mrs Janet Abel has produced beautifully stitched collages for events such as the millennium and for themed flower festivals. She conducts the choir and her husband was the organist for many years.

Bridal Exhibition and Flower Festival, August 1992

When Mrs Grace Stark (née Moulton) wandered into St Edmund's Church on her holiday from Texas, USA, she was astonished to see a photograph of the dress she wore on her wedding day! At the church Flower Festival and Exhibition of Bridal Gowns Through The Century, she saw Freda Nathan's (née Strowger) wedding photograph. Freda had lent Grace the dress when she got married during the war to an American serviceman, before going back to the States with him. The incumbent of St Edmund's refused to marry her, disapproving of local girls marrying GIs, so she was married at Beccles, in Freda's gown. The gown itself, although Freda still has it, was not on show, as it was subsequently dyed black for use as an evening dress.

At the exhibition, conceived by Freda two years earlier, a dress was displayed from each decade of the twentieth century. The oldest dress was from 1902 and was worn by the late Kathleen Tripp (née Sims). Many brides also displayed their photographs or albums, including those of Jill and Andrew Walker, which pictured a kilted bridegroom with a castle background! Karen Gooch (née Gardiner), who married Kevin at the Methodist Church, showed the white lacy dress she had knitted for their big day.

An earlier wedding gown.

Gowns through the ages.

Confessions of a Choirboy:
The Day I shot Revd Emms
By George Swan

I remember the first time going to Yarmouth with my mother. It was a Sunday School treat. This particular day, I was told not to go far from home and I was given tuppence to get my dinner at Charlie Bond's fish shop... I bought an ice-cream and some rock and with the money I had left over, I bought a water pistol. At four o'clock, I was reminded not to leave my mother's side, because at 4.30 we all had to meet for tea and cakes at the Ellis Tearooms... on the seafront.

Everybody enjoyed their refreshments and I was dying to try out my gun. The only liquid available was my cup of tea, so I filled the water pistol from my cup and squeezed the trigger. The contents shot across two tables, hitting the parson, who accompanied us on the trip. My new gun was confiscated, never to be seen again, but worse still, I was made to stand up and apologise in front of everyone.

Christening Robes Exhibition and Flower Festival, August 1993

With the added incentive of cream teas and ploughman's lunches, the Christening Gowns Exhibition and Flower Festival, organised again by Kathleen Knights, drew the crowds and raised over £1,200.

One of the oldest exhibits was a Christening 'vest' made in 1840 in a convent from a man's hem-stitched hanky. Each gown was complemented with beautiful floral displays. Christening presents were also shown. One ancient custom was to give the child salt, sometimes in fine salt cellars, for salt was once an expensive and valuable commodity (from which our word 'salary' is derived), along with eggs, a sign of fertility and silver, for wealth. Sometimes all three were combined in a silver egg-shaped salt cellar.

The newest gown was knitted by Ingrid Utting and given as a prize to the person who guessed the name of the doll modelling it; Mrs Yvonne Gardiner guessed the name 'Ada' and won the gown.

Personality Profile: Betty Wigg
(Taken from the *Kessingland Times*, April 2000)

If you go to any fund-raising event for St Edmund's Church in Kessingland, you'll probably find Betty Wigg, along with friend and fellow fund-raiser Daphne Brown, behind the teapot or selling her cakes.

She has lived in the same house at the beach end of the village for the last 50 years, but she was born and brought up in Warwickshire. She met her husband, Walter Wigg, in Stratford-upon-Avon when they worked in the same munitions factory at the start of the Second World War. She had left school aged 14 and gone into domestic service. They moved to Kessingland after the war and initially stayed with Walter's mother before finding a house of their own. Betty recalls:

When the children were small, I took in Bed & Breakfast visitors. I think everyone did in those days to supplement the low wages of their menfolk. Often all four of us crammed into one bedroom so we could let the others. Some people even slept in their sheds in the summer to let out their rooms! The visitors didn't seem to mind then that we had no bathrooms. They were used to having the big old ewer jugs of water upstairs on the washstands for washing. It was fishing in the winter and the visitors in the summer that kept the village going.

When the children were older Betty went to work at the Suffolk Wildlife Park and the Denes Holiday Camp, but many of her summer 'regulars' kept in touch. She enjoyed working at the camp and made a lot of friends there. One year she washed 1,300 blankets between September and the following

March, for which she earned £76 – a small fortune at that time.

Having had a pacemaker fitted Betty is a 'recycled teenager', able to enjoy life to the full. She has five grandchildren and two great-grandchildren to keep her young at heart. Her involvement at St Edmund's also keeps her busy and she tries not to miss a service. 'There's always a need to raise money to keep a church like St Edmund's going,' she says.

Personality Profile: Gillie Powell
(Taken from the *Kessingland Times*, 2004)

Gillie and David Powell moved to the village in 1989 'by accident', according to David. After working in Saudi Arabia he asked Gillie where she would ideally like to live. Her reply was 'By the sea'. David found a job as an Agricultural Engineer in Acle, near Great Yarmouth, and so they moved to Kessingland.

Gillie is very active in pastoral work, not only in the Benefice, but also in her capacity as Assistant Anglican Chaplain at Blundeston Prison. She also teaches music in her own home. At the time of writing Gillie is training for the Anglican ministry.

Personality Profile: Stephen Collier
(Taken from the *Kessingland Times*)

Born in Ealing, West London, Stephen has travelled a lot but feels at home in Kessingland, where he has been since his Induction in July 2001:

By the time I was 20 I was sure of my beliefs and was confirmed by the Bishop of Oxford. This happily came full circle last year, when I prepared a young lady for Confirmation in Norwich. She turned out to be the Bishop of Oxford's granddaughter.

After university Stephen went to Tobago, where he taught for a year and met his wife, Nola. Stephen worked at various jobs and the couple had three children, Hugh, Harry and Mary.

In 1980 they sold up and returned to Tobago. They stayed for ten years and son Daniel was born there. Stephen worked as a Schools Guidance Counsellor, helping children with study skills, sex education and deciding on different careers.

Ten years later they came back to England and stayed for four years in Stephen's holiday home in Cornwall. He worked with the homeless in hostels and became more and more drawn to the Church ministry. They had always been involved in Sunday school and youth work and other church activities, but in 1992, aged 45, Stephen started a two-year training course at Queen's College, Birmingham.

After this they spent the next four years at Thorpe St Andrew, Norwich. A second curacy at St Peter Mancroft followed and then they had to choose: either back to the West Indies, or to the West Country.

Procession of priests leaving the church after the induction of Revd Stephen Collier, May 2001. The lady on the right is Angela Morgan, whose late husband, Bernard, was a former rector at St Edmund's.

One night, on the way back to the West Country, the car broke down:

I had to call out the AA and the man said, 'I don't think you'll get to your destination. Take my advice and go back to Norwich.' It has been said that once you come to Norwich, you never move up or down again, only horizontally, and so it was. We came to Kessingland and love it here... There are so many activities in the village and such willing volunteers who run so many organisations.

Sadly, Stephen and Nola Collier had to retire in 2005 due to ill health, leaving the church once more with an interregnum. Retired priest John Blacker, with Joan Oddy and the Revd Peter Simpson, made sure that parishioners received the same pastoral care.

Personality Profile: Stella Knights
(Taken from the *Kessingland Times*, 1990)

Stella was born and raised in Kessingland. She attended the school in Church Road, then worked at the Lowestoft Silkworks until that was moved to Manchester. Her horizons widened when Mr Barrett, who then owned the Pakefield Holiday Camp, took in German-Jewish refugees as talk of war escalated in early 1939. They were coming over in their hundreds and needed help, friendship and eventually re-housing. Stella became involved because then, as now, she has a passionate interest in people and their welfare.

Stella has vivid memories of two thatched cottages catching fire in the village. She also remembers a one-roomed cottage in White's Lane where her grandfather once lived. Jack Mudd's grandmother, also lived there at one time.

She remembers the first bombs on Kessingland in 1942, when High Street baker George Bird's wife and daughter were killed outright in their bungalow in Church Road (Chapel Road as it was then). A shop was also demolished and Miss Dolly Girling (still of High Street) and Miss Cable from Benacre were dug

Church Road, early 1900s.

out of the rubble. This was Mr George Buckenham's general store. It stood in the High Street and trade had to be resumed from a back store (which was later Kessingland Antiques).

Four days later, Stella went to Leicester to join the ATS and was sent to Bulford Camp near Salisbury, and from there to Oxford, where she stayed until the end of the war. Stella went into the Army as a cook and hated every minute of the cooking!

After being de-mobbed, she joined the Church Army, working in a hostel in Victoria, London. Stella left the Church Army when her mother became ill and she felt she was needed at home. After her mother's death in 1951, Stella stayed with her father and worked at Catchpole's Holiday Camp for two seasons, then at Beecham's until her retirement.

Stella is an active member of St Edmund's Church, its choir, the Octaves and KESSIs, the Friendship Club and the WI. She enjoys her busy retirement, especially going around to old people's homes and hospitals with the choir as well as knitting the endless supply of toys which are sold for charity. She loves to travel, but when asked about her favourite place, there was no hesitation:

I've been to lots of places, but there's no air like Kessingland sea air. There's just something different about it. I'm always glad to come home to Kessingland. There's no other place quite like it.

The Mothers' Union
(Taken from an interview with Muriel Brown in the *Kessingland Times*, 1995)

Kessingland's Mothers' Union celebrated its centenary in 1995 with two special services, a ploughman's lunch and a tea. There were wonderful floral displays by Pat Honeywood, Pat Briggs, Julie Warner and Jean Purkis and friends came from far and wide.

The MU members have for years provided tea and entertainment for residents of Harleston House, belonging to the Church Army. Muriel Brown, an MU member since 1949, was instrumental in the centenary celebrations. With her love of singing and her good voice, she was in both the church and the WI choir.

The MU cloth, on which each new member embroiders her name, was started by Mrs Peregrine, wife of a former Kessingland doctor, who also started the first Young Wives Group in the village at her home in 1947. It attracted young mothers with toddlers, who played on the floor or in the garden with toys during meetings. When the children reached school age, their mothers joined the MU meetings instead. Unfortunately this group ceased when Mrs Peregrine moved until a different style Young Wives Group began, meeting in the evenings because many women worked.

Kessingland MU
(Taken from the Diocesan Newsletter, Spring 1992)

The first recorded list of names was dated 1895, when the meeting was held in a room at the Old Rectory; 20 names were recorded. There were 58 in the years to 1907. Throughout the First World War numbers remained steady.

Early on the MU was the only organisation in the village where women could meet together regularly, and in those days church congregations were bigger, with more families attending, so the membership of the MU was an extension of Christian family life.

Many names in the first register are listed in more recent times; older people today still remember names well known in the village: Chipperfield, Blowers, Thacker, Harvey, Spindler, Storm, Schilling, Bunn, D'Arcy, Aldred and Brown, to mention a few.

Between 1918 and 1943 records are rather sparse but it appears meetings were then held in the WVS canteen (since demolished). Mrs Curtis was the enrolling member, followed in 1946 by Mrs Peregrine.

The MU has always supported the Church in a practical way. In 1961 a project was started to make carpets for the sanctuary and in 1982 kneelers were made by members. There is no record of when the banner was purchased, but as it was falling into disrepair by 1979, it was renovated, using the original design. New green altar dressings were made and paid for by the MU and a member made and donated new purple hangings in memory of her husband.

The MU has a scrapbook recording 'Our Church, Yesterday, Today & Tomorrow', compiled by members. Mary Sumner, the founder of the MU, would be proud to know that from such small beginnings in Winchester, her dream has become a worldwide organisation, and members wear their badges with pride.

The Methodist Church

When Kessingland Methodist Church celebrated a centenary in 1991, the Minister, Revd John Fenner, wrote in the preface to the centenary booklet:

The Old Rectory.

When does a Centenary Celebration not celebrate 100 years? Answer: When it happens at Kessingland Methodist Church. The church was built in 1877, with the congregation being established since 1805. In 1891 a hall was built behind the church and it was this building that the Centenary celebrated.

In 1975 the old building was pulled down and replaced with a modern suite of rooms that front onto Church Road. At that time the hall was renovated and became the church worship area, with the new rooms for Sunday school, youth work, meetings and community projects. There was a grand opening of the new premises in 1976, which was 99 years after the original church was opened. The new work continued with the second floor of the new building being finished and furnished in the following years at a cost of £28,000.

A splendid new building was opened in 1887 and the schoolroom was added in 1891, which did service until 1913, when it was enlarged.

A tablet from the church wall, now in the present worship area, reads:

To the Glory of God and in Beloved Memory of JOHN MITCHELL, who died May 15th 1900, aged 80 years. And of PHOEBE his wife who died May 2nd 1901, aged 72 years. They were for more than 40 years consistent members of this Church. This tablet was erected by their children and members of the congregation.

Although people today still tend to sit in their favourite or usual seat, the seats are no longer rented! In 1877 seat rents brought in £5.16s., which more than paid for the lighting, heating and cleaning expenses for the year at £4.16s.4d.

The Sunday school was growing with Mr Sampson as the superintendent. Today his great-granddaughter, Karen Gooch, teaches in the Primary department. In 1897 a Mr Hall (Anne Adams's father) moved from Lowestoft to Kessingland and proved another strong leader. He was to forward both the youth and other church work for many years.

Wesley House, where early Methodists met in Kessingland.

Foundation-stone from the former chapel, removed and inserted into the inside wall of the 'new' chapel, made in the old schoolroom of the former building. It commemorates John Mitchell, 1820–1900, and his wife Phebe 1829–1901.

In 1905, with the Revd Tasker as minister, there was a great spiritual revival. Methodist hymns and preaching packed the church every Sunday and most week nights. Prayer meetings were also held nightly. By 1911, singing parties went out to neighbouring churches in wagonettes (covered over if the weather was wet). Mr J.R. Smith, local bootmaker and draper, acted as a human pillar to hold up the cover; his daughter Dorothy later succeeded him as organist, for 40 years. When revival services were held at Barnby Chapel, many Kessingland members even walked to Barnby and back to support the friends there. They obviously could not afford bicycles, although *The Guild* magazine of the Wesley Guild, in its issue of August 1897, offered 'The Wesley Guild Bicycle' at £13.13s.0d. Built by The Cranfield Cycle Co., Redditch, 'a firm of Wesleyans who build cycles for Wesleyans', it was described as 'a perfect marvel'.

As well as organist, 'J.R.' as he was called, was chief

decorator of the church or hall for special occasions and stall-decorator for the successful annual bazaars and sales of work. He kept the drapery shop at the Beach village and no doubt employed his window-dressing skills! On 13 January 1910 a bazaar raised £60 – a lot of money, especially just after Christmas! The Revd A.E. Sennet was Minister and his daughter was later to come back to the circuit as the wife of the Revd Clucas-Moore in the 1950s.

The Twentieth Century

In June 1911 King George V's coronation took place. In celebration Mr and Mrs Collen gave a tea on their meadow. Miss Pleasance Harvey remembers that her brothers, who attended the village school, were given a mug. The Collen family also arranged Methodist strawberry teas in their garden at Manor Farm. Later their daughter, Mary, married and did the same at Cliff Farm (now Heathland's Caravan Park.) Miss Harvey was to attend hundreds more Methodist tea parties; as assistant organist for many years, she sang and played on numerous occasions and, as a teacher at the village school next door to the church, she encouraged her pupils to attend Sunday school.

Storm clouds of conflict were gathering and 1914 saw the outbreak of the First World War. The hall was used as a canteen for soldiers stationed in the area; church members baked cakes and manned the teapots. After the war, the hall had different occupants when a class of pupil teachers trained five days weekly, from 1920.

Mr John Adams senr, who lived in The Ark, the oldest house in Kessingland, was society steward from 1915–49, and was succeeded by his son Chester, then his grandson John, now married to Anne, one of the circuit stewards.

From 1910 Mr Hall was superintendent of the Sunday school. The annual treat was eagerly anticipated, and the games on the meadow opposite the Shell service station, followed by tea, with ice-cream, were talked of for weeks! The Sunday-school anniversary was also a grand affair. The children learned recitations and new hymns, wore flowers in their buttonholes or in their hair and enjoyed the address which was just for them!

In 1933 came the Deed of Union and in Lowestoft three circuits amalgamated to make one large area manned by seven ministers. The Revd Raine Sunter served here and Kessingland had 21 members. The name on the arch over the main doorway was changed from 'WESLEYAN CHAPEL 1877' to 'METHODIST CHURCH'. Six years later, in 1939, there were 26 members and still a large Sunday school.

The Second World War found the Methodist Hall in use as temporary classrooms, but when, in 1941, a bomb dropped nearby, it was the community which offered accommodation to the church! Members

The new church building, opened in 1976.

joined in Sunday worship at both the Bethel and St Edmund's Church, whilst a beating shed, loaned by Mrs Tripp, was used for Sunday school and Women's Bright Hour meetings. Damage to the roof of the church caused water to pour in and ruin the newly installed organ, the result of much hard work and fund-raising. This was not the only bombshell. J.R. Smith, who held the post of Sunday-school superintendent and who had been chapel steward, secretary and treasurer as well, died that year. Mr Layton succeeded him in the Sunday school. The work went on, along with fervent prayer for peace. Praise services and parties took place when peace finally came.

Postwar Britain, and particularly Methodism, was charged with new purpose and fresh hope. For the fortunate, servicemen and women were returning, with their gratuity payments, setting up new businesses or going back to their old jobs. War damage was slowly being repaired. In 1945 there were 26 members of the church; by 1951 this had risen to 51. The Sunday school was headed by John Adams junr, who had succeeded Mr Layton as superintendent.

The Watson family were working with the youngsters in Guides, Brownies and Cubs. A Senior Youth Club was also started. Again, with an open membership, many were drawn into church life, mainly due to the worship element and the fun-packed weekend camps at Henham Park (in 1946 and '47), and were taking part in wider interests, such as the drama festival at Lowestoft, where members did well at the Sparrow's Nest Theatre. Drama and music played a large part in the church at this time and the Nativity Plays were resumed from 1945. Many of the leaders of those various youth groups are still involved with Methodism or with other churches, both at home and away.

In 1950 the back line of pews was removed and the lobby extended. There was then room for a small table of welcoming flowers, over which was the portrait of Christ, now hanging at the back of the hall and beloved by many members. There is also a deeply worshipful tapestry of Christ's face, embroidered and designed by Mrs Eileen Gourley.

It was during the 1950s that Kessingland churches seemed to draw more together. They had always supported each other's fund-raising activities and special services had traditionally drawn folk from other churches. The Step Forward Together campaign enriched the ecumenical bond, as did the programmes on the Parables, which followed. These united programmes continue today.

Beryl Williams and Bette Dobney have held many positions during the last 30 years, mostly in youth work or secretarial duties. Their memories include:

Sticking to the varnish in the old Church pews when it warmed to your back!... The dark, dismal church, with the brass stair rods and door knobs to clean when it was our turn... The Sunday school scholar who prayed 'deliver us from the eagle!... Remembering not to sit in someone's regular pew. Mr and Mrs Adams had one each!... The Revd Caink telling us 30 years ago of the danger of aerosol sprays.

Challenge, the church magazine, was started in the 1960s, was produced by Beryl and Maureen. Change and adaptability marked the 1970s. In 1973, for the first time in living memory, the bazaar date was changed from the first Thursday in November to the following Saturday. This was due to the wedding of Princess Anne and Captain Mark Phillips, which everyone wanted to watch on television. The change was for the better and it has stayed on a Saturday ever since! Mrs G. Wigg and her team used to collect bazaar items.

In September of that year a team of about 20 people, led by Revd Maurice Barnet, arrived from Westminster Central Hall to lead a Mission. House meetings during the next two weeks led to friendships and spiritual enrichment. The ecumenical scene was never the same again! Kessingland Christians were involved in introducing their friends and neighbours to the love of Jesus.

Christians went on meeting together, with four united services each year. The Partners in Learning church education programme was used successfully for several years. The local Anglicans joined the monthly teachers' preparation classes, which led to a greater sense of unity, as they planned and prayed together and shared joys and problems. In 1981, this led to the setting up of the United Christian Youth Club, with Bette Dobney, Angela Morgan and Mike Beales as main leaders for each denomination, backed up by others.

During the 1980s the church served the community with the new building. The hall was used for parties, meetings, the Mother and Toddler Club, the formation of the Waveney Eldercare Luncheon

Club, practice night for the local concert party, as well as choir and adult education classes. The closure of the old church building meant the discontinuation of those community events, so services were held in homes, mostly those of Mr and Mrs Grice, along with Mr and Mrs Purdy who, incidentally, had arranged the last Flower Festival in the old church building. Sunday school took place in Mrs Winnie Gardiner's home, which was next door to the church. Classes spread into various rooms. Youth Club members met at the Long household at Henstead, later at Kessingland.

Nationally, the Women's Fellowship was renamed Network, retaining the same format as the former Women's Bright Hour, a devotional meeting with a visiting speaker, followed by a cup of tea. Many members have connections to the church that stretch back through the last century, such as Mrs Ivy Sims and her granddaughter. Ivy's sisters and mother were longstanding members, likewise Miss Millie Studd's and Dorothy Smith's mothers. Mrs Olive Monk was president, and other past leaders include Mrs Vera Parker, Mrs Ablett, Miss Dorothy Smith, Miss Lily Gouldby, Mrs Maureen Long, Mrs Walker and others. The Women's Fellowship aims 'to bring women and girls into a knowledge of God's love...'

Kessingland Methodist Church Today and Tomorrow
(Taken from material by Beryl Williams, Doris Meadows, Bette Dobney and Tina Long)

The Adult Group and Local Arrangement has brought comfort and inspiration to its members. There are several different leaders that take turns and many summer visitors also get involved in Group Bible Study, discussion and learning. Mrs Tina Long, Sunday-school superintendent, recalls:

I have some wonderful memories of times during my childhood which were spent either in this church or at other activities organised by the Sunday School and the Circuit. Concerts, pantomimes, sports days and parties were looked forward to and enjoyed by all, not forgetting the yearly Scripture exam* and anniversary... The most memorable anniversary for me was when my sister, three brothers and I had to learn a verse each of 'All things Bright and Beautiful' and sing before the congregation. My verse was 'Each little flower that opens'.

As superintendent and a primary school teacher I hope to pass on to our children all the joys of belonging to a Sunday School.

Scripture exam rally, 1960s.

* Tina's sister, Julie, gained 100 per cent in the examination when a teenager.

Scenes from the pantomime Cinderella, *1985.*

Agnetta Meadows at the celebrations of the centenary of the Methodist Church in Kessingland, 1991.

Centenary celebrations, 1991.

Centenary tea party, 1991. The centenary booklet carried messages from some former ministers, including Revd David and Mrs Rosemary Caink, Revd Ronald and Mrs Margaret Kemp, Revd and Mrs Joan Simons, Revd and Mrs Val Richards, Revd C. Brian Cooke, Revd David (Tim) Pittock, as well as from Revd Norwyn Denny, Superintendent of the East Suffolk Circuit, Revd Richard Jones, Chairman of the District, John Adams, Circuit Steward, Canon Leslie Harris, rector of Kessingland and Gisleham and Miss Jane O'Brien on behalf of Bethel members.

Inter-church party game. In the centre is Miss Dorothy Smith, former church organist and treasurer and Beach village draper, daughter of J.R. Smith.

Bethel Friends, including Madge Roth, Roy Brown and Pat Brown.

More fun and games at the Methodist Church, 1990.

Part of the adult group, Sunday morning all-age worship, including Jean Holt, Karolyn Smithson, Doris Meadows, Miriam Murdoch, Bette Dobney and organist Laurie Haddock.

Mrs Mac's annual garden party, Lloyds Avenue. This picture includes: Mrs Elsie Traynier and Mr Gilbey, Mrs Mac (MacKibben).

Morning service at Kessingland Methodist Church, 1991.

Today, several years after the centenary, Methodist members carry on the work and witness of the church, still working closely with the other congregations. They still enjoy anniversary events and Harvest Suppers. Ministers since then have been the Revd Eric Potts and, currently, Revd Joanne Jacobs.

Panto

The Church has always had a strong young people's section (the Sunday school and Youth Clubs) and on the lighter side, each year it was a tradition to put on a pantomime. Such care and attention went into the making of the costumes by Mrs Barbara Eyre, and the enthusiasm of everyone involved, including the youngsters, was remarkable. The plays were usually written by the leaders, to ensure there was a part for everyone. Over the years, these, as with all Methodist events, have been – and continue to be – widely supported by the village.

Keith Durrant and little girls at the 1991 Methodist Church centenary party with the cake.

Personality Profile: George Dellar

There have been many outstanding members of the church, one of whom was George Dellar, never to be forgotten. Born a spastic, George overcame his difficulties to gain 10 A-levels and pursue an academic career. His faith was always the centre of his life and he went on to write his biography, *Unto Another, Two*, taken from the parable of the talents. Just before one Easter, he took a trip to the Holy Land. Although his hands were always shaking, he bought a camera to take with him (even though his practice shots were blurred). When on the trip, his interest and determination resulted in perfect concentration and co-ordination and he brought back beautiful slides, which were shown on the Good Friday afternoon service, before the usual tea. George even attempted the commentary, speaking slowly and clearly. Many people who had never bothered to listen to him or speak to him before, no doubt due to embarrassment, were amazed. The human spirit, especially when linked to a strong faith, can accomplish great things, as George proved.

The Bethel
(Taken in part from an article by the late Mr E.J. Hunter, former secretary)

With the great fishing bonanza in the 1800s after Lowestoft Harbour was built, the village burgeoned with new housing and amenities. As no real records were kept, the early days of Kessingland Bethel are a bit uncertain. A Mr 'Dip' Durrant, and Mr J. Kemp, a local builder, were among those who helped to lead home-based meetings before the Bethel existed. In around 1880 two maiden ladies by the name of Green were instrumental in getting the Bethel built for the local fishermen, their wives and families, and other people to gather together for regular worship.

Built of cobblestone walls in keeping with the village and seaside, it was a solid building, capable of holding a large congregation. After the Bethel was opened for Sunday worship, it was felt that perhaps it would be best to hand the deeds over to a Society, so that the work could continue when the original workers had gone. The British and Foreign Sailors Society, eventually took the Bethel under its wing.

In those days many lives were lost at sea. The sailing ships were often caught by sudden gales when way out on the fishing grounds. Life for the fishermen was indeed very hard, and sometimes their earnings were very small indeed, but when home for a week or two they would gather at the Bethel and raise the roof with their singing of 'All the storms will soon be over', 'Will your anchor hold?' and the 'Glory Song'. When a Kessingland boat was lost at sea with all hands, Archibald Brown, the great evangelist preacher, was staying in Kessingland on holiday. He visited all the relatives in their homes and conducted special services at the Bethel. Before he left for London he put up a huge tent at the rear of the Bethel and invited all the fisherfolk there for a substantial meal.

Around 1900 Mr Edward H. Hunter took over as local leader of the Bethel, with responsibility for Sunday morning services and the choir. He was also the Sunday-school teacher. The Sunday school had grown to almost 100 scholars, and there was a female choir of around 20 voices. The Sunday school and youth work thrived. Around 1920 Mrs Clara Hann, who had spent all her working life with the Salvation Army, came to live at Kessingland. She saw the need for a new building for the Sunday school. The money for this was raised in three years, mostly by her efforts and with the help of members of the newly formed 'Sisterhood'. Two former members of the Sunday school, the Revd Harry Catchpole and the Revd Kenneth Thacker, have since become active Ministers with the Anglican Church.

Despite the enforced blackout, the evening services

The Bethel, 2000.   (PHOTOGRAPH RICHARD CATCHPOLE)

Gerald Brown and Neville Skinner with their book, 2002.

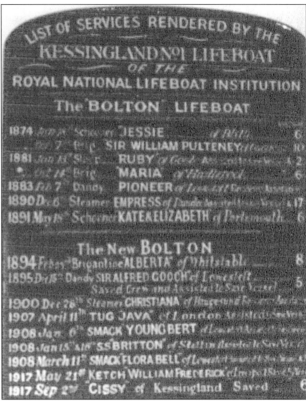

No.1 Lifeboat Record Board in Kessingland Bethel.

Exhibition in the Bethel at the launch of Gerald and Neville's book, 2002.

Pat and Gerald Brown with cheques for the Bethel and St Edmund's Church – proceeds from the first book on the war memorial, 2002.

during the First and Second World Wars were carried out as usual, although the Kessingland Friends were often called upon to take the services.

In recent years the Bethel has joined with the Anglicans and the Methodists in regular United Meetings. The RAOBs (The Buffs), whose meeting place is The Queen's Head, have helped the Bethel funds in recent years. They also attend the Bethel for their Annual Service.

The schoolroom now opens to the public most mornings, housing a comprehensive collection of Kessingland photographs and memorabilia, as well as second-hand goods, all sold for charities including MASK (the Maritime and Art Society of Kessingland), The Kessingland Working Men's Club,

The Sailors Society and the Bethel). It is run by Roy and Gerald Brown, both Bethel members. Roy, now aged 90, is still on the Parish Council and is the official beach warden, ensuring that the beach is kept free of litter.

Gerald is the village Recorder, and has produced records of all the parish births, marriages and deaths, from the registers. This is an invaluable service used by many villagers and visitors alike who are compiling their family trees. Gerald has also, in conjunction with Dr Neville Skinner, produced a book on the

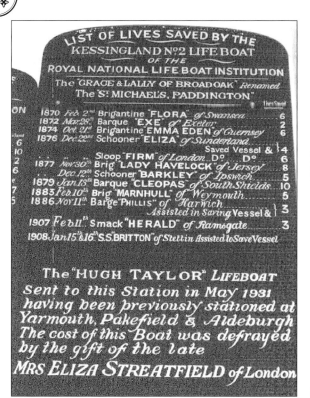

Lifeboat hero Harry Smith's framed photograph is displayed in the Bethel.

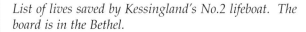

List of lives saved by Kessingland's No.2 lifeboat. The board is in the Bethel.

Above: Model of the *Welcome Home in the Bethel.*

Above left: Photograph of the Welcome Home.

"Welcome Home" - LT 256

The rudder of this model has been made from a piece of oak, which was part of the original rudder of the wooden steam-drifter "Peacemaker", LT 768, built by Richards of Lowestoft in 1911. Throughout her working life, "Peacemaker" was skippered by Alfred ("Mildew") Beamish of Kessingland. He was part owner of "Peacemaker" until 1919, when he became sole owner. His net-store, drying rails, tanning copper, etc., were situated in Green Lane, at Kessingland Beach.

Model by A.W. Thurston, a native of Kessingland.

Left: The Methodist chapel.

Left: Plaque from the model boat.

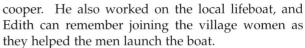

village war memorial names, which includes photographs and information on each.

A big thank you must be recorded for the local preachers who have conducted the Sunday Services throughout these last 100 years, as well as Ministers from the Lowestoft Bethel.

Personality Profile: Daisy Knights
(Taken from the *Kessingland Times*, 1993)

Daisy's large family moved from Westleton to Kessingland, where she attended school. The teachers were strict, but she had a good education and attended the Bethel Sunday School, where she sang in the choir.

Daisy enjoyed the Sunday-school outings, including a trip to Dunwich in horse-drawn wagons, singing all the way. At the end of the journey there would be fun and games and sweets, a luxury for most of the village children. Daisy particularly remembered the races.

Like many young women at that time, Daisy left school at 14 and went into the beating sheds. After she married, at 19, she earned a bit extra by mending nets at home.

Her husband was a fisherman and the couple had two sons. After her sister died at an early age, she brought up her niece. When her son Stanley died young, Daisy's strong faith carried her through her sadness, and he did leave her grandchildren. Her other son, Alan, also has children and the family is as close as ever.

Daisy lost her husband in 1963, but her faith pulled her through the bereavement. A loyal member of the Bethel, she was particularly involved in the Sisterhood meeting, being the leader for many years.

She always loved Kessingland, the countryside and sea, as well as the lovely views from the Manor Farm House windows. Daisy was loved and respected and although she has now died, today she is still remembered by her friends and fellow Bethel members with affection.

Personality Profile: Edith Dowe
(Taken from the *Kessingland Times*, 2000)

Edith Dowe watched a whole century go by. She saw everything from the invention of motor cars to man landing on the moon. Born at Kessingland on 14 May 1900, Edith (née King), remembered travelling to Pakefield by wagon. Edith was the eldest of six children, with five sisters and one brother; she outlived all of them.

Edith was interviewed on her 100th birthday, since she shared her date of birth with the late Queen Mother. Both women have since died.

Her father worked as a Kessingland sail maker and cooper. He also worked on the local lifeboat, and Edith can remember joining the village women as they helped the men launch the boat.

Being the eldest, Edith used to help her mother by doing what Edith called 'Just Jobs'. 'Mother would say 'Just run to the shop; Just wipe his nose; Just help him dress; Just set the table'. Occasionally her mother would take in lodgers as well.

Sundays were strictly days of rest.

I remember if my mother asked me to do any chores, I would say 'What? On my day of rest?' and she would reply. 'You get along and do it! What about MY day of rest?'

We went to Kessingland Bethel and my first prize for attendance was a framed text, which always hung in my bedroom. It had a picture of a little girl on a donkey and the text was: 'Kept by the power of God.' Well, I can honestly say I have been kept by His power ever since. I remember the Bethel Sunday School treats when we would have a picnic on a field. There was the Annual Bethel Tea when all the mothers would bake... The children soon realised which were the best cooks and would try to get on their favourite table.

Edith remembered Sir Henry Rider Haggard being at The Grange as he had a summerhouse near there where he used to write. One of his publishers once lodged with her mother, who also used to launder Lilias Rider Haggard's white silk blouses.

Aged 14, Edith went into service and worked for Benjamin Britten's parents. She would look after Benjamin himself, having a half-day off a week to walk home and visit her family. She took the young composer to his very first music lessons. After four years there, she worked as assistant matron at a children's home at Hedenham Hall. Another of Edith's claims to fame was that she knew Captain Sanders, who used to test his aeroplane invention on Kessingland Beach.

When she reached 26, Edith married William and moved to Marine Parade. She attended Kirkley Run Mission then before becoming a member of Lowestoft Bethel. A year after their marriage, they had a son, Ernest, who was later in the Mission choir. Edith began to do laundry for the local children's home.

And Finally...

The Bethel Church still stands as a witness to all those like Daisy and Edith who lived by their faith and their hard work to make a good life for their families. Today it is led by a descendant of the District Nurse Elizabeth O'Brien and her daughter Jane, Mr and Mrs Gerald Brown and, of course, Roy Brown.

Chapter 3

Farming

Farming and fishing had always been the two main industries in the village, before the silting up of the harbour, the Black Death and the decline of the population, and many men were involved in both, owning a small boat from which to fish from the beach as well as a parcel of land to provide food. Both world wars gave a boost to farming, when producing extra food was high priority, especially in the Second World War, when former food factories were used to produce munitions.

Although the village boasts no large house, estate or squire's seat, most of the larger houses were the centre of thriving farms, including The Grove House, now Livingstone's Restaurant and Public House, formerly the farmhouse to all the land now occupied by Kessingland Wildlife Park. It used to be three storeys high, but some time after 1917 the top storey was pulled down.

Memories of The Grove
George Swan

Some weeks ago I went for a meal at Livingstone's and very nice it was, too. Never in my wildest dreams did I think that one day I would sit in Grove House and have a meal! In my schooldays it was forbidden territory! It was owned by a Mrs Burton, the wife of the farmer at Grove Farm, opposite. After Mr Burton died, his wife and daughter Diane only came to the house in the summer time. I remember looking through the windows and seeing the furniture all covered in white dust sheets – more like Bleak House! They also owned

the meadow in White's Lane, between the house and the water-tower, known to us as Burton's Meadow, where, as lads, we played most of our football and cricket.

In about 1937 or '38, a Mr Burwood and his son, who lived at Corton, were hired to fell all but one of the trees, leaving one horse chestnut, which is still there today alongside the water-tower... The trees were literally pulled clean out of the ground, sawn up, and the roots used to fill in a pond which today is part of somebody's back garden.

Getting back to The Grove: we, as boys, when the coast was clear, would venture into the garden and scrump the apples, also take some of the medlars, bury them in an airtight tin, then go back to eat them later. You don't see medlars around today, but they are small brown apple-like fruit, which are eaten when decayed. I only knew of two medlar trees in the vicinity. This one was at The Grove, the other in Billy Bunn's orchard, way down the footpath, past the Loke (renamed The Avenue now).

After my recent meal at Livingstone's, I stood and looked around, remembering the Crinkly Crankly wall. (There was a similar one in Wash Lane, near the Rectory.) The beautiful Grove House gardens now a car park, but I walked up to the big beech tree, which stands in the grounds at the front and there I saw the initials of some of the lads cut into the bark, and marks where we would cut out a hole with our penknives and insert a halfpenny, preferably with that year's date on it. This all happened 65 years ago.

At the back of the restaurant, I looked across to where the Wildlife Park is and where a car boot sale is

An early picture of The Grove, revealing its original three storeys.

Livingstone's Restaurant, formerly The Grove, 2005.

held. At the front, looking across the main road, there is a new housing development. I wondered what Mrs Burton would have thought of all this...

Maureen Long also has memories of The Grove:

When my parents Fred and Dolly Bligh bought Mrs Lockwood's (formerly Layton's) shop on the corner of the Market Place in 1948, The Grove was owned by Mr and Mrs Waller, who kept the large restaurant and tearooms at Oulton Broad. As they were Methodists, the young people of the church were often at The Grove, where Mr and Mrs Cottingham and their daughter Beryl lived. Mr Cottingham ran Grove Farm for Mr Waller, who would attend the Methodist Church Harvest Festival Monday evening event each year to auction off the produce. This was an hilarious fun-filled occasion, after a short service, when small things could be run up to big amounts, all for the good of the cause. Mr Waller was always very generous to the church, where Beryl Cottingham was a member. She often invited the young people of the church to Grove House, where her mother cooked a beautiful meal, served in lovely china and silver. Beryl later married Ivan Davis the thatcher at Mutford, but sadly died at quite a young age.

The Grove was later turned into a public house, but before then it was the home of the late Mr and Mrs Wright. After her husband's death, Mrs Wright spoke to the *Kessingland Times*, recalling how she came to be living in her chalet bungalow just inside the gates of the Suffolk Wildlife Park, which she and her late husband, Laurence, founded in the 1960s. When deciding where to build their house, she chose the view she wanted from her balcony by climbing a ladder on top of a truck.

It was hard to envisage the house then, let alone where I wanted the garden, but since cattle were grazing here, the site obviously had to be fenced off and plans drawn. We had already obtained planning permission for the original site, but the view settled it.

Beryl, who came from farming stock on her mother's side and loved living again in the country, met Laurence when her mother rented a house in Saham owned by his father. When the couple eventually married, they farmed next door to Saham Grove and later at Fulmodestone, where Laurence already had the agricultural and motor engineering business, being a Ford agent. Later, when they sold Southgates (of Fakenham), they rented a house in Somerleyton for a while, as they looked at various places before buying Kessingland Grove House and Farm in 1954. Always looking ahead and sensing new developments, they came here because of the trend for growing for the fast-freeze industry. As well as seasonal jobs in the three holiday camps, women especially were needed

for bean-stringing, fruit-picking, etc., while the men had all the overtime they wanted with giant pea-viners becoming a fascinating sight on the fields. Four hours between farm and freezer meant sometimes working by artificial light to get the peas to the factory. They also grew late potatoes.

The original holding of 320 acres purchased, was mainly dairy, including third-class grazing and valueless sedge marshes, but the local drainage board planned to install a pumping system to drain the marshland. The Wrights seized the opportunity: the first two winters were spent laying pipes and under-draining the marshes, all by their own staff. In the summer of 1960 they were able to acquire 2,000 yards of a large disused council water main, already installed across the full width of the farm, which eventually gave them a complete irrigation system. The 70-strong dairy herd grazed on the reclaimed marshes in the summer and on by-products of the vegetables grown for freezing in winter.

As their two sons, Richard and John, finished agricultural college, Laurence decided to hand over the reins to John. Richard was already farming three adjacent farms they had bought in Barnby and Mutford. The couple were much too active to retire and, with the same farsightedness, watched with

One of the park's first postcards.

Mrs Beryl Wright in 1991, first owner and founder, with her husband, Laurence, of Kessingland Wildlife Park.

interest as friend Philip Wayre started the Norfolk Wildlife Park – so popular that visitors crowded it out every opening day. Many local people flocked there, although it was some distance away.

Laurence and Beryl opened a Wildlife Park at Kessingland and the first lion cub born there was named Kessy. Since then the Park, the first to be recognised by the Countryside Commission, has also catered for those who want to picnic or relax in the countryside.

After Laurence died, the Park was sold. Beryl, with the same attitude of overcoming difficulties and adapting to new circumstances which had carried her through as the wife of such an active and far-sighted farmer, now had to rebuild her life. She began to take foreign holidays with a school friend, eventually going to Australia; she started swimming; she enjoyed dressmaking and gardening and keeping up with six active grandchildren.

Always active in village life, Beryl often opened the Methodist Church Bazaar and provided the milk for that and other Church events whilst dairy farming. When asked if she had ever thought of moving from Kessingland, Beryl said, 'No... this is my home. All my family and friends are in East Anglia and I love it. Apart from that, I chose the view!' She died in 1999.

Today son John farms at Henstead, whilst The Grove is now Livingstone's Restaurant. The Wildlife Park, now owned by Banham Zoo, goes from strength to strength.

The Ark

Opposite The Grove, The Ark (right) is reputed to be the oldest house in Kessingland. The property housed farm labourers, and belonged to Grove Farm. Mr John Adams lived there, as did Billy Bird and his mother during the Second World War. Elsie Bullock, one of the village's oldest residents, spoke to the *Kessingland Times* just before her ninetieth birthday, claiming, 'I have had a very happy life, in spite of all the hard times and I don't regret any of it. I've a wonderful family who help me.'

Elsie was born at Oaklands Terrace, where she lived for most of her life. Her father, a fisherman, had been born at the beach end of the village, at High Path, and her mother came from Yarmouth. Elsie was one of seven children (four boys, three girls).

She attended Kessingland Upper School when Mr Storm was headmaster and enjoyed her strict schooldays, leaving at age 13 to go into service. But those last few months of schooldays were exciting! A young man, Arthur Bullock, moved into the house next door, No. 19, and even though he was nearly six years older, they had eyes only for each other.

I used to rush home from school at dinner time... and at first we looked out for each other. He worked at Moat

Farm (opposite Ashley Nursery) and we tried to walk home and back together, but we wasted time sometimes missing each other, so we devised a secret system. If I didn't see a stone on the top of the big white stone pillar at the farm gate, I would put a stone on top myself. Then Arthur would know I had passed and would hurry to catch me up. Or I would run to catch him up. Neither of us ever had anyone else, and we had a long and happy married life, bringing up seven children...

We went to Sunday school at the church, and mother always asked if we'd called to see Dad's mother, our Granny. She lived in a small black house which could only be called a hut, like a bed-sitter, near the Four Dwellers in White's Lane (now the site of Badger's Holt). It always amazed us how she managed there, but she did. Money was short and there were hard times, but everyone looked after each other and shared what little there was...

After leaving school Elsie worked at Cliff House, near Kensington Gardens, the home of the family who owned the Tuttles Department Store in Lowestoft.

I was there for six and a half years, until my father died and I had to go home to help my mother... We wore blue uniforms in the morning for the housework and maroon ones in the afternoon for the lighter duties. Mrs Tuttle was very good to me, often asking her sons to bring home some towels or other household items for me, as I was engaged to Arthur. When we eventually married when I was 20, I had all my linen, gifts from my mistress who appreciated what I did for her...

The bus fare was 5 pence return but we couldn't afford it. The trams ran in the town, but we mostly walked. I had every other Sunday off, but I had to go back at 4 to get afternoon tea, so Arthur would walk back with me from Kessingland, along the cliffs, and when I had finished tea duty we would meet in Kensington Gardens.

Her father had sailed with Mouse Catchpole and Ritson Tripp before joining the Navy, where he was blown up and injured in a submarine. He died aged 49. Elsie married Arthur and moved into No. 19 Oaklands with her in-laws. Her mother went out to work, so Elsie spent her time next door at No. 20, keeping house for her and cooking for the family.

Arthur was aged seven when his family had moved from Geldeston to live at The Ark.

Kessingland was mostly country then. You could walk across the fields from Field Lane to the church, across two stiles. There was the Beach village and the Street. Now there's hardly a green space to be found.

Arthur worked at Gisleham brickworks after the farm work. He was happy there, working with the large brick kilns, until one day a strong wind blew sparks out, which damaged one eye and made him totally blind in the other; he had to give up work.

The Ark was left empty for a number of years, until the site at the end of the High Street was redeveloped, when the owner modernised it. Although it retains its outward appearance, it is obviously very different from when it held the basic necessities for two farm labourers' families. It is commemorated in the adjoining area, Ark Close. The rest of the development has been named Noah's Drive and Heritage Green, so that the history will not be forgotten.

Harvests of the Past
Written by Billy Shipley,
Iris Morphew contributed this story

Harvest over, but the work goes on. There is no respite on the farm, Scot and Beauty the two bay mares, their foals forgotten, plough out the potatoes. In the next field a tractor-plough turns over the stubble, two furrows at a time. From a lofty pulpit at the top of the tall thatching ladder leaning against the roof of the barley stack, Bill surveys the busy scene, in his hand a thatching combe, leather pads on his knees. His assistant the boy Kenny, staggers up the ladder with a bunch of wheat straw bigger than himself. It's not just anybody's job, this thatching. Skilfully, methodically, strip by strip, Bill covers the stack with its golden wig of straw, and what more attractive sight than a line of neat ricks in a trim stackyard, each well built, well groomed, well thatched, the substantial products of a year's labour, the symbols of prosperity.

Bill, perched on his ladder, never pausing in his work, has something to say to every passer-by. It may be the village blacksmith, here to take a troublesome nail out of the old mare's foot, or the cowmen from the next farm, taking a short cut through the fields. Even the schoolchildren, attracted by the arrival of another huge load of wheat straw, stop to watch the thatching in progress. They stand and stare at Kenny as he throws pailfuls of water over the pile of straw, pulls it out in double handfuls, combs it into neat bundles with his nimble fingers, 'Wireworms', says Bill, in response to the blacksmith's grumbles. 'There is only one way to kill a wireworm. An ancient remedy.' A new discovery? Hopefully, we await the explanation. 'Only one way', repeats Bill. 'And that is to wait until he is lying asleep with his head on a stone, and then run the rib-roll over him.'

Never have the thatchers been busier. On many farms two stacks now stand where only one stood before. In bulk, or crop, if not in threshed-out weight of grain, the harvest has been a record one. In the village church great preparations are afoot. The Harvest Thanksgiving Service. Decorative sheaf-knots of corn, huge pumpkins and marrows, piles of fruit, pyramids of vegetables... there is thanksgiving in many hearts, in Bill's too, as he slowly descends the ladder, another stack thatched, another store of precious corn made safe. Let wintry winds and weather do what they will; Bill has pegged it well.

So he and his mate light up a fag and say, 'Thank the Lord we have done!'

Today there are fewer farmers, but Mr Podd still farms the Manor Farm land, Michael and Stephen Guymer operate at the Lowestoft end of the village, although their farm was sliced in half by the A12 bypass, when much of their land was bought under a compulsory purchase order. This meant that their milk production was no longer viable, as they were left with not enough pasture on the milking parlour side of the bypass. They had lost land earlier due to compulsory purchase when the Kessingland Playing-Field came into existence.

Such are the hazards of modern farming and those sons of the soil struggling on need to be appreciated.

Ponds
George Swan, July 2003

The ponds that have been filled in that I remember include the one at the end of the road leading down to the Heathland's Caravan Park. I remember once the families that lived in the Oaklands filling their buckets from the pond for their washing. Then there were two ponds across the footpath running from Field Lane to the St Edmund's Church. They are now somewhere under the Lloyds estate. The one nearest the church was where the working horses quenched their thirst after a day's work. Two more that have gone were on Grove Farm. The other, having just recently been filled, was beside the A12 and in front of the Ark. This was also known as the Horse Pond.

Another pond still here, although neglected, is in front of Pond Farm, aptly named and was once owned by a Mr Ong. I remember being a lad when this pond flooded after a very heavy storm. Some of us lads were catching sticklebacks on the main road.

The pond between Grove House (now called Livingstone's) and the Barn Road on the meadow known as 'the lawn', is where the chapel used to have Sunday school treats. In this pond there were goldfish put there by Miss Diana Burton, whose father owned The Grove Farm and house. So many lads had goldfish in their sweet jars as pets. This is where I spent many happy hours in summer catching newts, many of which were the great crested ones much talked about today. In the winter, when the pond was frozen over, we would run and slide from one bank to the other after making sure it was safe.

Then at fourteen I started work on the farm where lots of ponds had fish in them. It was then I saw the one and only wild otter... I often wish the children of today could experience some of the happiness we had as children.

Chapter 4

Shooting the Nets for the Silver Darlings: Living with the Sea

Fishing

Fishing has been a major industry throughout Kessingland's history. The associated tasks of net-making and mending, rope-making, barrel and fish box construction have also been predominant. When the 1950s saw the emergence of the fast-freeze industry, the Bird's Eye factory at Lowestoft gave employment to both men and women, producing frozen fish, fish fingers, fish cakes and the like.

There have been two fishing peaks for the village: one when Kessingland Harbour was a thriving port in medieval times, and again when the harbour at Lowestoft was built and opened in 1831, which led to fishermen walking from Kessingland to work on the old sailing boats, the drifters and later the steam trawlers. There were many who went on to become skippers, share owners and then owners and boat-builders – men such as 'Mouse' Catchpole, 'Friday' Beamish, 'Rock' Curtis, Arthur Beamish, C. and R. Harvey and William Tripp. Most Kessingland fishermen had far from flattering nicknames and such was their strength and staying power that they were regarded as the best the nation could produce. In the seventeenth century they became known as 'The Roaring Boys of Suffolk'. This nickname came from their occupation. In the days before ice became the method of keeping the fish fresh from the sea to the market, they were sprinkled with salt, especially the herring catch. The piles of fish were turned over with a 'roaring shovel', the job was called 'roaring' and the men who did it were therefore 'roaring boys'. It was tough wresting a living from the powerful sea, and those who fought it had to be tough too. The Roaring Boys were synonymous with courage, stamina and physical strength.

With the great herring bonanza of the early-twentieth century, prosperity returned to the area. Kessingland became known as 'Klondyke' and dubbed 'the richest village in England'. Peter Cherry has recorded much more of the village's fishing history in his book of that name.

Herring was prolific, cheap and even free if you went to the fish market at Lowestoft, or Kessingland Beach when the boats came in. You could pick up all you needed. All those slopped out of baskets on to the fish-market ground could be taken. They were easy to cook, but to get a variety of meals, they were fried, smoked, 'kippered' and baked (often in vinegar and pickling spice to preserve them for longer). The kitchens of most houses in the village, whether

An old boat on Kessingland Beach.

(PHOTOGRAPH RICHARD CATCHPOLE)

Fishermen's winch, Kessingland Beach, 2000. Sadly, the old 'beach furniture' has been cleared from the beach.

cottage or large residence, would smell of fish cooking at most meals. It was the same on the boats, with herring for breakfast, maybe again for dinner or supper. Meat was more expensive and did not keep as long during longer sea voyages, before the days of refrigeration.

Fishermen gained a reputation for the number of herring they could eat at a sitting. A Fraserborough man had set a 'record' of eating a dozen kippers in 15 minutes, but local men decided to beat that, since they regularly had as many each for breakfast! It is said that Amos Beamish, the 'Barnby Giant', an enormous man from a neighbouring village, had eaten

Kessingland fishermen: a busy day, c.1910.

Sea Row and the Lifeboat Shed.

100 spring herring at one meal for a bet. He too sailed out of Lowestoft – no doubt with a reinforced bunk for his bulk!

There were fishing 'seasons' and the autumn herring fishing was the heaviest for local men. Scots fishermen came to Lowestoft and Great Yarmouth as well, with their wives and daughters, the 'Scots Girls', gutting and packing the catch. The Scots fleet, like many local owners, did not go to sea on a Sunday, hence the large attendance at the Lowestoft and Kessingland Bethels for worship. At Great Yarmouth, only 50 or 60 years ago, it was possible to walk across the River Yare by stepping from one boat to the next on a Sunday, as they piled into the harbour on a Saturday and filled every available space. One elderly lady remembers how every bus or tram smelt of fish for months, because the fishermen and Scots girls used public transport to and from the harbour and fish market.

Those in the area who supplemented their income in the summer season by taking in tourists for bed and breakfast, would take in the fisher-girls during the autumn, while the men were away to the fishing grounds. Alternatively, local men would travel around the coast, following the seasonal fish catches, meeting up with other fishermen they knew at Scottish ports, as well as those in the south.

The village retains a few of the netting sheds, used for net-making and mending and many older women still have their needles and tools used in earlier careers. Many girls went straight from school to mending and making nets. Today the remaining netting sheds are used by businesses for storage, offices, the motor trade and some have even been turned into residential property. They were large wooden buildings, probably cold in winter when the work was prolific. Some women made or mended nets at home and many children would occupy themselves after school during winter evenings by filling the spools with string from massive balls that the owners would drop off to the houses. The Second World War brought even more work for them in the form of camouflage nets for the Army and Navy.

There were many tanning coppers around the village, where the nets were soaked in cutch (or catechu, an astringent resinous substance derived from South Asian plants, used in medicine and for dyeing and tanning) for preservation, then set out to dry on drying grounds, to make them strong and preserve them from the salt water. These were outdoor versions of the old-fashioned indoor copper. Reeds were also grown for the osiers to gather and make into baskets. The fishing industry used thousands of basketware skips, usually holding a cran (37.5 gallons) of herring.

At a meeting of the Maritime and Art Society of Kessingland, Ingrid Utting gave an interesting and informative talk on net-making and mending:

If you've complained about smelly socks in your dirty washing basket, spare a thought for the wives of Kessingland fishermen earlier this century. Men would often be away for long spells, following the fish to Scotland, Cornwall, Devon, etc. They would pack and sew up their smelly fishy 'shiftings' (clothing to the uninitiated) in hessian bags and post back home for laundering. Bags as well had to be washed before the clean clothes were posted back.

Ingrid once worked in one of the 20 or so beating sheds in Kessingland after she left school. Even when she started work, the fishing industry was past its heyday and after two years she went on to become first a dentist's receptionist, and later to work in the surgery.

After the Second World War about 150–200 Lowestoft boats and 150 Scottish ones worked from the port. Eight nets would be let down from each boat. Joined together they stretched from one and a half to two miles long.

Beating and Beatsters
By George Swan, 2002

The small herring net needles were used by beatsters, who either worked at the beating sheds or chambers or sometimes at home. My mother was one of them.

Left: *Beatsters outside a beating shed, early 1900s.* Left to right: *Mr and Mrs Knivett, Miss Hart, Mrs Studd, ?, C. Smith.*

Below: *The interior of St Edmund's Church during a Harvest of the Sea service.*

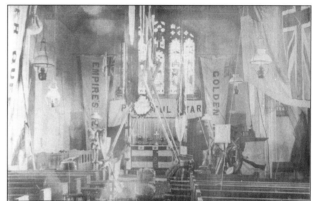

Left: *The beach in the 1950s.*

She would hang the net from the cupboard door handle, helped by my father, who would fill the needles from a ball of tanned cotton. Some weeks she could mend two nets: it all depended how badly they were ripped. For each mended net she was paid, I think, five shillings when Mr Jack Catchpole collected them on a Saturday.

The other beatsters, as I mentioned, worked at the beating sheds, which were situated all over the village, and most still exist today, but sadly not for mending herring nets. One is down Marsh Lane and Mr John Briggs the builder uses it for his workshop, like the one in Church Road belonging to the Brock builders business.

There was another one situated alongside the road, near to where the MASK shop is today. Incidentally, this is where, as young lads, we would go to the pictures. A man would bring his projector on his bike and charge us tuppence to get in. So for three-pence you could watch a film, they were silent and black and white...

Other beating chambers were: in White's Lane at the back of Wily Harvey's house and others in Chapel Road (now Church Road). Adjoining the ones in Church Road were the drying grounds which were posts with strong wire between where the nets were hung out to dry after being tanned. I can only recall one tanning copper, where the nets were tanned...

The number of beating sheds and the number of people employed was due to the many drifters sailing and fishing from Lowestoft, with each boat allowed to 'shoot' or cast I believe one hundred and one nets...

My mother, also along with many other women, made camouflage nets during the war as part of their war effort. Sadly, beating a net is no longer a skilled job on the scale that it once was when the herring was plentiful...

Fishermen are very superstitious and locally they wore no green-coloured clothing, no parsons nor pigs were allowed on board (so pork was off the menu whilst at sea). Local shops which stocked packs of socks in mixed colours would have to sell the green ones off in the January sales – usually to girls when the jeans era arrived.

But in spite of warding off all these signs of bad luck, fishing was a dangerous life. Apart from the obvious risk of drowning at sea because of storms, shipwreck, forgotten enemy mines and the like, there were also accidents on board, with scalds from the galley, burns from the hot utensils and injuries from using sharp knives to clean and prepare fish.

Personality Profile: Colin Burrows
(Taken from a 1993 interview by Lewis Watling, a founder member of Kessingland Writers)

Colin was ten years old when, in the late 1950s, he first fished for Dover sole in the Humber with his Yorkshire-born father. At 14 he was 'pleasuring' with his uncle, and then went to Iceland as galley-boy in the *Stella Canopis* for three weeks, repeating the experience in the *Ross Proycon* a year later.

Whilst working on the *Lochinver*, he found himself hauling nets with insufficient help, and lost the fingers of his left hand in the gallows of the ship's fore-door. He also suffered a crushed elbow and ripped muscles. The injuries landed him in Iceland's North Fiord Hospital for six weeks. Upon his return, Hillier Brothers, owners of the *Lochinver*, arranged for him to see their company doctor, who diagnosed gangrene, and he was despatched to St James's Hospital in Leeds for special treatment to remove the

View of Kessingland Beach.

Yawls on the beach.

Boats at rest, Kessingland Beach.

dead flesh. He received compensation, and rehabilitation followed in Chamberlain Road, Hull, but he was told he would never go to sea again.

Restless and dissatisfied, Colin heard that a tar-jump was wanted urgently by the *Loch Eriboll*, and immediately applied. He was allowed to work at gutting, but couldn't haul wire. The chief engineer suggested he serve in the engine-room, but he didn't like the pervading smell of oil; and radio communications proved not to be his line.

He therefore became a cook and worked for two years as galley-boy. For a further nine months he assisted Billy Adams, who was cook on the trawler *D.B. Finn*, and took charge of the galley during Billy's leave of absence. He went on to cooks' school in Hull from 1968–69.

Fishermen at work.

Success as a cook launched Colin on a full-time sea career. He was with Hellier Brothers' *Ross Orion* when it broke the world record with a catch worth £64,000, and later with Newington's *C.F. Forrester* when it broke the record with a £114,000 catch off Iceland. Then he was sacked for being drunk.

Sidewinder trawlers gradually gave way to freezer ships, to which Colin transferred as second cook, making trips to Iceland and Greenland.

Long distance fishing in the *Boston Lincoln* as far as Bear Island, Newfoundland, followed, and on a trip to the Falklands Colin and his fellow crewmen were rewarded with catches of 14 tons of fish in two months. He had been back at sea in the *Westella* for two days when he lost the end of his index finger on his right hand. No heroics; he'd been trying to knock down a tin which had been holding a skylight open. Once again he required hospital treatment, this time in Aberdeen.

After stints on the Norwegian factory ship the *Nor Global*, followed by the *Neuf Christiansen*, Colin returned to trawlers, which brought him to Colne Shipping in Lowestoft, who helped him to find a home nearby. He was able to save enough from his share of catches to buy his own 18 footer and, with the help of various shore jobs, became self-employed with a home in Kessingland. In the late 1980s, while he was away in Hull where his father had died, his boat was smashed in Lowestoft docks. The partner who had joined him in the venture was unable to finance his share of repairs, so Colin went back to beam-enders, intending to save and start again. Incredibly, perhaps, his love of the sea remains.

Passing the Time at Sea

There are long, sometimes boring hours at sea in some weathers, so some men make models out of almost anything lying around. One old salt made wonderful models of boats from shells he had collected all over the world. Others 'whittle' away at a piece of wood, carving small animals, or engraving letters onto wood. Roy Brown has a wooden plaque of the Lord's Prayer beautifully carved by an elderly fisherman ancestor. Another occupation to keep spirits up was to sing sea shanties or compose rhymes. Here is one that Roy taught to several members of the Maritime and Art Society of Kessingland:

Longshoreman's Rhyme (c.1933)

Listen awhile while in rhyme I will preach,
About all the Longshoremen at Kessingland Beach:
There's Lonnie and Ronnie and poor old 'Brick',
Who's only needed when the fish they are thick;
'Bucko' and Watson in Eight Eighty One,
With Teddy as Skipper, they all weigh a ton!
Lewis and Kitty, when their engine is chronic
Go out in a small boat they call the 'Bionic'.
There's 'Hips' and 'Ribs' in a creaky old boat –
They have to keep bailing to keep her afloat!
Bob, 'Ginger' and 'Woopy' are young Brownie's crew.
They hang onto their nets until all else is blue.
'Buller' and Bill and 'Caravan Joe',
Who slept in a tent and never said 'No'.
'Scrub' and 'Boy Fred', a couple of rummuns,
They warmed their magneto in Miss Taylor's oven.
'Huffis' and 'Yorkie' both fond of a chow
Their hauling hid at it when it comes to a blow.
Tommy' and 'Monkey' in a very big boat,
They have to shove hard to get her afloat.
George Harvey goes out in a boat called 'Handy'
You always know him, 'cos his legs are bandy.
These rhymes were written for me and for you.
If you don't like them, you know what to do!

Memories of the Fishing Industry
By Gerald Brown

There are times, particularly in October and early November when there is a sharpness in the air in the mornings and my thoughts turn back to the late 1940s and early '50s when the autumn fishing was still a big event. I remember that I used to stand on the corner of the Lowestoft fish market near the sale ring, watching the drifters unloading their catches. Then I would hear the sound of the hand-bell, rung by Arthur Mitchell and hearing him call out 'Herring buyers! Herring buyers!' meaning that the herring sale was about to begin in the sale room. Once the drifters had landed their catch, they went back to sea again, leaving only the odd herring on the lower landing for the gulls to pick up. The noise, hustle and bustle, comings and goings held a deep fascination for me then, and it remains with me still even though those days are long gone...

I remember getting up at four in the morning while still dark and walking down to [Kessingland] Beach with a bag which had a flask of tea and sandwich in it,

to herring catch with my uncle 'Hurricane' Hutch Brown, and great uncle Alfie. I remember pushing off from the beach (it was nearer the sea wall then) and seeing all the lights of the other longshore boats all around us, then shooting the nets 'in the name of the Lord'. Slowly the daylight used to come into the sky, then we hauled the nets into the boat full of the 'silver darlings', then coming ashore, boxing the catch, then loading them on Mr Manthorpe's lorry and home for dinner. Kessingland Beach in those days still had quite a number of boats, and a fair number of families depended on the fishing industry, both deep sea and longshore. Those members of the older generation can no doubt remember when Lowestoft Harbour used to be full with drifters from all the little ports down the east coast of Scotland, and how the town was swarming with the Scots fishermen and fisher-girls who used to gut and pack the herring into barrels for export to the continent. Happy memories!

Personality Profile: Roy Brown

You name it, Roy's done it – from chatting with Princess Anne, reading a Bible lesson from a boat off Kessingland for the BBC's *Songs of Praise*, ballroom dancing, amateur boxing, supervising Kessingland's Home Guard, helping found the Yacht Club, being auctioneer for Harvest Festival Sales and 50-50 auctions, MC at numerous village functions, metal detecting, boat-building, photography, council duties and raising money for the Shipwrecked Mariners Society, to name just some! He played bowls for Suffolk County for several years, winning the English Bowling Federation Championship at Skegness. He is a trustee of The Help-in-Need Trust and a former chairman of the boatshed committee. A hobby is collecting old photographs and documents, particularly to do with boats, and he is the longest-standing member of the Working Men's Club.

His only son, Gerald, a most knowledgeable genealogist, has helped trace their ancestry here back to 1570. Durrants Close is so-called after his grandmother's family. One of his proud possessions is the little wooden house, Woodcot, a former netting shed standing on the Cliffs; it was moved on large rollers

Clearing up after the 1934 storms.

to its present position. His grandmother raised 12 children in the house.

Roy was educated at the Beach School and the 'top' school in Church Road. He represented Suffolk in the All-England Athletic championships at Stanford Bridge and played football for Lowestoft Town Schoolboys. Leaving school aged 14 and serving a seven-year apprenticeship in a Lowestoft shipyard, he spent his entire working life building ships, eventually becoming foreman shipwright and chief safety officer. He acted as chief adviser to the Excelsior Trust, hence his meeting the Princess Royal.

Roy has come from a family of Bethel members and is himself one of the present trustees, as well as the longest-serving parish councillor.

Roy's closest dice with death came one Sunday morning as he stood on the deck of a minesweeper in Lowestoft Harbour. A German bomber flew low, dropping bombs on the fish market and killing ten men, including Bertie Thacker, a fellow Bethel member. Roy shouted to the sailors to go below. All obeyed bar the one standing next to him, who tried to man the gun and fire back. It was too late and he was killed outright, but Roy's shout saved the other lives.

Roy was Home Guard sergeant and recruited Kessingland fishermen of all ages to become nimble-footed 'soldiers' on sten-gun duty. He took on this onerous task after three weeks' training in Dunmow,

Fisherman's wooden cottage belonging to the Brown family. It is still in existence.

The Brown family, early 1900s.

Essex, and was then in charge of his 'Dads' Army' and their huge naval guns on the requisitioned Holiday Fellowship Camp grounds.

He married Hazel and they have two grandchildren, who love to listen to his stories, such as going to the Kinnodrome in London Road, shouting and singing to himself all the way through Wash Lane to stop his terror of the notorious 'ghost' on the dark path past the Old Rectory. The Kinnodrome drew boys like a magnet, in spite of the imagined horrors of the journey. After an evening of 'Elmo the Mighty', who was afraid of an old ghost on the way home?

He also boxed at the Rothesay Hall and wanted to turn professional but injured his thumb and lost that opportunity.

Now retired, aged 91 in 2006, Roy is the beach warden, and spends many mornings out with his metal detector. His interesting albums of photographs and cuttings chronicle a life brimming with love, past and present, a wonderful legacy to pass down through a family who share his zest for the present and his fascination with the past.

Personality Profile: George Knights
(Taken from a 1992 interview)

The late George Knights described himself as being 'Like an old ship... gone below the water line!'. As he got older his legs started to let him down, but his arms were as strong as when he was hauling ropes and nets aboard. His brain was keen as when he was guiding his ship into harbour or through perilous seas.

Although he travelled the world, he maintained that England was his favourite country and of course Kessingland the best place to live! He was born here in 1903 and went to Kessingland school, leaving at nearly 13 and going to sea at 14. That began a career of 52 years on the ocean waves, mostly fishing around the Irish Sea, with a break of six years in minesweepers and patrol vessels during the war. He need not have joined the Navy, since he was helping produce the nation's food, but volunteered and saw more of the world as a result.

As a boy at Kessingland school, he won an essay competition. He had to write a letter to Admiral Sir John Jellicoe, which Headmaster Mr Storm regarded as so good that he sent it to the Naval legend. George received a signed letter back, which resulted in George's picture in the local papers.

George's association with Kessingland's literary celebrity was, however, limited to scrumping apples from Rider Haggard's orchard, which ran down the north side of Rider Haggard Lane!

'I suppose I was one of the rough 'uns... I had more fights at school than Henry Cooper!' remembered George.

When the Navy was preparing a fleet of craft to invade Japan and George was in Australia, he met

Top and above: *Lookout sheds on Kessingland Beach.*

Reggie Killington of Kessingland, whom he knew well and who had left the sea to join the Australian Fire Service, at much higher pay. He also saw his own nephew walking towards him one morning! Neither knew the other was there. He met and used to breakfast with, after a night on duty, a young Lieutenant, Jack France, son of the coastguard who married Mildred Coy, whose family kept the Beach Post Office. They swapped memories of home.

George's heaviest catch was a German torpedo. 'It had been dropped to hit a ship, but missed... next trip I trawled it up and we landed it at Fleetwood.'

Twice George narrowly escaped death, when just after he had left a Naval ship for another, it was blown up.

Some say I was lucky. Well, in the war I was... but as for fishing, if I did well it was proficiency. I've known skippers who slept while the men worked, but I always guided my ship through myself, snatching sleep before we got to perilous seas, especially in the Irish Sea, where you often get a boiling sea and need to know the dips and highs. Once I woke to hear that the ship drove 'heavy'. No wonder, the hold was nearly full of water, but the bulkheads held. We limped to Llandudno Harbour, where we were pumped out, to find one rivet missing. We plugged the hole with a bit off a broom handle and came safely back to Fleetwood, for repair.

Lifeboats and Lighthouses

Personality Profile: Cock Robin
(Taken from a 1997 interview by Chris Barker, a member of Kessingland Writers)

Stanley 'Cock Robin' Brown was a legend in his own lifetime, who referred to himself as 'one of the old village relics!' Sadly, he died just two weeks after the interview. He explained the origin of his name:

During the First World War we were told to set traps to catch sparrows, because they ate so much grub, but we caught robins so I wouldn't set no more. I rather liked robins. We caught rats too. Cut the tail off a rat and you got tuppence for that.

His father was one of a large family born in Kessingland and he had a sister who was killed in a motoring accident.

Ten boys and three girls, the Brown family. There's a little wooden cottage, Woodcot, opposite the fish shop, that's where my father lived. All the boys went to war, in the Navy, and all came back, the only family that did.

Stanley himself had a close shave when on Lowestoft Docks, after training as a sheet-metal worker during the Second World War:

I was working on a trawler in the harbour and an enemy bomber, going over very high, dropped its load of bombs. One of them landed in the trawler's engine room without going off. None of them went off for some reason. Lucky for me.

Stanley was awarded a medal after he found a man, who was building a well, trapped at the bottom when it collapsed. 'He was covered with mud. I cleared the dirt away from his face and stayed with him for 17 hours until he could be dug out. It did seem a long time.'

Stanley's father served on the lifeboat:

My father, Arthur Brown, and all the brothers did... There were several boats over the years. One was given by a Surrey doctor who was blind. We had two boats from the Bolton people, it was with public subscription that they were bought for us. They were Bolton I and Bolton II... The first Bolton boat, before my time, she turned over and they had to cut a hole in the bottom to get the people out. In the end only one man was lost, Tripp his name, was only 26. He's buried next to the path in Kessingland churchyard. They bought us another new boat after that. That would be before the First World War.

We had a lifeboat here before the Institute was started. In the 1800s the fishermen got together and bought a boat from Southwold for 45 quid. That saved lives. There was no power in those days, all sail. It was a rough life...

Launching the lifeboat was a community affair:

We pushed it. They had a long rope out to sea with an anchor on and they'd pull it off with that. Nearly everyone in the village helped... Six pairs of oars, each oar about 18 foot long. The rowers sat waist deep in water for hours. There was a sail too. But lives were lost, beachmen and lifeboat men... The boat that was in distress put a rocket up and the coastguards spotted it. There was a lookout on the cliffs, day and night.

Stanley could recall the excitement after the famous rescue by the crew of the *St Paul*, lifeboat at Kessingland between 1897 and 1931, of the fishing smack *AJW* in 1919:

All the crew went to the Hippodrome at Lowestoft to receive their medals, the mayor gave it to them, but the coxswain, old George 'Tubby' Knights, and others... all received medals for different acts of bravery, they had to go to London... they met lots of different people: the King was there and Sir Ernest Shackleton, the explorer, you know? He sat near Knights, and he said, 'Excuse me, Coxswain, but your badge on your hat is sewn on upside down.' 'Is it?' Knights says. 'Well, my old gal she don't know any different.' So he cut it off and pinned it on with a safety pin for the rest of the time!

That was right after the First World War, December 1919. When that rescue took place, there were two boats launched from Lowestoft, one each from Pakefield, Southwold and Kessingland. All were looking for this smack from Rye, but they couldn't find it because it was blowing a gale of wind and snow. It was on the bottom, but they couldn't see it, it was on a sandbank. The Kessingland boat, they were just going about, to go round on the other tack... Well, when they were doing this, my Uncle Rue heard this fellow shouting from this wreck. He says, 'We must be right close to them, 'cos I can hear 'em lathering.' So they shout back, but they can't see them. So the lifeboatmen figured out where they were, with head wind and ebb tide sea, and got so far in and dropped an anchor and they paid out on this rope, and they let the wind and tide blow 'em down, right onto the wreck. They took the men off; they were lashed up there in the rigging, snow and ice on them. A good bit of seamanship.

Many of the Kessingland families were involved with the lifeboat. 'It was a part of the village. There's the Smiths, the Uttings, Catchpoles, Wiggs. Lots more.'

The beach has since been built up between the sea and sea wall. Stanley recalled the boat being pulled to the sea from the lifeboat shed:

A hundred yards or so it was then. The lifeboat shed used to be where the amusements are now. But there was a gale of wind that wrecked the lifeboat shed and damaged the lifeboat, that was in 1936, so they had to take the boat away. Lowestoft had a motor boat then, so they covered Kessingland from there. It was a big loss to Kessingland though, people were upset, that was a big part of village life gone. Good days to look back on though.

In his 1937 book *Storm Warriors of the Suffolk Coast*, Ernest Read Cooper pronounces G. 'Gaffer' Strowger as 'the most celebrated of the Kessingland coxswains... who retired before 1911, after having earned the Silver Medal and Clasp for long service.'

Generations on Call
(Taken from an interview with Betty Wigg by Chris Barker)

Mrs Betty Wigg has lived in the same house nearly all her married life. It is one of the cottages within reach of sand and spray from Kessingland Beach, a true beachman's home, at the narrowest part of Church Road. Husband and father-in-law are among members of the Wigg family that served on the Kessingland lifeboat.

Mr Edward Wigg senr (Betty's father-in-law's father) was awarded a special vellum in recognition of the exceptional services which he and his family rendered to the Lifeboat Service. He was a winch-man, and became a member of the crew in 1870. One of his sons was coxswain, another a signalman. Two others were members of the crew awarded the Institution's bronze medal. Three grandsons and one great-grandson were also members of the crew. A son-in-law was second coxswain, and one of his daughters and a granddaughter-in-law were members of the Ladies' Lifeboat Guild. The vellum was in the form of a family tree, with the various dates of enrolment in the Lifeboat Service.

The Wigg family in 1919, after Walter and Alfred Wigg received medals for their part in the St Paul's rescue of the smack AJW.

Wagon at a regatta. Mrs Wigg remembered regatta days in Kessingland: 'When we first came here to live, we lived with mother-in-law three years before we got the house... the first regatta I knew about... it was my boy's birthday. He was two and he thought it was all for him. They had fireworks and dancing in the street, he went round with his grandmother in a boat for a race; he loved it. We only had two regattas after I came here. It filled the street.'

Below: Kessingland Beach at the beginning of the 1900s.

Things for lifeboat men have changed: 'There wasn't any sort of uniform... they just wore what they called their 'slops', what the fishermen wore, they didn't have much else in those days.'

Betty's father-in-law was also on the lifeboat *St Paul* with Tubby Knights. He received the vellum and a medal at the Lowestoft Hippodrome. The *St Paul* is now in the museum at Chatham.

The End of an Era

The *Post Office Directory* of 1875 for Cambridgeshire, Norfolk and Suffolk records:

The coastguards have a station on the beach. There is accommodation for eleven families. [Later to be Kessingland Grange, home of Sir Henry Rider Haggard.]

The sea is making its encroachments upon the land; a piece of ground known as the 'Sea Row', a place thickly populated, was swept away about 1834 by the action of the waves. Two walls were left standing, which remained as turrets in the sand, but have now disappeared.

A lighthouse was erected in 1874, in place of two formerly at Hopton, for the guidance of mariners through The Gut, the sands of which have shifted.

The end of the lifeboat station was inevitable, as Ernest Read Cooper explains:

Since the advent of motor boats at Lowestoft and Southwold, the need for one at Kessingland had passed. The station was finally closed in 1937 when the Hugh Taylor was removed.

Memories of the 1953 Flood

George Swan: In Deep Water

On 31 January 1953 the East Coast of England, including Lowestoft, experienced one of the worst nights on record, due to the gale-force winds and flooding from the high tide. I can remember that night and the following week very clearly. I was courting Pam, now my wife, at this time and like many courting couples, we spent the afternoon at the pictures. We then met up with our friends for a drink in the Belle Vue, which was knocked down to make way for the new road.

At about ten o'clock, the police came in and said that if anybody lived in the beach area, they should make their way home at once, as the sea was flooding their homes. As we left later, we crossed the road, looking over a wall and could see water everywhere...

The following day, Sunday, we walked through the town and along the Esplanade, looking at the damage. I felt sorry for the people who owned or lived in the boarding-houses, as all the downstairs windows were smashed and the rooms filled with sand, stones and sea water, like several more properties in the town.

At this time I was working for the Railway, at the Harbour yard, and spent the next few weeks repairing and cleaning up after what was the worst flood in living memory.

John Blowers

At that time I was working in Lowestoft at the Fish Market as a fish auctioneer and as usual we worked on

Nicknames

Most Kessingland men had and some still do have a nickname. Peter Cherry wrote, 'Kessingland is a rare place for nicknames – few people escape without one and often they are far from flattering! Usually they are acquired from some trivial happening, and then they stick for life.'

No one could possibly set down all the nicknames which have befallen Kessingland men down the ages, but one fisherman contributed a remarkable list of those he can remember from his days with the fishing fleet. Here are a few listed family by family, in alphabetical order:

ALDRED – Tin-eye, Chicky, Nolty.

BIRD – Stumpy, Bunker, Birdie.

BLOCK – Lallar, Lil, Pum, Pedger.

BLOWERS – Tiff, Woody, Buff, Lue, Micky, Blood, Tash, Cucks, Slater, Gallus.

BROWN – Rue, Froggie, Buffer, Hutch, Nanty, Ollie, Dosser, Diddy, Cock Robin, Gobbler.

BUNN – Snick, Baze, Swifty, Stilry, Poley, Buller, Cockle.

CATCHPOLE – Truncher, Tidley, Light, Labby, Funk, Sly, Wilky, Pilcher, Boiler, Crop, Trunnie, Bucko, Pardy, Ike, Holele, Nash, Hinix, Hucker, Hundred, Starcher, Mouse, Lando, Dog, Hudge and Ebber.

COOK – Sparkey, Shellie.

DODDINGTON – Swose, Lar, Doddie, Boler.

DOWDING – Tinnie, Dowdy, Milph, Peas, Noisy.

DURRANT – Judy, Dill, Golls, Nossy, Brick.

FARROW – Scrub, Mop.

HART – Hufus, Boss, Paddy, Closh, Lodger, Yan.

HARVEY – Jitty, Skip, Fatty, Youger, Ponto, Billygoat.

JAMES – Spider, Whippet.

JULINGS – Tager, Greasy, Brush.

KEABLE – Friday, Rumbolt, Bighead.

KEMP – Mike, Beno, Spittems, Turkey, Bumch.

KNIGHTS – Tubby, Backer, Dish, Spuff, Dutch, Wonney, Egger, Ninety, Fritz, Lofty, Cuca, Munt Sot, Barley, Kruger.

MALLETT – Hicke.

MARJORAM – Chips, Manny, Batlie, Hecker, Rollie.

MOYSE – Gee, Pots, Hardies, Cuts.

MUTTITT – Tinks, Doff, Rugus, Zip, Pip.

ROTH – Yacker, Stut, Twot.

SPILLINGS – Wag, Titler, Brick, Fisher.

SMITH – Ready Money Bob, Boney, Skinny, Bucko, Flipper, Poacher, Bish, Longing, Ducky, Foby.

STROWGER – Rocks, Gardy, Brewer, Leo, Ossie, Fredadear, Feck, Woops, Tiger, Toots.

THOMPSON – Ducks, Buffer, Crusty,

TURRELL – Winser, Yellow-Iron, Bark, Jelly, Click, Fluffy, Pouch, Tarrie.

UTTING / UTTON – Monkey, Yorkie, Deaf Charlie, Twee, Curly, Rusty, Doddles, Shells, Twinie, Moffat, Drug, Rush, Stiff, Braddy, Benny, Yank, Beno, Austy, Nid, Skips, Chy, Peao.

WIGGS – Hinny, Brownie, Nitty, Hoe.

To complete the list, here are a few odd ones: Haunch Horne, Gunner Beckham, Tarbrush Cooper, Pilcher Sterry, Ticker Wade, Doey Hall, Marner Weavers, Dumps Davis, Steamboat Thacker, Dutch Sims, Mildew Beamish, Silly Manthorpe, Snuffy Polkard, Onespud Holbrook, Cockerdilly Edwards, Dreamy Smith, Kaiser Bond, Pork Manthorpe, England Reynolds, Toto Robinson, Peck'm Gouldby, Blind Horace.

Saturdays. Our first-floor office in Waveney Road gave a good view of the old trawl dock and the harbour entrance. At some time during that afternoon we noticed a peculiar event, in that the water-level in the dock was higher at low tide than it was at the previous high tide, which meant that instead of falling, the water had actually risen and was doing so fast. With another six hours to go until high water, it was obvious then that it would flood at least over the level of the dock. I eventually went home and later, as was usual, myself and a crowd of the local lads went to the Odeon.

At approximately nine or ten p.m., I'm not exactly sure which, we could hear sirens going, similar to the old wartime 'All Clear' and then a message came up on the screen asking everybody to leave the cinema and go home as severe flooding was imminent. On leaving the Odeon, we realised people were making their way down the street to the harbour area and we followed. On arrival at traffic lights near the Suffolk Hotel, we saw a car trapped there with water over the wheels and all the Station Square area flooded with water coming in from the docks. News got around that the water was then

over the old swing bridge. We then knew we would have a problem getting home to Kessingland. We then struck lucky, as an empty coach pulled up and the driver offered to get us over the bridge, which he did, with the water coming up to the wheel arches. We then got off and had a collection for the coach driver and on being told we came from Kessingland, he offered to take us home for a bit more cash. We duly arrived at the Sailor's Home pub car park, where crowds were watching the sea crashing over the sea wall and also saw the damage occurring at the Wave Crest Tearooms. We watched for a while and then went home, but were back again to see the damage in the area on the Sunday morning.

I remember one of our trawler skippers coming into the office on the Monday morning and saying he was fishing to the south of Lowestoft, when he decided to make a run for home due to the worsening weather on the Saturday evening and was amazed to encounter various wreckage and furniture floating past, as he steamed past Southwold, but did not realise the extent of what was going on until he arrived in port, much to his relief, safely.

Chapter 5

Village Health

Local Historian Peter Cherry used his vast knowledge when working through various parish registers to research and put together a series of articles for his book *From Stone Age to Stagecoach*, published in 2003. He found mention of doctors in the registers but it is not clear when they came to the village. Mrs Ellen Newson's book, *The District Nurse*, tells the story of her grandmother. The nurse, Mrs Elizabeth Utting (née Durrant), lived at Fern Cottage, where her great-great-granddaughter, Jane, now lives. She and her husband, Robert, had 12 children (six boys and six girls). Robert spent a lot of time at sea and died when fairly young of heart problems. They ran the Beach Stores (later called Rockhill Retail, but now a residential property).

Their youngest son, John, had been a very weak baby and Ellen had nursed him, although the doctor had not expected him to live. He turned out to be one of the strongest. Ellen also helped her neighbours, extended family and friends in times of illness and childbirth. As she took on more and more, especially after her husband's death, the doctor, who had relied on her help and expertise for years, recognised her as his district nurse from 1880, when her eldest child was only eight. Because times were hard, she was often paid in kind rather than cash, which helped to feed, clothe and warm her large family. Somehow all the nursing work and the shop carried on. Ellen Newson remembers as a child that, miraculously, Granny's cake tins, kept on the lower shelves for children after school, were always replenished. Granny always seemed to have time for them, too, as well as for gardening and for feeding the pig, which was fattened up each year for Christmas pork and hams.

The nurse was able to assist in the birth of even the smallest babies – not just in Kessingland, but also across the outlying villages. She used Lysol as the main disinfectant and Condy's Fluid, made up of bright mauve crystals, which turned pink when water was added.

Fishermen would suffer from boils on their hands and severe cuts, but the remedy was a poultice made of washing soap and sugar, which was infallible.

In those days, she also had to be the local dentist, pulling teeth when required and helping with operations on scrubbed kitchen tables, with the doctor in charge. Ellen, the author of the booklet, lost her own tonsils and adenoids in granny's front bedroom in

Arthur Vere's grave, photographed 2006.

this way! Other tasks were to inspect the school-children's head for lice and apply lotion to those affected. Outbreaks of diphtheria or scarlet fever saw nurse Ellen run off her feet, but she seemed to cope.

Accidents also had to be attended to, for instance when a village lad fell through the ice whilst skating on the river; after a fire at the wooden house near the church; when Maudie Hunn was run over by the bus as a child. Ellen smartly dispersed the bus passengers and had the driver turn it around and race back to Lowestoft Hospital with the casualty.

Laying out the dead was another duty. Her grateful clients would sometimes buy her a pair of black nursing stockings or teacloths, if they could not afford the bill.

Nurse Ellen worked closely with Dr Schillings, who lived in the doctor's house in Church Road (then Chapel Road) in the Street area. He also conducted a morning surgery in the nurse's front room for the Beach village residents and an evening one in his own house. When she retired, just over a year before her death, aged 82, residents presented her with a certificate and a purse of gold sovereigns in recognition of her devoted service to the village.

Nurse Ellen's sons became skippers and boat owners and a grandson, Arthur Vere Harvey, became an Air Commodore in the RAF, then an MP for Macclesfield. He was made Lord Harvey of Prestbury in recognition of his outstanding war service and is buried in Kessingland churchyard.

Mrs Guthrie took over the nurse's work. Another local health worker was Nurse Griffiths, who lived at Red House with her husband, Will, a teacher. Griffiths Close, in the vicinity, commemorates the contribution they both made to village life.

Personality Profile: Sister Elsie King
(Taken from a 1992 interview)

Elsie was Kessingland's last village midwife, before NHS changes meant that nurses were attached to groups of doctors rather than to a place. She helped many local people into this world and nursed lots of past residents at the end of their lives. Her area covered Kessingland, Gisleham, Rushmere, Henstead and Hulver, with herself and the Carlton Colville nurse covering each other's holidays and off-duty periods, adding Carlton also to her 'district'. By a remarkable coincidence, the first baby she delivered here became a mother on the day she retired.

Many older readers will remember those two snowy winters of 1946 and '47. During this period Elsie, fresh from city nursing, battled her way around this rural district, with 'snow up to the top of the telegraph poles.' With no roads visible, no lights and no directions, she certainly had a hard initiation into the job. Elsie recalls:

... how exciting it was, the arrival of a new baby after weeks of preparation... We always had to visit the newest baby first, then work backwards, with the general nursing being fitted in somehow through the day, but those reports had to be written straight away after a delivery, while the details were still fresh in your mind. You mostly worked alone, responsible for two lives, with the doctor coming along later, unless there were complications and you sent for him early. Therefore, every detail had to be recorded, in case it was needed later.

I started here with Dr Peregrine, with the surgery at his house. Patients would be sitting around waiting for surgery to begin, then at 6p.m. he locked the door, not like today with receptionists and appointment books!

In 1948 came the introduction of the National Health Service, which everyone greeted with delight. It would be wonderful to get free treatment and the District Nurse became the Community Sister. Not many people had telephones then and there were no answerphones, so an added chore was to put out a slate on her porch, on which were chalked her visits with approximate times. Anxious prospective fathers just had to cycle or run around until they found her! Before rushing off with them to the next job, she had to go home and update the information.

Sister King was known affectionately in the district as 'Kingie' and managed to balance that fine line between professionalism and friendship needed for the job in such a close-knit rural area. Many used her as a counsellor and source of advice, but she never seemed to mind the extra time and effort she put in.

On Dr Peregrine's retirement, the surgery was moved to a room in the house of Miss Mary Clarke, in the Market Place. Mary was to become a close friend of Elsie, especially as they shared a love for people and pets. Dr Hewson followed, then emigrated, and Dr Audrey King-Davis and Dr Bracewell extended their work into Kessingland. As the village grew, with the building of the Lloyds estate, a new surgery was built, followed by the present one. Elsie remembers that the first baby born on the new estate arrived on a Christmas Day.

She travelled to London after 21 years, to receive the Queen's long-service badge from the Duchess of Kent. She was also invited to Buckingham Palace for another special occasion.

Even before retirement, Elsie was involved in helping Mary Clarke and others interested in rescuing animals and finding new homes for them. She was involved in the upkeep of Bonny and Dinah, the two ex-working horses that lived on the Old Rectory Meadow. She has also helped goats, donkeys, dogs and cats, many of which were cared for on Mary's land in Church Road. (This has since been built on, following her death.)

Manor Farm Residential Home

Manor Farm Residential Home was started by Katie Hallsworth and her family. Katie was 'Mum', and daughter Caroline a senior care assistant helping with office work. Katie set up a real 'home' for 20 residents, with a sense of care and family feeling. Katie found it hard to contend with the death of any of her 'extended family' and attending funerals was the only side of the job she was happy to lose, after she retired. However, residents and those on the waiting list can be assured that the same staff have been kept on and the 'family' atmosphere is maintained by the new owners.

Katie maintained good relationships with residents and their relatives. She loved listening to older people and learned a lot from the fund of stories which they love to tell, especially about past life here in the village or in the neighbourhood.

With 24-hour-a-day care, staff is the main expense, and a good relationship with staff is another priority. The fact that so many of the staff have worked at the home for so long is a recommendation.

The home is now owned by Mr and Mrs Jackson, with Mrs Alison Palmer as registered manager. There have been extensive alterations and improvements to cater for more people. A summer fête is held annually in August and the residents enjoy several other treats, including celebrating birthdays and special occasions.

Kessingland Surgery

The surgery is now using a new appointment system, designed to allow patients to be seen by a doctor within one or, at the most, two working days from the request for an appointment. It now has a Patient Participation Group under the chairmanship of Jean Purkis, created to form a more structured feedback pathway for the patients' voice. It has been quite active on behalf of the patients in trying to re-establish a chiropodist in the village, among other things.

A Happy, Healthy Village

All of the people mentioned and many more have helped to keep villagers happy and healthy, but most of them put their natural good health down to sea air, good home-grown food and the peace and quiet of the nearby countryside.

Chapter 6

Kessingland At War

Gerald Brown and Dr Neville Skinner produced an interesting book called *Not Yet Forgotten* on the men from the village who lost their lives in the First World War.

The population of the village at the beginning of the First World War was about 1,800, of whom 52 men are recorded on the war memorial. However, the authors discovered four other names which, in theory, ought to have been included on the memorial but, for some unknown reason, were left off. The list of names does not include those Kessingland civilians or fishermen killed or drowned at sea because of enemy action by German U-boats. Many of those killed were in the Royal Naval Reserve, serving on specially adapted drifters and trawlers which had been taken on for military service.

The First World War

The First World War meant big changes in village life. With many of the men away at war, women had to take on new responsibilities. Farming and fishing had to go on, but it was usually left to the older men or the younger lads. The indomitable British spirit meant that in spite of the changes, people tried to ensure that life was kept as normal as possible. In October 1914 the local magazine, called *The Sign*, recorded that:

... the young men of our parish responded to the call of our King and we compliment them on their display of patriotism, as well as the praise accorded them by

The war memorial dedicated to those who lost their lives during the First World War. Second World War victims are recorded on the other side.

Colonel Graham at Bury St Edmunds, when he said, 'They are among the finest and HEFTIEST I HAVE EVER SEEN'. Our lads for the most part are attached to the 9th (Service) Battalion of the Suffolk Regiment, and are thoroughly enjoying the severe training they are undergoing at Shoreham...

Some families had many of their men missing, which was a cause of great anxiety. In November, the church sent nine baskets full of fruit and vegetables to HMS *Russell*, presumably still in the area. The Commanding Officer sent a thank you letter, printed in the magazine.

Interesting advertisements in the magazines show some of the items we can still buy today, such as Pears

---

Those Serving in the First World War

Many Kessingland men were attached to the 9th (Service) Battalion of the Suffolk Regiment, and trained at Shoreham. The following is a list of those who served their King and country during this conflict.

NAVY: Archer Butcher, RN, Chas Frank Williams, Frederick Kemble Williams, RN, John B. Jeffreys, Herbert Thacker, ? Blowers, RNR, Stanley Brown, Frank Brown, Sidney Brown, Lewis Brown, James Cutler, H. Foyster, B. Foyster, C. Foyster, Hy Weavers, C. Curtis, Herbert Nichols, John Goddard, Wm Goddard, E. Catchpole, George Brown, Albert Doddington, Basil Raven, Archie Brown, Harold Davis, Albert A. Swan.

COASTGUARDS: J.H. Thomas, S. Martin John, A.G.W. Baker, J.E. Harman, Mr Holme, Mr France.

ARMY: Victor Blowers, Hedley Catchpole, Chas E. Catchpole, Orlando Catchpole, Stanley A. Catchpole, John Wm. Catchpole, Chas Hy Crane, Leonard Hall, Harry E. Lane, William Lane, Hy Morse, Herbert Parry, F.G. Pike, F.O. Rumsby, B.D.G. Spindler, Alfred E. Summons, Fred Summons, Geo. Albert Self, Walter Jas Tripp, Clifford Wigg, John R. Wingfield, Victor Harvey, Geo. N. Staunton, Major Chevers, Wm. Bird, Robert Fannen, Victor Aldred, Frank Curtis, Jack Mallet, Thomas Davis, Edgar Riches, Arthur E. Kent, Donald Barker, Harry Snelling.

EXEMPTED FROM SERVICE, ENTITLED TO WEAR BUTTON OF SUFFOLK REGIMENT: Fred Strowger, Stanley Durrant, Reginald Holbert, Thomas Beamish, Lancelot Daines, Arthur Utting, Wm Mallett.

soap, and some that we can't, including corsets from Mrs Fleming's, the drapery shop in Church Street. Mr Aldridge, also of Church Road, made boots and shoes to order or attended to repairs promptly.

As part of the war effort, householders were encouraged to be as self-sufficient as possible, keeping chickens and rabbits, as well as growing fruit and vegetables. One of the rector's tasks was to visit every household, by order of the Government, to make sure that they were doing all they could to produce food.

Normal church life went on, with the Lord Bishop of Thetford confirming 18 candidates from Kessingland at St Peter's Church, Carlton Colville. In July 1916 sympathy was offered to Mr and Mrs E. Kemp, whose eldest son, Frederick, was drowned when fishing off the beach on 9 June. He had been in the choir, and confirmed the previous April.

The magazine recorded a long list of those who had received free coal from the Poor Land Trust (now the Help-in-Need Trust, which still operates today). Those eligible were widows, aged people, labourers, deserving cases and soldiers' wives. The coal would have been very welcome in those days of hardship.

In 1918 the war was over and by August 1919 there were plans for suitable war memorials. The magnificent memorial in Kessingland churchyard was produced by local stonemason Mr Guthrie.

The Carlton Colville Chronicles by Canon Bignold, edited by J. Goffin, produced from diaries kept at the back of church ledgers, records the price increases that came about because a war was on. It was recorded that between July 1914 and October 1918 the price of all principal foods had gone up by 129 per cent; textiles, leather, etc., by 213 per cent; coal by 77 per cent, soap by 133 per cent, candles by 248 per cent.

After compulsory rationing came in, one never heard a word of complaint. Instead, the sentiment was along the lines of 'Think of the boys in the trenches and what they have to put up with!' Those boys in the trenches would try to get news home wherever possible. George Swan has a large collection of wartime postcards.

**A Family Pulls Together
(Taken from material supplied by Ellen Newson)**

Ellen Newson was a small child when war broke out. Her father, John Turrell, was a Naval officer in charge of the *Golden Rule*, based at Dover under Sir Roger Keyes, who asked for volunteers for minesweeping across the Dover Straits, to allow safe passage for British gunboats to enter Zeebrugge Harbour and blow it up. Heavy enemy gunfire caused nine out of ten boats to be lost, with her father and the chief engineer the only survivors on the *Golden Rule* They limped it back to Dover, both badly injured, and were

taken to Deal Naval Hospital.

Ellen's mother and grandmother travelled to Deal and found John in a bad way. Ellen's grandmother stayed for several weeks, while her mother, John's wife, stayed for six months. He had six operations and made slow progress but was awarded the DSC (Distinguished Service Cross). As he was not well enough to go to the Palace for his medal, King George V and Queen Mary went to Deal. John was so heavily bandaged that the King did not know where to pin the medal! Ellen's mother curtsied to the Queen, who said, 'You must be very proud of your husband.'

John was scarred for life, but eventually returned to Kessingland, where Granny once more cared for him until he recovered. The whole village was there to welcome him and rejoice in his homecoming.

The Second World War

Although the First World War was supposed to be the war to end all wars, just 20 years later the country was gearing up for another international conflict.

**Wartime Memories
By Gordon Blowers (aged 77 in 1999)**

The 1939–45 war had started and I volunteered to join the RAF. I was accepted and after training was posted to RAF Hornchurch and Southend, both fighter-stations, Hornchurch being the Headquarters of 11 Fighter Group. After a time I was posted overseas to Malaya... A beautiful country! Japan entered the war and within a few weeks most of our aircraft had been shot down. They were too slow, badly armed and were no match against the modern Jap Zero fighter planes. We were moved further down Malaya, just keeping ahead of the enemy and reached Singapore. Here I had a surprise meeting with Fred Dowden, serving in the Royal Navy Submarines. Fred was off to Australia, but it was great meeting him 9,000 miles from home. That was the last time I saw him until after the war... We left Malaya by ship and reached Java in the Dutch East Indies, but with no possible way of escaping the Island. It was a hopeless situation for all our Forces. Surrender came shortly after and we all became prisoners of war in 1942. Walking through the POW camp, I met a good friend from Kessingland, Bob Durrant. We talked and talked. We were split up and sent to different islands to work and I never saw him again. Later I heard that he had died. He was a grand chap...

After three and a half years the Japs surrendered. I was flown out in a hospital plane to Singapore. After several weeks in hospital, having intensive treatment, my weight increased to 7 stone 12 pounds... I had a lift in a truck to the dock area, full of Naval Craft. As I walked past the ships I thought I recognised Sid Watson from Kessingland. He was a Petty Officer on a Royal Naval Cruiser. To meet in those circumstances it felt unbelievable. Sid shouted out, 'Come Aboard!' which I did. He filled me up with food, cigarettes, etc.

He has passed on, but I will always be grateful for his kindness... He was a friendly face from my home village called Kessingland. Shortly after this I was on my way home on a hospital ship. My weight had now improved to over 8 stone. It was a lovely journey home. We were treated very well, nothing was too much trouble for the crew and medical staff in helping us. We were being treated round the clock, with medicine and special food to help our stomachs recover from the malnutrition. It was a slow process and the medics said that it would take time.

We arrived at Liverpool, were taken to hospital, where we had more treatment and wrote to our relatives. After three weeks most of us had responded well to the wonderful treatment and the doctors said those that could travel would be sent home on sick leave. I was one of those. We were seen onto the train and travelled to London. Here the party was split up and we went our different ways. I travelled to Lowestoft where I was met by Mr Boughton the photographer, with a car to give me a lift home. On arrival in Kessingland the flags were up and friends and relatives were there to welcome me. I was HOME, a place I thought that I would never see again. It was November 1945.

After my leave, my weight had increased a lot and I returned, to be assessed in hospital. More tests, more leaves and finally my discharge from the RAF in March 1946. By then I had met a young lady who was to become my wife. Her name was Tilly Catchpole. She had served in the WRENS during the war and was a local girl...

Tilly and I married in Kessingland Parish Church in November 1946. We had a son, Michael, born 1951. I obtained a job as a plumber, first with W.J. Taylor of Norwich & Great Yarmouth (plumbing and heating engineers), where I worked for eight years. I then left to work with R.G. Carter, a builder, of Great Yarmouth for 16 years, still as a plumber. It was a good job with a big company who carried out large contracts. The work was good but hard... so following that for 12 years I worked at Pye Television factory in Oulton Broad as a maintenance fitter, until the firm closed and I went to Pontins at Pakefield for the next four years until I retired. One job was to fit 200 new basins into the chalets.

Tilly and I had a happy marriage and after Michael started school she went to work at Catchpole's Holiday Camp where she became manageress. Michael married Marylyn and in a few years we were blessed with two grandchildren, Michelle and Steven. In 1987 Tilly became very ill and died within a few months. She was a very dear wife and mother and I was devastated. Tilly's friends and my family helped in every way they could, but it was a hard time for me. After three years, I met Mary, a widow who lived locally and we married in 1990 and are very happy...

God has blessed me so much over the years. Little did I think during those bad POW years that I would be around at 77 years of age. There we lived for the day and in closing, I would like to say that those POWs who died in the Japanese hell-camps, will never be forgotten by those of us who were so lucky to make it back to our homes.

Gordon has done a lot of work for St Edmund's Church over the years, including serving as deputy churchwarden. He was instrumental in collecting the money for the plaque (made by LEC Marine, Lowestoft) recording the names of those who died in the Second World War, with the help of other church members. Tony Warner made the frame to match the top plaque, commemorating those who gave their lives in the First World War.

Personality Profile: Fred Studd
(Taken from a 1994 interview)

A total of 31 years in the Navy meant long separations from his wife, Violet, especially during the war, when Fred only managed to get home three times. Fred and Violet had married when Fred was with the Fisheries Protection vessel HMS *Dee*.

After growing up in the village and working at a variety of agricultural jobs he joined the Navy in March 1926. Fred says he wouldn't have changed life in the Navy for anything. He travelled all over the world and met many lovely people. After returning from China before the war, he and Violet went to Chatham on holiday. They decided to move house, to spare the journeys back and forth. However, they'd just settled when war was declared.

Fred, qualified as a coxswain, was on HMS *Eskimo* for four years and was involved in the Second Battle of Narvic. They were torpedoed and brought the ship back to Barrow-in-Furness. With a new skipper and crew, they set sail for Malta, were bombed on the way to Salerno, came back to Immingham for repair, then departed for the USA.

He managed to get two weeks' leave and visited an aunt in Minnesota. She and her husband, a fisherman, had emigrated from Suffolk in 1920. Fred enjoyed seeing the Mississippi and the ancient Municipal Building with its rich history. Much later the relatives were able to come to England for a reunion.

He found Americans friendly. He and his friend met a man one night who invited them home for the weekend in Canada, where they visited the Victoria Falls. Another weekend was spent in Boston with emigrants from the Lancashire cotton mills.

As the war finished, Fred was on the American ship *Papua*, checking on U-boats trying to return to Germany. He loved all the travelling, 'But your homeland is always the best'. Fred was awarded the DSM and mentioned in dispatches.

Later moving from Chatham to Strood, Fred retired from the Navy in 1955. He and Violet set up their own window-cleaning business and later his son joined the firm.

For 13 years they spent their holidays camping on the North Denes at Lowestoft and catching up with the family. Eventually Fred retired and moved 'home', to Kessingland. They spent holidays in Norway, Belgium and Holland, but that was the extent of his seafaring.

A Boy's Memories of Kessingland At War
By John Blowers

Kessingland was... in the front line, as we are, I think, the closest point to mainland Germany in Britain. As historians will tell us, 1939–40 was a relatively quiet time, known as the Phoney War [but]... it was not long before things were hotting up, with the occupation of Holland and Belgium and subsequently France, followed by [the events at] Dunkirk.

We were now in an invasion situation and things started moving in Kessingland. Soldiers began to arrive and accommodation had to be procured. The Holiday Fellowship camp was taken over, followed by The Grange, Sir Henry Rider Haggard's second home and any other large houses having been vacated by owners who had moved to a safe place.

All sorts of exciting things (to us boys) started to happen and urgent anti-invasion preparations got going. As I remember, the first coastal line of defence was installed, this being massive steel spikes set in concrete boxes, which were set into the beach at the low-water mark. These were known as 'dragon's teeth', and stretched, according to our limited knowledge at the time, from Lowestoft to Southwold. They did, of course, go all along the eastern seaboard of the country. Next came the 'tank traps', consisting of rows of steel pipes, similar to today's scaffold poles, latticed together to stop enemy tanks, although I fear the German Panzer Tanks would have made short work of them. Next came the land or beach mines, which were buried in the sand to stop invading infantrymen. We lads noted the positions of these. Then came masses of coiled barbed wire all along the beaches and cliff tops and even inland around the fields. Finally came miles of trenches and pillboxes with gun emplacements occupied by troops. More ominously, at least to my young mind, were the huge landmines buried at strategic points along the then Beach Road and Church Road. In the event of an invasion, these would be blown up from a common point to, hopefully, make the road impassable.

These mines were located outside the Sailor's Home pub, the Kessingland Beach Post Office and, to my horror, outside the junction of Green Lane and Beach Road. We were told that if these mines were blown up, all the houses in the area would disappear and my

house was one of the nearest...

I must explain that items such as shrapnel, bullet cases and live bullets were vigorously sought after by us boys at that time and a pile of 0.5 calibre machine-gun bullets had arrived on the beach at the bottom of the cliff near where D'Arcy's house stood.

Our gang was most intent on recovering this valuable prize, despite the mines and barbed wire. The plan was to procure some rope, we already knew of a supply, and make a rope ladder. Coincidentally, I was the youngest and therefore the lightest member and by popular vote I was elected to make the descent down to the beach. Unfortunately the bullets were some way out into the minefield, but I was assured by those more knowledgeable than myself, that after lowering me, I would be quite safe by crawling to the booty and probing the sand with my fingers to locate any mines, just as the Sappers do with their bayonets and I would therefore be quite safe and avoid them. The story obviously had a happy ending, or I would not be here to tell the tale.

I was now quite famous as a mine crawler, although I cannot remember my mother finding out or my fate would have been worse than being blown up!

My experience held me in good stead as, at a later date, a pal and I were watching an aeroplane towing a drogue target along, parallel to the beach at Kessingland, when it became detached from the tow wire and landed on the beach in that area. News had got round that if anybody could get their hands on one of these drogues, which were made of nylon, the long-shore fishermen would buy them to make sails.

We decided the target should be ours, but it had fallen into a minefield. No problem! I was the local expert in minefield object retrieval. In I went, the barbed wire being a bit of a nuisance on this occasion, got the drogue and made my way back, using the tested and well-tried finger-probing method.

Unfortunately, all did not go well this time. Before I got back to mine-less territory a number of soldiers had observed my actions and were yelling and hollering for me to stay perfectly still until they got me out. This advice was ignored and I got back, but the sad end to the story was that after a ticking off in terms I cannot put into print, they relieved me of ownership of the drogue.

The Liberator

It was, as far as I can remember, sometime in the late spring of 1944, at the height of the American bombing of Germany mainly from the East Anglian bases, when the Liberator came down.

The sky was continually filled with Fortresses and Liberators forming up before going off on their missions. I was at the tender age of 11 years and war to us boys was just another exciting time...

On the early evening of one Saturday myself and friend Conrad Turrell had 'borrowed' a canoe each from unsuspecting pals and decided to paddle from Benacre Sluice along the River Hundred towards the Latymere Dam.

It was coming in dark when we got back to Kessingland marshes where we were to leave the canoes and go home by the lane... the bombers were returning to their bases and it seems that the German fighters adopted a tactic of joining in with the bombers to confuse our radar. Coming across the marshes we began to hear machine-gun fire and saw the flashes as the bombers were being attacked and we saw what looked like an aircraft on fire out Lowestoft way. This, as we say in these parts, put the wind up of us so we ran all the way home.

On arriving at my home at Kessingland Beach the sky was full of activity with gunfire going on everywhere and suddenly an aircraft got hit badly and was on fire... within seconds. It was a Liberator and flakes of burning metal fell all around and fortunately nobody on the ground was hurt.

The Liberator then spun out of control to eventually crash on the marshes and appeared to burn most of the night. On reflection I realise that we were watching the crew of the plane dying as there was no way they could have escaped by parachute as it all happened so quickly.

The next morning myself and Maurice Turrell (Conrad's brother) went to the crash site and found the wreckage burnt out and as nobody was about we looked for souvenirs, as Plexiglas and bullets were great prizes.

I will never forget the next part of this story as in my excitement I found a belt of machine-gun bullets and started to pull them out of the wreckage but to my horror a human arm dropped on me and I could see a body attached. I called Maurice over and we could see other bodies there. By that time an American Serviceman turned up. He had been looking for the wreckage, and we showed him our grim find. He thanked us and then told us to leave the site.

There was one following event in that a gang of us went to the site area on the Monday and discovered a 0.5 calibre machine-gun in a dyke which we recovered and examined. At that time it was rumoured that the crew of American bombers started dismantling and cleaning their guns on approaching the English coast thinking they were safe but I confirm this could not have been the case as we found a belt of ammunition attached to the gun with a live round in the breech as if it was being used before being hit... I cannot remember what was done with the gun but it was probably thrown into the River Hundred as I can remember the rusted remains coming to light years afterwards when the river was dredged.

Wartime Reflections
By S.J. Partridge

When one has passed the age of four-score years and ten,

one tends to slow down and sit about more, though the body may be idle, the brain keeps ticking away. All sort of thoughts and memories float past...

I was born in 1914. Food rationing was brought into being. Meat, butter, cheese and other items were rationed. It did not cause our family any hardship. We lived on a farm. We had a good supply of eggs and milk and all the fresh fruit and vegetables we needed. Also there was always someone in the village killing a pig or a sheep. My mother always stocked up on any pork on offer. Apart from the roasts, she would always buy a leg and two or three bellies of pork to cure. The leg was for ham and the bellies for streaky bacon. They were first salted in brine and then treated with dark brown sugar and spices. They were then placed in muslin bags and hung on the hooks in the kitchen ceiling over the kitchen fire to finish curing. So we always had bacon and ham to fall back on. Mother was also known to make butter on occasions.

As a child I was fed on home-cooked, wholesome food. There were no school meals. I came home for lunch. At the age of ten I transferred to Grammar School in the neighbouring town. I cycled the four miles there and four miles back in all weathers every day. My mother gave me a packed lunch, but there was always a hot meal on the table when I arrived home.

At the age of 17 it was time to leave school. I decided I would not take up my chosen career, but should get out, support myself and no longer be a burden on my parents, as my mother had suddenly become seriously ill. There was an advertisement in the local press: J. Sainsbury's needed young lads to work in their shops. I was accepted and the lads lived in the hostels over the shops. They employed a cook/housekeeper and two maids to look after us. We had our own room and there was a communal room and dining-room and also a bedroom, something I had not had the use of up til then. All the food was sent up from the shop. We had three cooked meals a day, with morning and afternoon breaks in between. The housekeeper really mothered us. I think she enjoyed her job. The work was hard and the hours long. It was a good training home from home.

When I joined the RAF... we were well fed. When I was married, my lovely wife was a very good cook. When she was alive, I was never allowed in the kitchen, so when she passed on I had to start training if I wanted to stay alive. Now I consider myself a bit of a gourmet chef...

There were times when I was singled out to evade death. Whilst in the RAF in the early days of training, I was on a course of about 30 lads. On completion of the course, we all passed out and I was asked to be the Wing Commander and stay on and take further courses. The remainder of the squad flew out to North Africa. The plane was shot down and they all lost their lives.

Another incident comes to mind. Whilst in the

RAF, I was home on a weekend pass. We decided on the Saturday evening to pay my married sister a visit. My wife was living in Ilford and my sister at Barkingside. During the evening we decided to take a walk down to the pub in nearby Chigwell. When we got there, there was a wedding party in progress. The place was packed... No hope of reaching the bar. So we decided to give up and make for home, and finish the evening over a cup of tea or coffee. On the way home there was a terrific bang and a gust of air which brought us to our knees. On Sunday morning my brother-in-law arrived on his bicycle to inform us that the big bang was caused by a landmine, a direct hit on the pub. Everyone lost their lives. On the Sunday afternoon, the wife and I took a bus ride out to Chigwell. The building was completely flattened. Pieces of clothing were fluttering in the breeze on the branches of what was left of nearby trees. So I think it is clearly 'Count your Blessings' time... Who's a lucky lad!

My Wartime Service

In 1939 lads in their 20s had a choice. They could volunteer or wait to be called up. I was a deputy manager in the food trade and my employers wanted to hold my services as long as possible. Eventually I was conscripted. At the interview the recruiting sergeant (looking at my records) said 'cook and butcher' 'Oh no' I said, 'haven't you something a bit more mechanical?' Such a nice sergeant. 'Alright then: armourer'. The date finally arrived for me to report at Cardington in Bedfordshire for my initial training in the RAF... I think this did me the world of good. Out in the open air all day I felt so much fitter. A change from being in a shop 12 (or more) hours a day. The only unpleasant part was the firing range. Thank goodness it was only a target we were firing at. I don't think I could fire at a person.

Training completed, a squad of 30 were posted to Melksham in Wiltshire for a five-week armourers' course. I really enjoyed the training here, I found it very interesting and did rather well. After passing out I was selected to attend a 22-week fitters' course at Weeton in Lancashire. The rest of the squad were posted to North Africa, where they all lost their lives. So off to Weeton. It was a bit bleak, being under canvas in November. We were six to a bed tent. The No. 8 School of Technical training was in its infancy. They had built the workshops but not the huts to house the troops. The course was great fun. We spent 8a.m.–12 noon and 1p.m.–5p.m. in the workshops, then after a good meal back to our tents. We were fed really well. We made all sorts of things from mild steel and aluminium using files and a hacksaw. Here again at the end of the course, I found I had done rather well, my test piece gaining fairly high marks. I was interviewed by the Wing Commander who suggested I should stay at Weeton and become an

instructor. I had already gained my LAC and was now promoted to corporal. I had only been instructing for a few weeks when I was posted to a number of bomber stations to gain experience with the various bomber aircraft – Blenheims, Hampdens, Whitleys, Wellingtons, Lancashires, Halifaxes etc. I spent a week at various stations in Yorkshire, Lincolnshire and Norfolk.

After this I was sent on another course at Porton Down in Wiltshire. This was about chemical weapons. Apparently it had been suspected for some time that Germany might use chemical weapons. Supplies of various chemical weapons had already been secretly stacked at all the main bomber stations. None of the armaments staff knew a thing about them. A school was set up in the wilds of Wiltshire to train all armaments personnel. I was posted here to deal with the practical side. I was giving live explosives demonstrations, and giving training on handling and preparation of the bombs and other weapons. Apart from the various bombs there were attachments which could be used for spraying. They could be used for laying a smokescreen or spraying liquids such as mustard gas. I took the squad to Boscombe Down (Experimental Aircraft Station) one day a week to experience the fitting of these weapons to various aircraft...

Wartime Kessingland
By Robert (Bob) Niblett

I was stationed at Benacre as a young soldier in the Artillery and worked on building the radar tower on Kessingland Beach. We had to cycle through the minefield to get to work. Afterwards, we used to go to Mr Roth's Fish shop, the best fish and chips you could get!

The Utton family were very kind to me, as I was sweet on one of the daughters, but I left and I heard later that she was married and moved to Lincolnshire, incidentally not far from my own home. At Kessingland, the family lived on the road that went uphill to the beach.

I went back to have a look when I first moved to Halesworth 40 years ago and was instantly recognised. Somehow we youngsters used to get to Lowestoft and go to the dances at a hall somewhere near the fisheries laboratory. Everyone in the village was so friendly and good to the soldiers.

Whatever Happened to John Bell?
By Graham Payne

John Bell was quite a character in the late 1930s and the early war years. He was the only son of Mr and Mrs Bell who lived in one of the large houses opposite the church. Though he was a clever lad, he was also well known as a prankster and if there was any trouble in the village, even if he was not involved, which was very rare, he was often blamed for it...

When John left the Lowestoft Secondary School, he

volunteered into the Royal Air Force. The last I remember of him was the time he brought the entire village out into the street, by nearly taking the chimney pots off his mother's house with a Spitfire! His mum was said to be out in the garden shaking her fist at him shouting 'you'll kill yourself you young idiot!' or words to that effect.

I left the village in 1943, but I seem to think there was some talk of him being lost later on in the war; I often wonder what really happened to him.

Barbara Todd's response to Graham's question, as it appeared in the *Kessingland Times*

John Bell was killed during the war. His plane was brought down over the sea in Holland. His body was found and he is buried in a village there.

A few years ago a man from that village got in touch with some of John's family. He had turned a room in his house into a little museum in memory of those lost there during the war... like so many of the boys, he was only in his early twenties when he was killed.

Winnie Adams's Wartime Memories

One of the minesweepers which operated out of Lowestoft during the Second World War was captained by Walter Adams. Towards the end of the war King George VI inspected the minesweeper.

Mrs Winnie Adams remembered that her husband, Walter, a Kessingland man, was on one of the last fishing boats to leave Lowestoft for minesweeping duties with the Naval Reserve Patrol Service, based at the Sparrow's Nest, and the last one to return to fishing after the war. He spent part of the time also on the *Sea King*, which was blown up, but he was in hospital at the time, so escaped that. After the war he was sent to Norway, to train young German sailors for minesweeping.

Linking the Village with Former Wars
By George Swan

Several houses in Kessingland are named after places and events associated with the Boer War. One such place is Pretoria, a house that stands on the corner of Church Road and Whites Lane. Another is called Kimberley, referring to the place where British troops guarded the diamond mines. Another well-known name is Mafeking, where Lord Baden Powell, the founder of the Boy Scout movement, was besieged for seven months. Its relief in May 1900 called for celebrations in this country. This house stands in Whites Lane. There is also a row of cottages known as the Zulus, named after the race of people living in Africa. All these premises were built around the turn of the nineteenth century.

Two more cottages come to mind – Lucknow and Alma – in London Road, Kessingland. Alma is a river in the Crimea, the location of the first battle of the war that took place in 1854. Lucknow was where the British Army was besieged during the Indian Mutiny in 1857.

An Overview
By George Swan

Out of all this carnage [the trenches of the First World War] came beautiful postcards which I have in my collection some of which are hand embroidered with silk and a small pocket where a message could be placed. The others are glossy or coloured and on most is a printed verse of a hymn or song...

There are about 200 cards in my collection, one for every week the war lasted. The nicest thing about these cards is that they were all sent home to the Connett Family, living in Cricklewood, London, by the same soldier. Each card has a little bit of family history written on the back of it.

King George VI at Lowestoft during the Second World War.

I do hope the soldier who sent these cards home had a long and happy life with his family. But the peace lasted just 21 years and in 1939 it all started again. I was 13 at the time and singing in the church choir on Sunday morning, when war was declared. After the service, I was told to get home as soon as possible. I ran all the way, scared of what might happen. I remember my mother saying, 'Thank God we are all together.' Little did she realise that my oldest brothers were soon to be called up, one of them serving in Burma. Men and women of the three Services were sent to serve halfway round the world.

Those of us left behind were all called on to do our duty in helping the war effort... fire-watching, air-raid wardens, fire-fighters and the Home Guard...

The women left behind took over the jobs of men who were called up. They worked in the factories, on the farms and the buses. Some helped by making camouflage nets, to name a few. This war was supposed to be the war to end all wars. I remember how empty the village felt when all the young men and women were called up.

Then by contrast, hundreds of soldiers and the ATS moved into the village, taking over the village halls and the holiday camps. I recall the East Surrey and the Sherwood Forrester Regiments. Every day you saw them training, going on route marches and driving their Bren-gun carriers. This went on until early June 1944, when every able-bodied man suddenly left. I remember standing in the High Street waving as trucks full of soldiers with their equipment were, as we found out later, heading to the ports for the invasion of France and eventually peace.

However, some of those soldiers did return – some of the village girls married soldiers who were stationed here. The peace has lasted 60 years. Let us hope that we and ours never have to experience the horrors of war again.

Sweet Memories of Bitter Times: Rationing
(Taken from an article by Peter Cherry)

Clothes, tinned foods and soaps had all gone off ration by 1950, but most staple foods were still in short supply. Tea rationing did not end until October 1952; chocolate, February 1953, eggs, March 1953; sugar, September 1953; coke (as in fuel, not soft drink!), February 1954; margarine, butter and cheese,

May 1954, meat and bacon, July 1954, coal, July 1958. Bread was rationed in May 1946 because of a world shortage of grain. This included cakes and bread and the normal ration was nine ounces a day, rising to 15 for a manual worker and going down to two ounces for an infant. Identity cards finished in 1952.

After the war, Sir Winston Churchill, worried that the public on the whole were living on rations worse than they had been in wartime, demanded that a typical ration should be laid out on a dish so that he could assess them. He was pleasantly surprised by the display of meat, sugar and other rations. 'Quite satisfying!' he remarked. However, he was aghast when told that this was not a day's rations but had to last a whole week!

Sweet and sugar rationing had ended in 1953 and many will remember the great 'free for all' when sweets became freely available. From the moment that they opened, sweet shops were besieged by customers, many of them children. By nightfall the shelves had been stripped bare. 'They were like a horde of locusts,' one Kessingland shopkeeper remembered.

Maureen Long worked from 1948 in her parent's shop, (F. & M. Bligh, on the corner of High Street and the Market Place). She remembered:

The choice was pretty limited. Just a few brands were available, Cadbury's Dairy Milk small blocks were among them. When we did get bigger bars in, there was one customer who was always coming in and out ready to grab them. She had no family, but she always had plenty of spare coupons, already cut out of the books. She did a job which entailed collecting money and when people could not pay, I was told afterwards, she asked for coupons and put in the cash herself...

There were great celebrations and burning of ration books when it all ended in July 1954. The temptation was great, but many people kept their books as a reminder of those days of austerity, during which we pleaded with the butcher for a little 'offal', ate sponge cakes made with liquid paraffin in place of butter or margarine, tried and rejected such points-free delicacies as tinned 'snoek' and those endless boiled carrots which the Ministry of Food assured us would help us to see in the blackout. Shopkeepers, who seemed to be out of everything, reminded people 'Don't you know there's a war on?'

Chapter 7

Building and Builders

Village Foundations

There were times when Kessingland was literally at 'rock bottom' after the Dissolution of the Monasteries, when, with the church in ruins, some of its stonework was removed to help build other places in the village. The pair of thatched cottages opposite the end of Field Lane were demolished in 1923 for road-widening improvements, but many are convinced that a big piece of village history went with them. Experts believe that they were the oldest buildings in the village, apart from the church tower. They were built around 1580, from stone and other materials 'borrowed' from the ruined church. The ashlar stone for the massive medieval buttresses came from the ruins, as well as a lot of other material. A similar cottage, demolished some years ago, bore a date on a plaque of 1664. News of the demolition brought Suffolk archaeologists out in force to protest and examine the remains. They said it had been an ancient hall or chapel, used as a toll-house on the turnpike road, as a courthouse and perhaps as a guildhall. Their protestations were to no avail, but

they did win one concession, that the massive stonework should be left on the site and at some time returned to the church. It stayed until 1948, when more road improvements necessitated its removal and Revd Chitty was given permission to transport it back to where it had been 'borrowed' from, 360 years earlier!

When the Old Rectory was sold and the newer, smaller Rectory built around the corner in Wash Lane, the Rectory became a much-needed bed-and-breakfast establishment.

There has been much debate about the suspected old guildhall. All we have left now is a photograph and what George Knights can tell us of what he remembers as his family's home. He writes:

The cottage near the road was definitely built from stone from the ruins of the church, which I was always led to believe, was when Cromwell destroyed the original church... The cottage on the left was built of Suffolk handmade red bricks and contained a dairy.

My parents moved there in the late 1890s. My youngest sister was born there in 1900 and myself in

The Old Rectory and rockery, 1990.

Above: *The guildhall.*
Right: *George Knights's father outside Old Guildhall Cottage, early 1900s.*

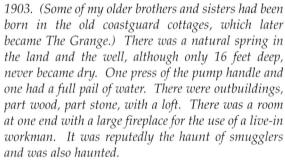

Left and above: *Giant stones in the Old Rectory rockery thought to have come from the guildhall.*

1903. *(Some of my older brothers and sisters had been born in the old coastguard cottages, which later became The Grange.) There was a natural spring in the land and the well, although only 16 feet deep, never became dry. One press of the pump handle and one had a full pail of water. There were outbuildings, part wood, part stone, with a loft. There was a room at one end with a large fireplace for the use of a live-in workman. It was reputedly the haunt of smugglers and was also haunted.*

When the cottage near the road was demolished, the gable end was rebuilt. The busts which are now in the church were identified by Mr Guthrie, the stone-mason, as those of St Edmund the Dane and his wife. The two properties were owned by Mr Chipperfield, of the well-known family of butchers. The rent, inclusive of rates, was £6 per year.

The blacksmith's shop opposite was very old. When it was destroyed by a German bomb, the walls of the old cottage were not damaged as they were so solidly built. The wheelwrights' place was behind the two cottages. I planted the sycamore tree now standing on Blacksmith's Corner...

When I was a boy there were older houses in the village: The Ark in the High Street, the old cottages at the east end of the church which were burned down and others to the south of the Sailor's Home which were swallowed up by the sea. Probably the oldest of all was the cottage at the far end of the Loke (now the Avenue). The house was officially in Kessingland and the large garden and orchard in Gisleham. My dad's grandparents, the Bunns, who lived there, had to pay the tithes of two villages!

As well as various archeological finds made over the years, Peter Cherry discovered more about the origins of the old blacksmith's shop. Despite being destroyed in a wartime bombing raid, the site is still known as 'Blacksmith's Corner'. At that time the blacksmith's was run by the Wade family and the youngest son, Lancelot, died when it was hit by bombs on the evening of 12 May 1943. The Wades also had forges at Mutford and Gisleham.

In the days when most work on farms relied on horse power, there was plenty of work for black-smiths, who were called upon for a variety of skills. The forge at Kessingland must have had a long history but the first tangible evidence seems to date from 1895, when it was among a variety of properties that came up for auction at the Suffolk Hotel on 8 July. Other lots included 10 acres of arable land at 'Mill Mount', which was also described as suitable for building development. Presumably the cottages still known as 'Mill Mount' date from this period when, it seems, building developers were beginning to meet the need for new housing in a village which, because of the booming herring industry, was becoming 'the richest village in England'.

The White House is Moved

A remarkable 'house removal' occurred early in the 1900s when there was a terrific storm and the sea came within yards of the White House on Kessingland Cliffs, just past where Sea Row once stood. That row of houses had been washed into the sea in 1834, when storms and high tides battered the coast.

William and Vera Sampson were a newly engaged couple house-hunting on a small budget. On the morning after the storm, the owner of the White House told Willie she did not know what to do as she could not rent out the house as before or sell it in that condition, with the knowledge that it could be swept

High Street, Kessingland, early 1900s.

Eric, Lancelot and Fred Wade at the blacksmith's shop.

Left: *Builder Charles Brock at home, November 1992.*

Below: *Russell Gage, carpenter and undertaker, 1991.*

Left: *The White House.*

into the sea with the next high tide. Willie told her he would buy it, but only had £40 in savings. The owner thought £40 was better than a heap of rubble, so accepted the offer. Before the next high tide the couple, along with family and friends, dismantled the house and moved the lot to a piece of ground in Wash Lane. They successfully rebuilt it, got married and lived in it until they retired. The adjoining land was used as a market garden, greenhouses were added later and Willie ran a weekend mobile round with a lorry in the village with fresh fruit and vegetables in season.

Amazingly, with Rider Haggard building up the beach, planting marram grass at one end, and Mr Staunton planting lupin plants in the sand at the other end where the White House had stood, the roots were able to hold the sand and the tides never reached that point again.

With Wealth Comes Property

When the fishing bonanza of the late 1800s brought more wealth to the village, building began in earnest. Many extended families that had been forced to live together were suddenly able to move out into their own homes; those early builders had plenty of work. More wealth meant more spending and new shops sprang up as well. Builders such as Mr Catchpole, Mr Kemp, Ernest Marjoram and Mr Brock expanded their workforces.

The Hart family during the war.

Although the Second World War disrupted village and family life, those men fortunate to survive came home with their horizons broadened, longing to get back to civilian life. Tony Hart and his brother Eddie both came home wanting to put the war behind them and forget the horrors of it. Eddie had been in Burma. Tony, in the RAF, gained seven medals and was commended by a US Brigadier General. Both brothers obtained work with a building firm and helped to build council houses at Kessingland and Reydon. Eventually, in the 1950s, the brothers set up their own building business and stayed together until Eddie retired in the 1970s. Tony was ten years off retirement age and not able to manage without Eddie, so he sold the business and began working as a bricklayer at Morton's food factory in Lowestoft.

More builders, plumbers and electricians were needed when farming declined and the land was turned over for building. In the 1970s, when Mr McLean's farm was sold, the Lloyds Avenue estate, including McLean's Drive, sprang up, joining the Beach and the Street 'villages'. The area was dubbed 'Little London'.

After the main development, further building took place between the new estate and the cliffs, with the building of Cliff Park, on both sides of Rider Haggard Lane, until the whole area was occupied. This inevitably put extra strain on services and infrastructure in the village, such as sewerage, health care and education, but these problems are slowly improving.

Later developments have been the estate surrounding The Ark, adding Heritage Green, Noah's Drive and Ark Close to the village map. At the time of writing new building work is taking place on the former Hutson's Meadow.

Kessingland is a growing village, yet somehow manages to retain its community spirit and build links with the existing residents. The variety of carpenters, painters, plumbers and electricians who help maintain property in a good condition follow in a long line of true craftsmen.

Chapter 8

The Post Office

It appears that there has been a High Street Post Office in Kessingland since at least 1858. The house and shop, along with four cottages, were purchased by a Mr James Woolnough, a builder of Lorne Road, Lowestoft, in that year.

From early photographs it seems that the Post Office first sold groceries, and possibly drapery as well. In 1860 the property passed to his son, John, then again in 1865 to a James Woolnough. In the 1880s, on the death of James, William Henry Woolnough inherited. The properties were then valued at £300. He died in 1934, having owned the site the longest, whereupon it was sold the following year to Mr Tom Battrick for £250.

However, none of these owners ran the Post Office themselves, and in 1868 the postmaster was Mr Edward Rackham. He had married Miranda Dann of Shotesham three years earlier. Elderly residents will remember one of his daughters, Nurse Evelyn Rackham, of Courtney House, High Street, born in 1872. She had brothers Wilby (who died in infancy), William (born 1868) and Everard (1870) and sisters Kate (1873) and Ada (1878). The *Post Office Directory* of 1875 records that the village had a Post and Money

Telegram sent to the High Street Post Office after 100 years of sending telegrams, December 1961.

Chris Satchell, postmistress, at the High Street Post Office, 2005.

High Street Post Office, December 2005.

Order and Telegraph Office and Savings Bank. Kate and Ada helped their father and then Ada, who became Mrs Kittle on marriage, continued to run the business. She was later helped by her married daughter, Joan Calver, whose husband, Frank was away at war.

It was in 1940 that the automatic telephone system came into operation. Jean Studd (née Swan) worked at the Post Office from July 1946:

Mrs Ada Kittle was postmistress and her sister Kate lived with her as housekeeper. Telegrams were telephoned through from Lowestoft and then copied onto forms by hand. I had to deliver them by cycle to the outlying villages... If I was lucky, the postman would sometimes take over. There were two postmen Sam(?) and Charlie Brown. The letters were collected from the Post Office and stamped by hand, also the parcels, then put into a big bag and sealed with sealing wax, to be collected by the Lowestoft postman.

I took over the job from Ethel Fiske (now Mrs Newell, of Lowestoft) who lived in Green Lane. When I left, Isobel Brock, wife of Charles Brock, local builder, carried on the job.

Some time during the early 1950s Jack Gage bought the Post Office from Mrs Kittle, running it for the next 30 years. In 1961 he received a congratulatory telegram from the Post Office commemorating 100

years of the National Savings Bank being operated there. After Jack Gage retired, Mr Needham bought it and ran it for two years, when it passed to Stephen Holden in 1984.

Christine Satchell: Life as a Postmistress
(Taken from a 1996 interview)

On moving to Kessingland in 1985 Christine worked at the Beach Post Office, followed by managerial positions at Belton Post Office and Safeway's in-store Post Office, before moving back to Kessingland.

Although the outside of the building has not changed much in the last century, the living quarters have been modernised. The Post Office was also installed with more security and offered more services.

Although born in Braintree, Christine and her family had longstanding ties with Kessingland as they used to visit the area on holiday. When they saw the house in Church Road for sale, complete with its own small orchard, they could not resist it. In due course both Christine's parents and grandmother moved to the village as well. 'We found the people here so friendly when we moved in.'

Christine became heavily involved with village projects, the Parish and the District Councils, the Playing Field Association and Community Council.

The Beach Post Office in the 1920s with Barbara Eyre's Aunt Mildred.

The Beach Post Office in earlier times.

The Beach Post Office

The Post Office at the beach end of the village sadly closed in September 2004, but a satellite branch was opened in January 2005 by Christine at the MASK shop, which sells local arts and crafts and operates a tourist information service. Mrs Barbara Eyre's grandparents, Mr and Mrs Coy, owned this general store and Post Office. Her Aunt Mildred served there until she married Jack France of the village.

Barbara's mother also lived at the Post Office (known as Ceylon House), until she met and married Walter Turrell, nicknamed 'Tarrie' and moved to Leicester, in 1924, where their children were all born. They returned to the Lowestoft area in the 1940s.

After the Coy's ownership, it seems that Mr and Mrs Mallett bought the Post Office. There have been other owners since, including Parish Councillor Paul Chapman and his wife Helen in the 1980s, followed by the last owners, Mr and Mrs Ricketts.

The Beach Post Office and house in the 1920s with Mildred outside.

The King's Head, Kessingland High Street, 1905.

Kessingland High Street, 1905.

Chapter 9

Traders of Former Times

The retail outlets of the 1930s and '40s differed hugely from those which survive on the High Street today. George Swan provided a list of some of the businesses he recalls, some of which have been included below – perhaps this will jog your memories too:

'Lucky' Layton on the corner of the Market Place; Miss Mary Chipperfield who taught the piano; Mallet's Workshop; 'Hurdles' Moyse, who made canoes; the butchers Sidney and Frank Chipperfield; the Queen's Head public house, with Holi Catchpole as landlord, then later Harry Lewis; greengrocer Lily Girling; Eddie Catchpole's shoe shop; Green's Electric Shop, with a clock hanging outside; Slug Shipley's coal yard; Louie Raven who sold homemade ice-cream; the bank, open one day a week, at the house of Mr Watson (later Barclay's built a new bank on the corner of the High Street and the Avenue, but when many rural banks closed, it was sold to the Three Rivers Veterinary Surgery); the bakery, owned by Mr Williams; Pifco Johnson's (who got his nickname from selling Pifco lamps); Judy ('screw your nut') Durrant, who sold newspapers; the fish and chip shop, owned by Charlie Bond and later, Arthur Betts; the harnessmaker's, belonging to Mr Easy; Mrs Bush's (later Mrs Eyre's) clothes shop; Diddy Buds hairdresser's and sweet shop;

George Lee, shoe repairer; Mrs Baker, the dressmaker; the King's Head; Moulton's Café; Bunker Bird the baker's; Clarke's Garage; Bruce the butcher's; Wade's the blacksmith's (bombed during the Second World War); Bertha Strowger's shop; Ernie Marjoram the undertaker.

Memories of Trade at Kessingland
By Colin Durrant

Miss Grace Gertrude Durrant, who was my Aunt, kept the grocery shop (now Costcutters) opposite the King's Head. She had an older sister, Mabel Mallett, and a younger brother, Norman, all of whom were brothers and sisters of my father.

Mabel kept a grocery shop down the beach (later Carol's Newsagent). Norman, who was blind, had a wooden structure shop with a smaller wooden structure store beside this, both of which were situated opposite Mabel's store. Norman made stools and cane baskets of many descriptions, using the knowledge he learned at St Dunstan's. He also sold sweets, etc. Many a Saturday afternoon at Kessingland United Football ground, next door to Podd's farm and opposite the allotments, I would sell on his behalf oranges a penny each or two for three half-pence, plus drinks, sweets and chocolate. Not only the locals, but often the visiting

The top of the High Street, 1905.

59

Sim's Fish Shop, Church Road, 1905.

supporters asked who I was selling for. When Norman's name was mentioned, purchases followed.

Lockwoods was formerly Layton's shop at the entrance to the Market Place. He was known as 'Lucky Layton ' in the village. I saw this gentleman daily, when delivering his copy of the News Chronicle. He regularly wore a long white coat with a white starched apron almost down to his ankles. The shop was heated with a paraffin stove: the warmth was welcoming but the smell off-putting.

Chipperfield's the butchers opposite, had a slaughterhouse at the rear. Often I have seen cattle purchased at Beccles Market being driven back to the village on foot, before being taken to Chipperfield's meadow at the rear of the High Street. The entrance was next to the fish and chip shop, opposite the King's Head.

Chemists in Kessingland

The original owner of the chemist's shop in the High Street, John Wallace Dent, obtained the land from a Mrs Christine Broom in September 1904, and had the shop built in November of that year. He died at the early age of 37 so Mrs Dent took over the shop in 1909 and it was in her hands until she sold it to a Mr C.H. Stevens in 1930.

Some of the older Kessingland residents remember a chemist called Longmate – was he a manager for Mrs Dent at some stage?

In 1935 the shop changed hands again; it was bought by the Perrèdes family from the Channel Islands. Mr Perrèdes conducted some original

research into the use of plant extracts (specifically Reserpine) to reduce blood pressure in hypertension

Chemist shop, 1904.

60

and tranquillise anxious patients.

On the death of his parents, Paul Iago Perrèdes ran the shop from 1950. Dick Carter became the proprietor in April 1965.

Personality Profile: Kevin Knightley
(Taken from a 2004 interview)

Kevin and Jackie Knightley bought the business from Dick Carter, who had spent the previous 30 years running the shop. Born and raised in London, for a while Kevin worked in Customs and Excise, analysing the alcohol content of preparations going in or out of the country. He also worked in the poison unit at Guy's Hospital before undertaking a pharmacy degree. Kevin qualified in 1976 and for a while worked in Australia:

One day a man came in and asked what I had for an eye infection. I could see nothing wrong with his eyes, but he brought a large Australian lizard from behind him. That cleared the shop pretty quickly! I just hoped human eye salve cured him! It probably did as I didn't see him again!

We also were suppliers to the Flying Doctor Service, so had to keep up full stocks. It was a good time and we were able to travel around the country a bit and see something of it. From there I changed to doing a time in hospitals in both Adelaide and Sydney. We spent a year touring before returning home. It was interesting, different and a marvellous experience to fully get acquainted with the Australian people and their ways of life, as well as enjoying the changes of temperatures and stunning scenery. I returned to Basildon Hospital,

where I worked in drugs information, before going into retailing. There followed jobs in pharmacies at Brentwood and Southend, followed by a partnership in Dovercourt, near Harwich for six years... I eventually had the opportunity to purchase this pharmacy in Kessingland...

Kessingland Pharmacy has joined the Numark Group, so it is able to offer monthly special price discounts and packages. All this, plus the experience and training of the proprietor, means a superb service for the village and the outlying region.

Jackie and Kevin implemented the modernisation of the Kessingland chemist's shop, which is up-to-date and efficiently run, but the friendliness and caring service has been continued. The chair for waiting customers may be an up-to-the-minute director's model, but the smiling assistants and customer-friendly hours retain the tradition of the long-established shop.

The pharmacy has been further extended and improved with a resident chiropodist and acupuncturist on site for one day a week. There is also a programme to help smokers give up the habit.

Butchers

Historian Paul Scrivens records the fact that his great-great-grandfather was a butcher here for about 50 years until he retired to Gisleham and later, in about 1901, to Southwold.

A Richard Hammond, butcher, was married at Gisleham in 1837 and is listed in directories of the mid-1800s. He died at the age of 96 and his death

Chipperfield's butcher's shop at Kessingland Beach, 1920s.

Hutson's butcher's, Kessingland Beach, September 1998.

Other notable butchers with a long trading history in Kessingland are the Chipperfields and Hutsons. Sidney Chipperfield made the famous Kessingland sausages to a secret recipe, and perfected home-made chutneys. Ken Hutson became errand boy to Mr Chipperfield, working his way up until he became the owner on Sidney's retirement. He extended the business with shops at Pakefield, South Lowestoft, Southwold and Beccles, before going into the meat packaging business in the 1980s. Hutson's special sausages then became known countrywide. His son John succeeded him until his own premature death, when John's son took over. Ken became well known for giving, carving and presiding over the St Edmund's Church Harvest Suppers during his years in the village, a role which John continued. Hutson's butcher's is still operating in 2006, next to the Queen's Head, but today is managed by John Giles and Hilda Bird, who have introduced bread from Glendower Bakery, fresh fruit and vegetables from Stradbrookes and milk and dairy products from Marybelle. A modern shop with traditional goods continues to succeed in a village like Kessingland, where people have been raised on home-produced, home-cooked food and know what is best for their health.

certificate described him as a 'master butcher, retd'. The 1841 Tithe Award for Kessingland shows a butcher's shop opposite the King's Head owned by John Mower Nickes and occupied by 'Nickes and others'.

General Stores

The small shop listed as Aisie Durrants was later run by sisters Ada and Grace Durrant and later sold to Mr and Mrs Hall, parents of film actor, director

Aladdin's Cave, at the beach, 2005. This site was formerly occupied by Hutson's butcher's and Kessingland Estates took over the property in 2006.

and impresario Sir Peter Hall, on their retirement. The family used to holiday in Kessingland and Mrs Hall said that Peter cut his first tooth in the village! The Halls extended the shop, then Raman (Ray) Patel and his brother purchased it, extended it and modernised it further. It is now a Costcutter mini-market still run by the Patels, whose family was originally from Kenya.

When the Lloyds estate was built, a row of new shops were also constructed, just off Field Lane. A new doctors' surgery was also provided, as well as a hairdresser, newsagent, fish shop and mini-super-market, run by the Prentice brothers, who later moved to Carlton Colville. In an interview in 1996, brothers Ivan and Austin stressed the importance of personal contact with customers in a family business – a sentiment they learnt from their father.

Their parents ran a greengrocery business in St Peter's Street, Lowestoft, and the boys both helped in the shop on Saturdays and holidays, or travelled with their father on the mobile shop he took around the Gunton estate. Ivan left school and went full-time into the business, while Austin, a bit younger, went into the motor-repair trade for seven years. They recalled:

I suppose Dad was forward-looking, because in the 1960s he could see how things were going. Much of the top end of Lowestoft was being pulled down. People were moving out into the outskirts of town. He saw plans of new shops to be built in Kessingland, a growing village, and was keen to move. However, it took two years before the shops were ready. The site of the proposed Shopping Parade was moved three times... until finally there was agreement on the present site.

Eventually in 1971 the new supermarket was ready and the Prentice family moved to Kessingland. Austin left the motor trade and the four of them worked hard to make it a success, helped by Mrs Prentice's sister, who quickly became 'Aunty Mary' to all the customers. Both brothers had married in 1968 and moved into bungalows on the estate (Ivan married Christine and they later had three sons, while Austin married Pat and they had twin daughters).

We've seen lots of changes in Kessingland, problems too that made the job harder, like bread strikes, sugar short-ages, oh and the electricity go-slow... the electricity was off for several hours each day. At first we rigged up lamps which we ran off car batteries. As soon as the power returned we had to recharge the batteries for the next day. This was such a bother that we decided to invest in Calor gas lighting. And just as we got it installed the electricians went back to working properly! During the bread strike we had to halve loaves and try to be fair to regular [customers] and large families.

Same with the sugar shortage, but most customers are grateful and reasonable and you learn to get on with the 'awkward' ones, although you have to have a sense of humour with those.

In 1979 the Prentice brothers bought the fruit and vegetable shop in the parade, run by Austin and Aunty Mary. Three years later the neighbouring hardware shop was added, with Christine's father running that. Four years later both Mr and Mrs Prentice died. The family had to reassess their busi-nesses, eventually opting to knock them all into one in 1991. Prentice's Supermarket, later to become Londis, was now all under one roof and much more convenient for the customers. As other smaller village shops closed, items of clothing and other necessities were added to the Prentice range.

We have never believed in opening for extra long hours or on Sundays, because the quality of family life then suffers. We like to give personal service and as much as we can to the community, but not at the expense of our wives and children.

It's been a recipe that has worked well, with long marriages and happy families, as well as a well-earned respect from Kessingland inhabitants.

Upholstery
(Taken from a 1998 interview with Dale Rogers)

Dale Rogers was born and bred in the village and says he wouldn't like to live anywhere else. The son of a Kessingland girl, from the Catchpole fishing family, and a London musician, Dale always wanted to be a carpenter:

When I left school I remember going to Lowestoft and trying all the local firms, but the recession was just starting to bite and no-one was taking on youngsters. Coming back, I saw a notice in Mr H. Burrows's upholstery shop. I soon realised it was for a trained upholsterer... I started on trial as a trainee upholsterer, at £10 a week. After three days they decided I would do and made the job permanent, with a rise to £12! I stayed there for 13 years until the firm moved away.
The next three months were awful, on the dole until I went to Jeckells, the sail makers. Here, whilst using my carpentry and upholstery skills, I learned a whole new side to the business, marine upholstery, fitting out boats and caravans. It was a new trade that has been useful to me... After several different jobs over the years I decided to start up in business on my own...

Dale is supported by his wife, Jackie, a part-time ancillary worker at Kessingland Primary School, who has business experience from her work with a Lowestoft solicitor, and deals with the bookwork.

Ashley Nursery, March 1993.

The house from which Ashley Nursery started, selling bunches of flowers at the door. Today the house is all that is left of the complex, having been sold for housing.

Carol's Newsagent, with her husband Tony, 2000.

(PHOTOGRAPH EVE HADDOCK)

Stuart Kerr's fish shop, with the winners of an art competition, 2004.

Below: *Former Rockhill Retail, where the district nurse used to trade when it was the Beach Stores. It is now a private residence.* (PHOTOGRAPH EVE HADDOCK)

Kessingland Carpet and Bed Centre, London Road, 1990. It was formerly stonemason Mr Guthrie's workshop, then Mr Burrough's upholstery business.

Trade Today

There are many other thriving businesses too numerous to mention here, and others that have closed down or changed hands. It seems that now, perhaps more than ever, traders need to adapt and diversify to stay afloat.

Kessingland has a great variety of modern stores and services, including hairdressers, beauticians, mobile chiropodists, travel consultants, florists, a tanning and tattooing shop, gift shops, arts and crafts, fish shops, mini-markets, a carpet and beds firm, pet shops, art galleries, carpet cleaning and flue clearing services, as well as driving instructors, electricians, plumbers and builders, to name but a few. A Sunday market on land near the Wildlife Park upsets local traders with high business rates to find, and a supermarket down the road has also closed small shops, but the pioneering spirit still seems alive and well and as one business closes, another seems to take its place. It seems that where family businesses flourish, the community spirit is alive and well.

The Waterfront, formerly Wavecrest Café, with owners Tina and David Wall, 2001.

Right: *The Sailor's Home and Restaurant with former owners Helen and Peter Devey, 2001.*

The marram grass at The Grange, 1905.

The Grange and garden, 1905.

Artwork at the HRH Festival, 1990.

Chapter 10

Sir Henry Rider Haggard KBE

After the success of *King Solomon's Mines*, Rider Haggard's most famous book, which has not been out of print since it was first published in 1885, the author bought two rows of former coastguard cottages on the cliffs at Kessingland. He turned them into one house, The Grange, by adding a passage at the end, creating one building in the shape of a square with the seaward side missing. There were 16 bedrooms, each named after a British Admiral, but the master bedroom was called 'Nelson', Haggard's hero.

His wife, Louisa, disliked Ditchingham House (where she had been born and brought up) in the autumn because she said it was 'cold in the fall of the leaf'. Consequently, each autumn she would take a suite of rooms at the Hotel Victoria in Lowestoft. Rider must have realised that his own second home would be less expensive!

There is no Hall or 'big house' in the village, so after his knighthood in 1919, he must have been the nearest thing to landed gentry that the village could boast. He certainly loved Kessingland and would cycle from Ditchingham or take the train from Bungay to Lowestoft and then cycle from there, in all weathers, to keep an eye on his 10 acres of farm land which surrounded the house, and to have peace and quiet to write. Much of his acclaimed work on gardening, such as *The Gardener's Year* was written at The Grange. He wrote:

I have another garden at a place by the sea, Kessingland in Suffolk, quite a humble one, but with certain qualities of its own. Thus the vegetables grown there have a better flavour than any others with which I am acquainted and the asparagus is superb. Carnations flourish like weeds, all of which things I suppose are to be accounted for by the excellence of the soil and the abundance of salt in the air.

A croquet court was laid, an added attraction for his many visitors when the beach was too cold. Rider wrote: 'There is nothing between my house and the North Pole.'

The house had 'wandering passages, queer cubby holes and unexpected rooms'. He renamed the house Kessingland Grange. Soon the walls were adorned: the drawing-room with religious pictures, the dining-room with pictures of the kings and queens of England and paintings by Sir Edwin Landseer, and the morning room with samplers. Those wandering passages became a monument to his African journeys, with Zulu assegais (spears), native war horns, ox-hide shields and knobkerries (a South African weapon). Framed Maurice Greiffenhagen originals of the illustrations for his books adorned the joining passage. It was a strange atmosphere, yet his children and their cousins loved the house and there were many family gatherings there. Some remember a cherished bust of Nelson, dated 1812, which was said to have been carved from timbers of the *Victory*. A pewter plate dated 1802 was another favourite.

Kipling frequently visited the house and one elderly lady recalled that he recited his famous poem 'If' in the village church. He was in the house just before the First World War when Haggard was away on a tour for his work on the Royal Commission on Penal Reform. Apparently some villagers thought Kipling to be a German spy, since he was interested in all that went on and asked a lot of questions! They were reticent, apparently, but he must have written some of the poems in his *Fringes of the Fleet* collection while on that visit, namely 'In Lowestoft a boat was laid...'

Writing to a friend on 4 August 1914, the day the war started, Kipling described The Grange as:

For all practical purposes like the side of a ship. The garden runs about fifteen feet to the cliff, then the sea and all the drama of the skirts of war are laid out before us. Destroyers going up and down in twos and fours – then a gunboat or so...

Although Haggard was ten years older, the two friends had much in common. At one time Kipling lived in the Elms at Rottingdean, near Brighton. The cliffs, old smugglers' passages, wrecks, fishing, farming and village life focused around the church – very similar to life at Kessingland. Rider had lost his only son, Jock, from measles when the child was only nine. Rudyard was to lose his only son, Jack, in the war which he had dreaded, and the coming of which he had written about in such poems as 'The Dyke'. Both men were keen gardeners, ardent churchgoers, fiercely patriotic and willing to give time and energy to their country and their local communities. They both had inventive minds that did not rest until the book was completed or the problem solved. But although Rudyard was an early motorist, Rider kept to his bicycle, trains and boats.

Kessingland probably saw its first Rolls-Royce in 1913, when Rudyard visited The Grange and brought both a Silver Ghost and its newly acquired chauffeur.

Rider had added garages to the property, for the convenience of his guests, even though he only needed a bicycle shed!

There are also suggestions that the first mobile telephone was invented in Kessingland! The opening chapter of *Stella Fregelius* was definitely written as Rider looked out from his garden wall over the sea. The book tells the story of an inventor who designs an 'aerophone', the first cordless telephone. Essentially a love story, the tale ends with a tragedy involving the sea.

Haggard was knighted not for his literature, but for his sterling work on penal reform and sea defence. He was greatly ahead of his time in these subjects and sat on Royal Commissions which took him abroad on fact-finding expeditions. A prolific writer, he would use every opportunity to absorb local knowledge and customs, which made his adventure stories so intriguing and exciting.

It was the destruction of the cliff and properties at Pakefield in 1905 which led Haggard to consider ways of protecting his own property. He wrote in his diary for 27 December that year:

Today a fierce gale is blowing from the sou'west and against it – having business there – I struggled to Kessingland, accomplishing most of the journey upon a bicycle. The ride from Lowestoft, in the very teeth of the wind, was the hardest I have ever undertaken. Very frequently indeed I was obliged to dismount and push behind, a duty that was not made more entertaining by the sight of a curate, cigarette in mouth, sailing past me in the opposite direction, his feet reposing on the rests...

At length I turned into the lane which leads to Cliff Grange, the very easternmost dwelling, I suppose in the whole kingdom, and as the wind was now upon my side, got along much better, until a most ferocious gust blew me and the bicycle several yards into a ploughed field. The sight from the cliff was very grand – a sullen-fretted sea raging beneath a low and sullen sky. But a gale from the sou'west is not that which does damage on the eastern coast – it is the nor'easter that we dread, especially if it be accompanied by very high tides. This is what happened in the great storm of last December, when the tide and the sea rose higher than they are believed to have done for the best part of a century. The damage at Lowestoft, Southwold, Pakefield, etc., was enormous and as I have come into possession of this Kessingland property, my state of mind until I heard that it had taken no harm, can be imagined. I think however, that if our cliff can still resist the worst of the onslaught of two generations, for the future we may sleep at ease. As a fact indeed, the beach at Kessingland is increasing in width: in front of my house it has risen more that five feet in a single year. This is consoling, but he who has to deal with the sea can never be quite certain of anything. If old Ocean wishes to have a thing, he will take it, and

at present he is taking Southwold and Pakefield, with other places; also large stretches of marshland are being ruined by the continual advance of the tide along the rivers.

But the inhabitants of East Anglia still do little or nothing concerted. Every man for himself, is the cry, and let the sea take the rest.

Conservationists are still arguing about the most efficient ways of dealing with coastal erosion.

Rider remembered that when he was in Africa, where plants were rooted, the storms and torrential rains did not sweep away the soil. He therefore experimented with various types of seed from strong African grasses, growing them in his greenhouse in Kessingland. Marram grass flourished and spread the fastest, so he transplanted little tufts out onto the beach. He records that in five years he had built up the beach by 12 feet under the cliffs. Before that the waves would lap at the bottom of the cliffs. It was painstaking work, but he persevered and today most of the coast of England is enhanced by marram grass.

Coastal erosion is still very much on the local and national agenda, although Kessingland's beach continues to build up, with sand and gravel swept in from the erosion at Benacre, just around the corner.

Sir Henry Rider Haggard 1856–1925
By the late Commander Mark Cheyne, 1989, Haggard's grandson, President of the HRH Society

If anyone was asked to quote six names associated with Haggard, I think it is likely they would include Allan

Sir Henry Rider Haggard, a great reader and writer, pictured in the early 1900s.

Haggard with his mother and sister.

(PHOTOGRAPH SUPPLIED BY ALAN GILL)

Sir Henry's barrister's wig.

Quatermain, Umslopo-gaas, Gagool, Chaka, Cetewayo and Captain Good. The interesting feature about these names is not that they are all characters from some of his 59 novels, but that half of them were inventions of his own fertile mind and half of them were real living people, and therein lay the secret of his phenomenal success as a spinner of adventure yarns, for he had the knack of intermingling fact and fiction so skilfully together that his readers suspended belief to such a degree that, under the spell of his writing, they became perfectly willing to accept the unaccept-able and believe the unbelievable.

Rider was born in 1856 at Wood Farm, Bradenham in Norfolk, part of the estate owned by his father, William Haggard. It has always been believed in the family that Rider acquired his fertile imagination from an ancestor who was reported to have been a Begum. A green and gold inlaid Indian brooch, supposed to have belonged to her, is still handed down to the eldest daughters in the family. Rider himself believed that he owed much of his literary ability to his mother.

After three years at Ipswich Grammar School, followed by private tuition for the Foreign Office Entrance Examination (but before this could be taken) William Haggard arranged for his son to be attached to the staff of Sir Henry Bulmer of Heydon in Norfolk, who had been appointed Governor of Natal.

In due course he arrived in South Africa to be faced

with the uneasy complications arising out of the existence of two white peoples – the English and the Dutch – who were hereditary foes and only waiting for the removal of a common danger – the Zulus – to spring at each other's throats.

After four years he returned to England... He lost no time in becoming engaged to be married, but the path to the altar was not an easy one. The young lady's guardians (she was an orphan heiress and owner of Ditchingham House in Norfolk) did not approve of the penniless adventurer from Africa as a suitable husband, and made Miss Margitson a ward-in-chancery. This delayed the ceremony for about a year, after which the pair returned to the Transvaal to farm – amongst other things, ostriches – which the groom described as being troublesome and ferocious birds... Within two years he and his wife, together with their firstborn son, returned to England where he was called to the Bar and made his first assays in authorship...

He was the epitome of a country squire and the 'English Gentleman' – an upholder of the village and all it stood for, including the local church...

The pattern of his life was to spend long periods at home followed by months of purposeful travelling. His travels provided him with material for many of his novels. He was something of a mystic.

To my mind he achieved more in his life than could reasonably be expected of 20 other men. He died on 14 May 1925.

Haggard and Hollywood
(Taken from an article by Shirley M. Addy, Rider Haggard Society)

Many film versions of Haggard's books have been made – even as early as 1899. In true Hollywood fashion, the screen goddess Theda Bara played the title role in Cleopatra in 1917. The film makers plagiarised

Haggard's book of the same title and it was some years before he was given payment for it. At least 12 of Haggard's works were used in movies but some were so wildly removed from the books that only Haggard's well-known title in the credits linked him to the work!

The Grange

The Grange was requisitioned for army barracks during the First World War and much damage was done to the décor, furnishings and fittings. Rider had no heart for the house after the war, seeming slow to get it repaired and refitted. However, his daughter, who had married Captain Reginald Cheyne, lived there with her young family until Haggard's death in 1925, when it was sold to Mr Catchpole, who turned the house and land into a holiday camp.

In its heyday, the house and its visitors certainly made an impact on the village, bringing employment and excitement to village life. Haggard joined in community affairs when in residence, opening fêtes, giving out Sunday-school prizes, chairing meetings, donating to good causes and caring about the environment. Famous visitors included, as well as Rudyard and Carrie Kipling, Andrew Lang and Sir Max Aitken, later to become Lord Beaverbrook, as well as other renowned MPs, writers and artists.

Rider Haggard's Legacy

Today he is remembered in the names of Rider Haggard Lane, Kipling Close and the hearts of those who appreciated his life and literature. After Catchpole's Holiday Camp was sold, the new owner tore down the house and replaced it with holiday cottages – quite a shock for the village. No one had thought to put a preservation order on the property.

However, the Maritime and Art Society of Kessingland (MASK) held a Rider Haggard Festival in 1990 to commemorate over a century of Sir Henry Rider Haggard's involvement with the village. A commemorative booklet was written by Gill Grey and Maureen Long and published by Michael Knights, who had dreamed up the idea of the festival; and a video was made by Ken Brickell. Haggard's grandson, Commander Mark Cheyne, and family gave generous assistance and permission to use photographs and excerpts from his work and the Rider Haggard Society held its annual meeting in Kessingland, where many more friends and links were made. Today the MASK tourist shop and information centre continues the work, selling books and various souvenirs linked to Kessingland's most famous home-owner.

The village is proud to have had HRH as a resident. He was commonly called HRH after finding that when travelling abroad, he was often mistaken for the Prince of Wales, because of the initials on his

A wedding present bought by Rider Haggard for an employee.

Bottom of the above vase.

The Grange commemorative vase, early 1900s.

Rider Haggard rare books at the HRH Festival in 1990.

Top right: *Paul Routledge of Norwich Record Centre speaking at the HRH Festival in 1990. Mrs Nada and Commander Mark Cheyne are in the front row.*

Above: *HRH Festival exhibition, 1990, with copies of* The Noonstar.

Left: *Items for sale and display at the HRH Festival.*

A resident shows his HRH collection.

cases. This gave him prompt and excellent service wherever he travelled, and tickled his fine sense of humour. He even planted a bank of daffodils at Ditchingham House in the form of the lettering, which has been preserved to this day.

Personality Profile: Mark Cheyne

Mark Cheyne lived at The Grange as a small child. Later, after 26 years' service in the Royal Navy, having been awarded the Distinguished Service Cross in 1943 for action in the Mediterranean during the Second World War, he retired back to Ditchingham to farm the family estate, as Sir Rider had done before him, giving himself unstintingly to community life. As well as his church duties at St Mary's, he served on Norfolk County Council, the District Council and the Parish Council, and was Deputy Lieutenant of Norfolk and Port & Haven Commissioner at Great Yarmouth.

Generous in spirit, with a wide knowledge of the world and his past family's varied talents and exploits, Mark is greatly missed by all who had the privilege to know and respect him. He was pleased to accept the Presidency of the RHS because he so greatly admired his grandfather's achievements, as both a writer and a public servant.

Mark had mobility problems for a long time, but always persevered to keep appointments and turn up at events, however painfully. However, hip operations and other treatment did alleviate them somewhat until his last illness. Commander Mark Cheyne, DSC, RN, (retd), DL, lives on in the hearts of those who loved him, in the prolific writing legacy he left behind, including letters and articles on all kinds of subjects, but especially about his grandfather, and in the influence he had on so many people who came into contact with him in his varied career.

Waveney MP David Porter (right) *visited the exhibition in 1990, seen here with* (left to right) *Maureen Long, Michael Knights and Evelyn Mathias.*

Chapter 11

From Shanks's Pony to Aviation and the Hovercraft

At one time, stagecoaches called at the King's Head, an ancient inn with a toll-gate, on the way to London. It was here that the charter of the Suffolk Humane Society was signed by the 1st Earl of Stradbrooke and by Sir Thomas Gooch. This was the forerunner of the RNLI.

In 1875 it was recorded that there was other, more local, travel. The Morning Star coach operated from Southwold to Lowestoft during the summer season, passing through at 10.15a.m. on Mondays, Wednesdays and Saturdays, returning the same day. The local carter was James Woolnough, who went to Lowestoft and back daily. Later Mr Harvey conveyed goods to Lowestoft.

At the beginning of the railway era, a line was planned from Lowestoft to Southwold, passing through Kessingland, but the cost of this eventually brought a halt to the project, although old sleepers have been found underground at Pakefield, showing that the work was started. There were horse-drawn wagons that carried passengers to Pakefield and Lowestoft in the late 1800s, followed by motor coaches later. The trams stopped at Pakefield, but buses eventually serviced the village.

The advent of the motor car meant that petrol was needed, as well as motor repairs. Mr Percy Clarke decided to help things along by running a taxi service and eventually sacrificed his front garden area by putting petrol pumps onto a forecourt in front of his bungalow. *White's Directory* of 1937 lists Clarke Bros as motor engineers and Thomas Clarke & Sons as 'cyclemakers'. Further along from the petrol pumps, they had a shop in the High Street (now the Tanning Centre) selling made-to-measure bicycles with the motor repair shop next door. Ivan Clarke, Percy's son and the last family member to run the business, has the last stamp which was put on the specially hand-made cycles.

The local service station, now a Jet outlet for fuel and general goods run by Richard and Lyn Pont, is still on the same site as the bungalow, whilst the motor-repair business is still operating a few yards further along, now renamed Kessingland Garage and MOT Centre and owned by Mr Gary Bligh.

Today this service station is the only fuel outlet in the village, but in Percy Clarke's day there was competition on the other side of the High Street, where 'Pifco' had a similar outfit, except that he did not make cycles! His extra services included charging up accumulators for old radios.

Clarke's Garage, early 1930s.

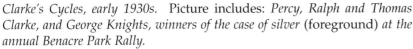

Mr H. Johnson ('Pifco'), 1950s.

Clarke's Cycles, early 1930s. Picture includes: Percy, Ralph and Thomas Clarke, and George Knights, winners of the case of silver (foreground) *at the annual Benacre Park Rally.*

Mrs Gladys Harvey remembered that Mr H. Johnson's Garage had a petrol pump almost on the pavement, an 'office' at the front of his cottage and an Esso sign. Motorists would pull up on the road outside and 'Pifco' would come out to serve them. He did a good trade from Kessingland and surrounding villages. Mr Percy Clarke, on the other hand, had a forecourt in front of his modern bungalow.

'Pifco's' was in a row of cottages next to the old bakery. Mr Johnson started off by mending bicycles and the first pump installed was for paraffin in a day when, even if you were fortunate enough to have discarded your oil-lights for electricity, you still used paraffin mainly for heating, cooking and for the Tilley lights used outside. Around 40 years ago Maureen Long would come in from Henstead to bring the children to Kessingland Upper School and pay 5s. (25p) a gallon of petrol for her 1936 Austin Cambridge, complete with running boards. It was often necessary to pick up an 'accumulator', which ran her father-in-law's wireless set. She was much more modern, having acquired a battery-powered radio as a wedding present; Pifco sold those, too. They were a necessary luxury in the depths of the countryside before television was widely affordable, with radio the only entertainment if you were at home with small children or too old to partake of the occasional social activities of Henstead, Hulver, Gisleham, Rushmere and other neighbouring hamlets. What a disappointment if the battery ran out in the middle of *Much Binding in the Marsh* or *Hancock's Half-Hour*!

Modernisation led to improvisation and most former cycle-makers (like Percy Clarke) or repairmen (like 'Pifco') had to learn the rudiments of simple car maintenance and repairs.

Transport at Kessingland
By Colin Durrant

My memory of village life through the mid-1930s until I left in 1944 remain vivid.

Living next door to Pifco, I saw and conversed with him daily. He was a quiet man, supplying and repairing cycles, serving petrol from the old hand-wound pumps, checking the engine oil of the few cars at that time, and inflating willingly, free of charge, with air the tubes of cycles belonging to the local youngsters who did not possess, or whose parents could not afford a cycle pump. During the war years he produced components for the war effort on a lathe inside his workshop.

Like Gladys Wyatt, I remember also the occasion that the cat was rescued from the well. This person was also a neighbour of Pifco's. Gladys, I recall, had two sisters, Honour and Lilian. Their mum, I believe I am correct in saying, was occasionally called to 'lay out' (prepare someone for burial), possibly performing this task for Mr Ernest Marjoram, the local under-taker. The black horses pulling the hearse, with the mourners' carriage following behind, or the mourners walking behind to the church, was a frequent sight. Mrs Kittle, the High Street village postmistress, and Williams the baker's opposite, with the front room of the adjacent house being used by Barclay's Bank every other Thursday morning, makes one realise how much life has changed.

Transport of Yesteryear
By George Swan

I recall the use of horses and other modes of transport in the village when I was a lad. Sam Weavers had a horse and covered-in cart, selling hardware and paraffin oil, as most houses did not have electricity. There was Bunker Bird, the baker, who also had a country round. His cart shed was in Chapel (now Church) Road, where the police house now stands. Another baker came in from Lowestoft. I helped him after school for a few pence. Then there was Slug Shipley, the coalman, so named because there never was a slower horse. The milkman was Bob Spindler from Gisleham. Milk was served from a large can into jugs. Dougie McLean – all he had at first was a bike (McLean's Drive is now named after him). Doreen Cook (later Doreen Ellender) did a milk round in the village for Dougie with a horse and cart.

Frank and Sidney Chipperfield, butchers, had a pony and cart for delivering their meat. The pony was kept down the Loke past the Working Men's Club.

Then of course there were the night-soil collectors. They were known by the awful name of scavengers, but more usually called 'The Honey Cart', not because of the sweet smell, either! They used a horse and covered-in cart. All that they collected was dumped on land where The Nordalls now is...

Then there are lorries and cars that I remember. Mr Percy Clarke at The Garage owned a silver Lagonda. Williams the baker had a two-tone brown and cream car to take the two sisters to the Beach School, where they were both teachers. They also had a small van for delivering bread. Mrs Chipperfield had a car, as did the dreaded headmaster, Henry Caston. I can still remember the registration number: BRT 142.

The lorries belonged to Wily Harvey, Hundred Catchpole, Willy Sampson, Nosey Durrant and of course Knat Bunn from Wrentham. His had spoked wheels, solid tyres and a claxon horn... How times have changed!

Making History

A more recent but highly successful business is Church Motors, run by Fred Sewell, whose wife Jill runs The Knoll bed and breakfast accommodation. Fred's son-in-law also operates a valet service behind the large premises off Church Road. There have been other smaller repair businesses, run by Trevor Murray, Mick Sutton, who now operates the vital local taxi service, and David Long. David specialised in older and veteran car repairs and restoration. As more men, women and young people acquired cars, the facilities grew accordingly to keep people mobile.

However, not all transport comes with four wheels and there have been pioneers in other fields. A notable one was Captain Sanders, who invented an early aeroplane; he built it in a shed and tried it out on the beach. As Peter Cherry recorded:

Motorbus, 1905.

Former Land Rover Centre in an old beating shed, now converted to a residential property, 1990.

David Long's workshop at the back of Trevor Murray's Land Rover Centre, 1990.

Top and above: *Church Motors with owner Fred Sewell, 2000.*

Inside David Long's workshop, 1990.

Top, above and right:
Captain Sanders at Kessingland Beach, 1909.

It was an historic moment at Kessingland when, in October 1909, the first man to fly in Suffolk or Norfolk took off from the Denes just to the south of Benacre Ness. Crowds gathered to watch Captain Haydn Sanders and his team trundle the biplane along the beach to the primitive airfield on the Denes. There was jubilation when the machine was seen to take to the air and carry out a successful flight.

Captain Sanders, a former Merchant Navy officer, was one of the very early pioneers of flight. Early in the century his home was at Croydon, where his father was a journalist, and there he formed the Croydon Aeroplane Co. Ltd.

Just why he chose to shift his plane building to Kessingland is not clear – perhaps it was the flat country-side and the expanse of sea. It was while he was living in Kessingland that he met and married Maud 'Dumps' Davis, the daughter of coastguard Francis Davis. Maud was a tall good-looking lady and why she was known as 'Dumps' is something of a mystery!

Captain Sanders set up a workshop where he began his plane, which was powered by a Brooke engine from Adrian Works in Lowestoft.

He made a number of trial flights in his flying machine, but one, in February 1910 ended in disaster. He had flown along the Denes as far as the Lifeboat Shed and was on his way back when a sudden gust of wind forced the plane out of control, its skid caught the telegraph wires and crashed. The plane was a total wreck but Captain Sanders escaped with bruising and a severe shake-up.

This persuaded him to transfer his flights to Beccles Common. Here he had a large wooden hangar where he built new models. When I talked to him in the 1950s he recalled that on one occasion he took on the challenge to race a train from Beccles to Lowestoft. 'I didn't make it', he told me, 'A hedge got in the way'.

His aeroplane company was wound up in 1914 when he joined the Royal Flying Corps. Here again he had a miraculous escape. He had swung the prop to start the engine and it was ticking over when he fell head first into it. 'I got some injuries to my head', he recalled 'but the propeller was smashed'. When I knew him in the 1950s he was growing carnations at his commercial nursery in Somerleyton Road, Lowestoft. Looking back on his pioneer days of flight, he told me, 'I feel now that aeroplanes were something the world could well have done without'.

There was great excitement the first time a charabanc was seen in the village – early coaches brought visitors to see the lupins at the beach (see Chapter 12).

Cycling Around Kessingland

Even up to 50 or so years ago, bicycles were the most common mode of transport. With the village having its own cycle makers in the Clarke brothers, it was better served than most villages. Later, when Clarke's was totally motorised, Reg Huggins came into his own, as he had a cycle parts and repair shop in London Road. Reg also sold accessories and general necessities for cyclists, gardeners and local handymen. He attended the local weekly auctions at Beccles Saleground, where, as well as second-hand cycles, he picked up other 'bargains'. He was sorely missed when he eventually retired. After his death, his wife moved and the property became residential.

Travelling in Style
(Inspired by a 2001 article, with additional research supplied by David Long)

Even today we do not see a lot of Rolls-Royces running around Kessingland. Your editor often sees a beautiful pale blue one in Lowestoft, with her initials on the number plate, owner unknown. (We can all dream!)

As far as we can ascertain, the first one spotted in the village was in 1913 or '14. Prolific writer and poet, Rudyard Kipling, great friend of Sir Henry Rider Haggard, was one of the pioneers of motoring. Always adventurous, he first hired a car from a Brighton agency. He described it as 'a Victorian hooded, carriage-sprung, carriage braked, single cylinder, belt-driven, fixed ignition Embryo, which at times could cover eight miles an hour.' Next, in 1901, he purchased a Locomobile Steamer, which he called the 'Holy Terror' when she played him up and 'Coughing Jane' on other occasions. It was American, as was his wife, but he once said, when it broke down only 100 yards from home, 'Carrie, my Dear, American girls are the best in the world but American cars – damn them'. Pretty strong words for the time! He said it had the 'most beautiful and excellent carriage' and 'her lines are lovely, her form is elegant'. He wrote to his mother-in-law in the States:

You won't know Brighton or Brighton seafront so you will never understand the joy of breaking down for lack of fuel under the eyes of 5,000 Brighton Hackneymen and about 2,000,000 trippers.

Kipling owned a Daimler, but finding repairs so expensive he eventually acquired a Rolls-Royce. Michael Smith, secretary of the Kipling Society, told us that Kipling kept a motoring journal. This, along with other documentary evidence, suggests that the first sighting of a Rolls-Royce in Kessingland could have been Kipling's Silver Spectre. We know that the Kiplings, who loved staying at The Grange with Rider Haggard, spent part of the summers of 1913 and 1914 here.

Traffic Today

Today traffic has become as heavy in the village as

Hovercraft and 'beach furniture' now sadly removed, 1999.

Beached hovercraft, 1999.

everywhere else, especially in the summer season. Towards the end of the twentieth century a bypass was built, rerouting the A12 road to the side of Kessingland, and traffic-calming measures were introduced near the school in Field Lane.

Although there have been no more flying experiments on the beach, there was a hovercraft which was blown off course a few years back, spending several days on the sand until it could be refloated. The craft was transporting some golfers from the South of England to Scotland, but they were diverted and spent the waiting time in a nearby hotel, which just goes to show that even with the most up-to-date and original modes of transport, things can go wrong and 'time and tide wait for no man!'

A Snapshot of Kessingland:
The Ford Jenkins Collection

The village owes a debt of gratitude to the late Ford Jenkins of Lowestoft, who photographed most of the village in the first decade of the twentieth century, at a time when not many people owned a camera and there would be little in the way of pictorial records passed down through families, except perhaps wedding or christening portraits. Ford photographed the village as it was: the beach, boats, boatshed, streets, with people or early transport, old prams, bath chairs, houses, the church, chapel and schools.

Ford's son, Peter, followed him into the business and has copied many of the Kessingland photographs, from original glass plates, for use in the village.

Ford himself turned most of his photographs of Kessingland, Pakefield, Lowestoft and neighbouring places into postcards, which he sold to tourists. As soon as he had developed a picture, he turned it into a postcard which he sold outside his shop. Such postcards are quite hard to find now (and, indeed, rather expensive at postcard fairs or collectors' shops), but with a good selection of the photographs in the hands of villagers, Ford Jenkins left us a valuable legacy of what the village looked like a century ago.

High Path, 1907. Note the wooden former beating shed, behind the gentleman.

Beach village, early 1900s.

Cliffs around Kessingland, early 1900s. D'Arcy's House is to the left with Cliff House behind.

Beach cafés, 1907.

Cyclist in Church Road, early 1900s.

South Cliff, 1905.

Belvedere Drive, early 1900s, with Bethel Drive in the foreground.

The top of Church Road, looking down the Beach village.

Visitors have enjoyed the beach for generations.

Cliff House, 1905.

Dunes.

Church Road. The shop belonging to J.R. Smith, local bootmaker and draper, is on the right, with the sheeting sun blind.

The view opposite the Sailor's Home.

Red House, North Cliff.

Ocean View and Sea View on Coastguard Lane, with an old beating shed to the right.

Church Road.

Above and right: *Cliff path.*

Caledonia, 1910s. This was a beach hut from which bathing huts could be hired.

Sandhills.

A popular spot for a country walk – 'Lupinland'.

Chapter 12

A Holiday Haven

Kessingland is part of the Suffolk Heritage Coast. Within reach of the beautiful city of Norwich and with sand, sea, countryside and wildlife, holiday camps with chalets and caravans for hire and nearby market towns, , it is no wonder that Kessingland is a favourite place for holiday-makers. Being the most easterly village in Britain, where the sun shines first, it was also a favourite place to be for the millennium New Year.

The Land of the Lupins
Taken from an article by Peter Cherry

Lupins have been blooming on our denes and beach for getting on for about 100 years, attracting visitors to admire and pick the flowers. How did the lupins arrive on our beach in the first place? Legend has it that a ship carrying lupin seeds as part of its cargo was wrecked on this stretch of coast and some of the seed was washed ashore. However, it seems that we owe our heritage of lupins to two men – the Revd J.C. Vawdrey, who was rector from 1900 to 1909, and Mr George Staunton, lord of the manor, who lived in the White House close to the beach. Revd Vawdrey had noticed lupins growing in the rectory garden. Mr Staunton also admired them and the rector gave him a couple of plants. He planted them in the garden of the White House and was so impressed by the way in which they flourished in the sandy soil that he began saving the seeds. In addition to growing well in the sandy soil they helped to bind the sand and shingle together and also acted as a fertiliser. Mr Staunton set himself an annual task of threshing out the seed and broadcasting it on the beach. Eventually he was sowing over a stone of seed every year.

Kessingland Grange, Catchpole's Holiday Camp in the 1940s.

The brilliant display drew crowds of visitors who could not resist tearing up the plants and taking bunches home. 'Lupinseed' Staunton eventually lost heart and when he moved away from the village it was feared that the lupins might die out, but somehow they managed to survive.

The White House eventually became the home of Colonel and Lady Violet Gregson but the increasing threat of sea erosion during the 1930s forced them to leave. It seemed that the White House was doomed to become a victim of the sea when local market gardener, Willie Sampson bought it for £40, knowing he had to demolish and remove it in six weeks, before the next spring tide.

Happy Campers

Since visitors first started coming to see the lupins, many coaches have dropped off loads of holiday-makers, many of them bound for the three main holiday camps operating in the twentieth century. These were Catchpole's Holiday Camp, the Youth Holiday Fellowship Camp and Denes Holiday Camp.

Outside The Grange, 1905.

The Grange, 1905.

Catchpole's Holiday Camp

Sir Henry Rider Haggard's house, The Grange, was sold on his death in 1925 to Mr Catchpole, who also owned Cliff House, further along the coast. The combined house and land became 'Catchpole's Holiday Camp'. He built wooden chalets on the land and both houses were used for holiday lettings. The dining-room was housed in the long 'passage' that Haggard had built to join the two rows of original coastguard cottages together when he bought The Grange. Other rooms were used as lounges and entertainment venues. A brochure tells us that the camp was completed and opened in 1929 and was affiliated to the National Federation of Permanent Holiday Camps (NFPHC). Visitors were promised that they would 'meet friendly folk, enjoy good food in pleasant and clean surroundings and be invited, but not forced, to join in the entertainments...' It also stated that 80 per cent of the camp's visitors returned time and time again.

It seems that Mr Catchpole gave a comprehensive service to meet the needs of those who visited, his success being reflected in the fact that huge numbers of satisfied customers returned year on year.

Holiday Youth Fellowship Camp

On the next part of the cliffs, coming back towards the Beach village, was the Holiday Youth Fellowship Camp. This was used by parties of young people, some from deprived areas, for cheap holidays at the seaside.

Visitors to the MASK shop frequently ask for information and old photographs of the camp, as it was requisitioned by the Army during the Second World War and many former soldiers, as well as the school-children who camped there, revisit the village and search for clues as to where it was situated. John Keetling from Derbyshire visited several years ago and was invited to write of his experiences for the *Kessingland Times*. His account is included below:

Any involvement between father and children in our family was minimal, but that was nothing unusual in those days. The war had not long ended and you were lucky to have a Dad who had not been killed in the war.

Our father worked five and a half days a week. Saturday afternoon and Sunday lunch times were spent in the public house or fishing, while Sunday afternoon and evenings were spent sleeping off the drink and getting fit enough to start a new week in the foundry. Cigarettes and beer took care of all spare cash, in fact it took priority over everything. Never, in all Dad's working life, did Mum ever see a wage packet or have any idea what proportion of his wages went towards her house-keeping money.

I do not recall going on holiday with my parents. With six children and only one bread-winner, Mother had little chance of taking us anywhere that cost money. The nearest coast was ninety miles away from Derby, which put even an individual rail or bus ticket out of reach.

What I do clearly recall is the day Mother informed me that, as a prize for good effort and results at school, I had been selected for a week's holiday by the sea. A holiday by the sea meant that at thirteen years old, I was to see the coast for the first time.

I was pretty 'street-wise' at that age, but treated this 'prize' like a gift from Santa. The holiday was a week's stay with school mates and staff at a place called the Holiday Fellowship Camp at Kessingland.

Children who have not had a holiday abroad before starting school these days are classed as under privileged, but here was I, almost old enough to leave school and overjoyed at the thought of going on a holiday by the sea. It was some 40 years later, at a school reunion, before I saw it recorded officially in school documents that the holiday was for under-privileged children. Under privileged! I had seen and done more in my short life by the age of 13 than many had in twice the time.

Mother told me that I had to go to my final interview with the Education Committee before being officially accepted on the holiday. She insisted that I had a good wash and turned me out in a reasonably clean condition for this 'interview' that just happened to be at the School Clinic. A full medical was carried out, literally from head to toe. Head for lice, feet for verruca and everything else in between to make sure that I had nothing that was catching, or a danger to other members of the party. That was it then. No money to pay, so that danger was out of the way. I was on the list. School staff pleaded that we do nothing to tarnish the name of the school. There were about 30 kids and eight staff in the party with children and staff of both sexes.

Preparations were made for the holiday but it was more a feeling of excitement and urging the day to come than preparing material things. What material things had we got, anyway? If we had a couple of decent-sized suitcases between us we could have got all the kids' luggage into them as one set of clothes on and one set in the wash was an accepted wardrobe for kids in our street.

Hall of the Holiday Fellowship Camp, c.1940s.

All that was required was the standard one clean and one being washed change plus the navy blue PT shorts, white vest and plimsolls for the beach. Even at that the shorts and vests could be within three or four sizes of your own. The plimsolls were not much closer to the correct size on many occasions.

Sunglasses were not even thought of and sunburn was treated when you had got it rather than loads of cream being pumped into your skin before you dare go outdoors. A towel was multi-purpose and no doubt was in a bit of a state by the end of the week, having been used after washes, showers, as a ground sheet or drying towel when on the beach. If the sun was not fully out the towel was constantly wet without being washed for the week. Departure day eventually arrived and it was an early start from school.

Mother walked down with me and it was only when I saw the coach waiting that I was satisfied that it was definitely going to happen. I was going to the seaside! All the kids had small parcels or bags of clothing. We didn't have carrier bags then or we would have well managed with one each for our possessions.

Teachers were there with broad smiles on their faces, explaining to the parents that all would be fine but even at my age I could sense that they were still wondering what they had volunteered for!

The staff offered to take care of any cash we had, rather than risk losing it. Mother had already explained that it would be a couple of days before she would have any money to send on to me so losing cash was not a problem for me. I did not have a penny to my name and was as happy, if not happier, than anyone else on the coach. I must say that, most surprisingly, a letter did arrive halfway through the week and in it was a ten shilling note. Fifty pence that was and I could blow the lot if I wanted!

It was like a madhouse on that bus, with everyone waving and shouting as we drove out of the council-house estate. We were going to the coast and as not many round our way did that it made us, probably for the first time in our lives, the privileged few.

Excitable chatter was replaced by community singing for the first few miles but that slowly faded out as those who had not slept all night for excitement, dozed off. We had a stop at about the halfway stage and packed lunches with the standard bottles of school-issue milk were distributed from the boot of the bus while the engine had a chance to cool down.

It was about 20 miles from the coast that the competition started: a good move by staff, who realised we were beginning to wake up again. An apple for the first one to see the sea was the prize and it worked as we had never been this far from home and had little idea of how close we were to the coast.

Signs for Kessingland appeared and caused uproar as we travelled down narrow country lanes before turning into our holiday camp destination, the Holiday Fellowship Camp.

The Camp was, I think, a disused Coast Guard Camp with about eight wooden huts, or billets. It was a typical coastal observation post set in isolation. Each hut had a dozen army-type tubular framed single beds with a couple of wash-basins, baths and toilets set at one end. Everything was so basic yet so ideal for us.

Six huts were used for living quarters, one for catering and the other for administration staff and a general meeting place.

Camp staff came onto the bus to greet us and we were out to impress, as instructed by our teachers. 'Good afternoon' by a member of the camp staff was repeated by all on the bus with enough volume to deafen anyone. We would have done anything the camp staff asked. It was Sinfin School we were representing and those people who had just boarded our bus had made a dream come true.

Into the living quarters we were marched and beds allocated. Our small parcels of belongings were placed on the allotted beds and we got changed into our PT shorts, vests and shoes. The sound we had dreamt about for weeks arrived: 'OK. Go and have a look at the beach.' A mass of kids piled out and headed for the beach, which was right alongside the camp.

Kenny Merry, a small and stocky lad who was as hard as nails, was first out and well in front. He was one of those lads who was always better than anyone else in the class at anything physical. The campsite was raised by about 20 feet of sand dunes from sea level and the sand-dunes made up a hill of about one in three. Kenny was certainly agile, but the sight of a 20 foot drop about 5 yards ahead of him while running at full speed caught him out and he went over those dunes like a lemming. Two or three others landed on top of Kenny and he had become the first casualty, with a broken ankle, within an hour of arriving.

Though difficult to imagine these days, I feel no embarrassment at all to admit that I was one of many in that group that just stood on the beach and stared in total amazement. Here was I checking to see how fine the sand was as it ran through my fingers. There were real seashells lying around to be collected. I can recall sitting on those sand-dunes as if it was yesterday. How different it was in those days! Hours upon hours were spent either alone or with a pal watching, wondering and discussing where these ships on the horizon had come from, what they had in them and where they were going. Imagination was allowed to run wild. We could imagine seeing the crew on the ship, people of all nations, when the only coloured people I had seen up til then were the American Servicemen in the war. Those ships are still in my mind, on the horizon, which was my first proof of how round the world was. I watched them come into sight from one side and my imagination flowed until they went out of sight on the other side.

Almost every shell, every piece of driftwood or seaweed was removed from the beach that week to be taken back to Derby as proof that we really had been to the coast. Anything we could salvage became a souvenir. Even seagull feathers and bottles that had been checked for messages appeared back at Derby. It must have been one of the cleanest beaches in England by the time we had taken anything that would remind us of those hours spent day-dreaming on the beach.

A walk along the beach as a group, ball games or sitting and generally passing time away as a sociable group cost nothing and was good enough for us.

Souvenirs could be purchased if you had the money and I certainly had. Ten bob that was all mine! A wooden hut just down the road was the village store but as the camp gate was the limit it meant that a member of staff would take two or three of us at a time if we asked. My turn came and in I went. There seemed to be everything you could want in there. The biggest surprise was the shopkeeper who stood behind the counter and greeted us like long-lost pals. He was totally blind! His wife spent some time in the store but seemed to spend most of it sunbathing and talking to passers-by as she posed in a chair outside the store.

That poor bloke would have had his shop stripped within the first week of opening it to a crowd of schoolchildren these days, but he was as safe as houses with us. We had respect for people and property. Not even an odd sweet went out of that shop without being paid for.

I bought Mother a small pressed brass plaque with a galleon design on it before I spent anything on myself. Not grovelling, but it was how we were in those days. You couldn't spend all the fifty pence on yourself, could you? Mother died many years ago but that same brass plaque is still cleaned regularly and rests on top of the fire in my lounge to this day, to cause my mind to wander back to Mother and that holiday from time to time.

The end of the week came and it was time for the return journey. Passengers, luggage, packed lunches and thousands of memories went onto that coach and camp staff came aboard to say goodbye. As the coach went to drive out of the camp a recording of 'So long, it's been good to know you' blasted out of the tannoy speakers that were

Blind Norman Durrant's shop, which the camp boys frequented, was taken over by Betty Bagot's Auntie Ivy, who is seen in the shop. (COURTESY BETTY BAGOT)

Betty Bagot (née Aimes) and Wendy Potts

fitted to telegraph poles at each end of the camp gates. We turned onto the road and as we did, probably as he had done many times before on hearing that tune, the blind chap came to his shop door and waved in the direction of the coach.

You could have cleaned that coach with tears from both staff and children. All went very quiet for the first few miles of the homebound journey.

I'll never forget that holiday. If those people of Kessingland got a quarter of the enjoyment they gave, then I am sure it was well worth all their effort.

Thank You Brian

Strong and pleasant memories of that holiday in Kessingland were still with me 40 years later when I took my brother-in-law and his wife on a long weekend break to Great Yarmouth. He had been forced into early retirement by illness and Jenny and I decided to take them away for a few days.

I must have mentioned going away to Brian Clough who had become the best friend and neighbour a family could have wished for. Brian insisted that we use his Mercedes car for the weekend, as he often did. With a tank full of petrol and a reliable car the world was ours to explore. Kessingland, which could not be too far from Yarmouth, came to mind.

We decided to see if the Holiday Camp was still there. Locals in the area were questioned regarding the camp and sure enough one was able to direct us to where it had been situated. We arrived at the site which was now a small modern chalet-style holiday camp, but this was certainly what we were looking for, as that wooden built shop still stood in good condition over the road.

I drove into the site and explained to the other three about Kenny Merry diving into the sand-dunes.

We walked around the site and onto the beach before I started to make my way back to the car, which was parked near the entrance. The others must have suspected how I felt (wives are good at that) and they held back as I arrived at the car on my own, while they wandered about for a few minutes.

Set on each side of the entrance were telegraph poles and on each one could be seen well-rusted remains of brackets which had previously supported loud speakers, out of which 'So long, it's been good to know you' could be played... I could almost hear that tune. I looked over the road and I could almost swear that the blind man was standing at his door.

I stood with my elbow on the open door of an almost new Mercedes car, in the exact spot that some forty years previously I had waited for fifty pence holiday spending money to arrive...

The Mercedes was probably worth more than the total site, buildings and coach would have fetched the last time I was there. Staff were looking at me from the *reception area. It passed through my mind that they may well be wondering whether I was a potential buyer of the site, as the car gave every indication that I was worth a few bob. I felt like going into the reception and saying, 'No, girls. This is the same person that your relations, who worked here all those years ago, felt sorry for, when he carried one change of clothing into a disused wooden army hut for the best holiday of his life.'*

'That sea breeze catches the sand, don't it?' I said to them, as I rubbed my eyes with a handkerchief. There was no wind about, but I had a stack of memories and the realisation of how life can change. I couldn't get it round my head how I had gone from the underprivileged kid with next to nothing to being there again in a car owned by a celebrity, who not only introduced himself as a personal friend of all my family, but did all he could to ensure that he and his family were the best friends and neighbours our family were ever to have.

They say that lightning does not strike twice in the same place, but I know that dreams can come true twice in the same place. Well, they can if you have a mate like Brian Clough.

The Hollies

As you approach the village from Lowestoft, on the left is The Hollies, a large house in front of several acres of meadowland. This was acquired by a retired Captain and called the London Boys' Camp, because at first it only gave holidays to boys, although during the 1970s girls were allowed as well. Three camps of over 100 children came each year, each group staying for two weeks. When the Captain died, others took this on and the trustees of the charity sought helpers and leaders (such as teachers and university students) who would be free for the summer. Some gave their time for the whole of the seven weeks, as there was preparation to do before and clearing up after.

When Rosemary Long was there as a leader in the 1970s, the changeover day was hectic. Over 100 children had to go to Lowestoft on buses to catch the train. Some of the staff would go too. Then, when they were all safely back with their parents or guardians, the next group had to be welcomed. Meanwhile the staff back at camp cleared up the site and the beach. A visit to the wholesaler in a large van then stocked up for the next contingent.

As well as the house, where the cooking was done, there were long shed-like buildings where discos and film shows were held in the evening. Each leader was responsible for eight youngsters. They were able to take them onto the beach, into the village or town, often two groups pairing up with the two leaders. As well as these smaller groups, whole-camp games, bonfire parties, treasure hunts, a visit to Great Yarmouth Funfair and other treats were arranged.

On the middle Thursday of the two weeks, there was a walk along the beach to Southwold, by which time the youngsters were quite tired, but still able to enjoy time on the beach, boating lake and amusements there before returning on coaches.

Often boys who had enjoyed holidays in the past would come back as helpers, doing some of the cooking. Young people from Kessingland village also helped.

Obviously, with so many children from homes with problems, they brought their own problems, such as shoplifting or fighting, but it was an adventure holiday and many returned the better for the experience. However, they were not used to country life. Some of the lads, about ten years old, saw a donkey in a neighbouring field. They were genuinely worried, because the only ones they had seen were on the front at seaside towns with their owners, or in enclosures in zoos. Believing the animal to be lost, they set about trying to catch it. To be suddenly pursued by several small boys frightened the animal, which took off across neighbouring wheat fields, causing hundreds of pounds worth of damage to the harvest about to be gathered. There were, therefore, delicate negotiations that sometimes ensued between organisers and local farmers or shopkeepers. Another lad, who had been given orange squash and chocolate biscuits in the garden of a shopkeeper, managed to steal a cheap powder compact because he had no pocket money and all the rest of the lads were taking home presents for their mums. On the train the following day his conscience got the better of him and he burst out crying, confessed all to his leader and asked him to return the compact to the shop-keeper because 'she gave me chocolate biscuits'.

There were heart-warming and heartbreaking stories, but overall there is no doubt that many lads have cause to look back on once-in-boyhood experiences of running free on Kessingland Beach and singsongs around the camp fire, with potatoes baked in the ashes and sausages roasted to go with them.

The Denes Holiday Camp

Tom Lyne built the Denes Holiday Camp, later Parkdean, almost literally by himself. He dug and laid the foundations and made concrete blocks himself, as and when he could get the materials, during the war years. The Denes House was built in 1936–37 and the camp opened in 1947. Half a century later, his grandson, Michael, ran the Alandale Holiday Bungalows site in Bethel Drive. Mike spent all of his school holidays at the camp, where his grandparents and parents worked to build up the business, employing around 165 staff at times. After his schooldays, he worked mostly in costing and estimating, but Mike was soon ready to float his own business assembling light fittings, when the family intervened, asking him to manage the Sea House Bar and caravan site at the Denes Holiday Camp.

The dance and dining-halls at the Denes Camp, 1960s.

The Denes Holiday Camp dinner, 1960s.

The camp would organise two half-day trips out: to Great Yarmouth and to Oulton Broad. The family sold out to Major Mason at the beginning of 1971, but Mike stayed until the end of the year. After Major Mason retired, the Denes became Parkdean Holiday Park and entertainment was put on there, especially by 'resident' artists Kenny and Caron Cantor, who now run their own Dance and Drama School. Kenny also ran the Mini Olympics for the Disabled at the Camp from 1979 to 1983.

The Lyne family ran a caravan park in Wales for seven years before Mike ended up at Alandale in Kessingland. In a 1997 interview he remembered: 'Laurence Wright had owned this land here, then sold it, complete with planning permission for holiday bungalows. The first one was built in 1965...'

Mike's father died in 1990 and his mother moved back to live with him until her death five years later.

Mike certainly saw a lot of changes in the holiday trade from the days of his childhood, when he lived at Seashell, then at Praetoria, 'further inland' along Church Road:

From the time when people expected full entertainment, the pendulum has swung until holiday accommodation is used as a base, from which to see other places in the area. We are attracting more foreign visitors and most people come because they want a quiet and peaceful holiday in lovely surroundings. Many of them just stay here and relax...

When I started, if you weren't 80 per cent booked up by the end of February it meant a bad year ahead. Today [1997], if you're 10 per cent booked then you are feeling optimistic. Cheaper foreign package holidays and our traffic problems, including Lowestoft Bridge, do not help.

Mike has now retired and is enjoying life, spending much of his time on his boat.

Other Places to Stay

Heathland's Beach Caravan Park, run by Mr and Mrs Bernard and May Reeder, is situated on the site of the old Cliff Farm, where, early in the twentieth century, owners Mr and Mrs Collen held Methodist Church strawberry teas in their garden.

The Heathland's Camp was started by Mr and Mrs

Denes Camp staff in the 1950/60s. The group includes: Mary Weavers, Hilda Hart, George ?, George's wife, Ivy Catchpole and Olive Long.

Mike Lynes at Alandale Chalet Park.

Heathland's Caravan Site, 1960s.

Aerial view of Heathland's Caravan Site, 1960s.

Heathland's Caravan Site, 1960s.

bordering the cliffs as the only place in the village where the elusive wild bee orchid could be found (although one visitor photographed a plant further along the cliffs). Although there is a swimming-pool and a modern club house, many visitors still come for peace and quiet and a chance to see the local flora, fauna and birdlife.

There are other sites in the village – one at White Gables on Beach Road, leading to the Holiday Camp, formerly the Denes, which is now all self-catering static caravans. Another site is near the Suffolk Wildlife Park, just off the A12, another beautiful venue, although you may hear the lions roar in the night! This is more than recompensed by the sight of the peacocks strutting up and down the lane by the camp, much appreciated by the campers and an incentive to visit the Wildlife Park, which is fast getting a reputation for its breeding programme, as well as its excellent facilities for both animals and visitors.

The camps gave much employment to both men and women in the village, especially when the Denes did all their own catering. Many hands were needed in the kitchen and the local ladies, who already did all their own home-cooking, were more than qualified. Others were employed in the office, while the men worked as maintenance staff or drove the buses that picked up the workers daily or transported the guests to and fro.

Alan Ladd, with a shop on site. May and Bernard took it over when the Ladds retired and have extensively enlarged and modernised it in past years. There are now facilities for tourers and static caravans, many luxury ones, and with fields running right down to the cliff and the sea, it is a popular venue. Elderly residents remember the field

Broadcaster John Eley from Radio Suffolk at the MASK shop, Mother Hubbard's Cupboard, with Evelyn Mathias and Yvonne King, 1997.

The Octaves choir entertaining at the Waveney Eldercare Christmas party in the Community Centre, 1995.

Chapter 13

Entertainment and Leisure

Entertaining the Community

The village boasts good amateur entertainment, including that by youngsters. The Scout and Guide Gangshows put on each year at the Community Centre are enjoyed by all who attend. It is not only the more professional artistes who deserve a mention (such as Ian Hale, the Chalkley family, Jane O'Brien, Kenny and Caron Cantor, John Eley from Radio Suffolk, The Octaves and other musicians such as Avril Coote and Dennis Richardson

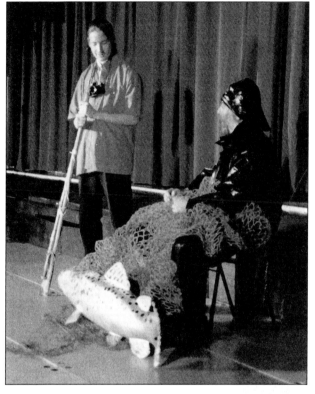

Stan, veteran fisherman, tells the 'young un' how it's done as part of the 1997 community play.

Kenny Cantor.

Community play – Girl Guides' camp fire.

to name just a few) but all the children who have taken part in school plays, members of the Scout and Guide movements, local church congregations and WI members who have all, over the years 'trodden the boards' to cheer up Kessingland, especially in the dark winter months.

Kessingland residents are members of Lowestoft Players and of various choirs and other groups putting on entertainment. The KESSIs played a large part in cheering up not only local audiences but also

A community play, 1997.

residents of residential homes, hospitals and the like under the direction of the late Peggy Ling and Gladys Recas.

In 1997 a community play was rehearsed and put on by John Hale, with a local cast, telling the history of the village, especially the fishing aspect of it.

The Passion Play

Many villagers were involved in some way with the Passion Play, put on in Lowestoft on a Good Friday in the 1980s, by the Lowestoft Council of Churches.

Passion play in the streets of Lowestoft, 1980s.

All three congregations took part and if folk were not learning lines, they were making props, sewing costumes or coaching children in their parts, all under the enthusiastic direction of Liz Stevens of St Edmund's Church (who went on to marry Arthur Edgely and who founded the Waveney Eldercare organisation with her friends Pauline and Hugh Wilding).

The impact and brilliance of the Passion Play was that it was performed in the town centre during the day on Good Friday and it was difficult to tell who were normal shoppers and who were those cheering or jeering the trial and crucifixion scenes. Kessingland's Sid Wigg was one of the two thieves crucified with Jesus, but earlier, in a Passion Play put on by the three churches in the village and directed by Miss Rosa Wake, he had been cast as Judas and forever after was called 'Judas' in the village, since many did not know his proper name. His wife, Angie, had been in the play and more men were needed. Sid was 'volunteered' and has been a fervent Christian ever since. Miss Wake is mentioned in the chapter on writers, as she was a prolific writer, as well as a drama teacher.

The KessWIs

This all-female group of pensioners was born over coffee at a meeting for new WI members in the 1980s. At that time there was no drama group in the village. The general feeling was that Kessingland wasn't the place for it, but new member Peggy Ling, a lifelong member of one concert party or another, knew that everyone loves a laugh, so took on the challenge of presenting a variety show for the WI at Christmas. She had just eight weeks to find the artistes, costumes and content. That first event was an overwhelming success and the KessWIs was launched. They have never asked to go anywhere, but have been invited to old folks' homes, charity concerts, hospitals, churches and the like in Kessingland and far beyond. At Christmas they have done up to three shows in different places in one day, so as not to disappoint anybody. A few years back, when non-WI members joined, their name was changed to The KESSIs, omitting the WI in the centre of their name.

Everard Wigg and The Kinnodrome

Maybe the most notable of all local entertainers was Everard Wigg, who built, maintained and ran The Kinnodrome, Kessingland's only claim to cinema fame. Everard was an eccentric, who devised and tried to market the game Solotogo, but it never achieved the same success as Monopoly or Trivial Pursuit. The Kinnodrome is fondly remembered by many elderly residents for the early films that were put on there. Local magazine contributor 'Hill Billy' from Beccles remembered:

Above: *The Kinnodrome's 'house rules', 1903.*
Left: *The Kinnodrome photographed in the 1960s. It was the home of the first Cinematograph Shows.*

Interior doors in the Kinnodrome.

Above and left: *Interior of the Kinnodrome, as it was in 1903. The picture on the left is thought to show the box office.*

Eve Haddock, a Kessingland artist, appeared with actor Robert Hardy in George Eliot's Middlemarch, *filmed at Somerleyton Hall, Suffolk in the 1990s.*

There were such exciting places of entertainment as The Kinnodrome in Kessingland. I went there from the age of seven and well recall the wooden seats! Everard Wigg, a brilliant engineering pattern-maker by trade, built and operated this ramshackle cinema in the early 1930s. A lovable eccentric, he was a man of good ideas. Unfortunately, they did not always prove realistic. His ambition was to build a lavish and safe cinema with a collapsible wall, allowing people to exit quickly in the event of fire. This was never realised, but the village continued to enjoy magic-lantern shows and early films without having to journey into Lowestoft or Beccles.

The building later became the workshop crammed full with other inventions, such as the automatic shoe-shine machine made from an old bicycle and shoe brushes. It should have revolutionised the streets of London but it never got further than Kessingland!

Everard did, however, invent and market a game called Solotogo, more complicated than chess and requiring great concentration... Maybe it was too clever to succeed as a relaxing and entertaining game.

The village owes much to Everard Wigg, though, for bringing exciting entertainment to the village when it was most needed.

Evie, as Everard was sometimes known, will long be remembered and loved in the village. When the old Kinnodrome was cleared and his house sold, after Mrs Wigg's death, the large garden was sold separately and new houses were built there. When the Parish Council asked local people for suggested names for the new development during the year of the Queen's silver jubilee, Kinnodrome Close was suggested, but Queen's Terrace won the day. Many people feel this is a shame as future generations may not now be aware of the brilliant Everard Wigg and his work.

Kessingland on the Silver Screen

A film version of *David Copperfield* was filmed in 1969 just along the beach towards Benacre.

On another occasion, in the 1970s, an episode of a James Bond film was shot there, with Roger Moore, using the cliffs for the scene. A local shopkeeper was speaking to a customer in the afternoon, who said she had been down the Beach village in the morning and 'it was lovely'.

'Oh, have you been to see the Saint?'* she enquired.

'No', came the answer. 'Is he preaching at the Bethel?'

Suffolk humour, however innocuous, is alive and well!

*'The Saint' was a TV character played by Roger Moor in the 1960s.

All the Fun of the Fair

Travelling fairs and circuses have also been a feature in the village over the years. Painter Dame Laura Knight, OBE , a great admirer of circus people, wrote: 'I have often tried to analyse the Circus appeal. It is the display of indomitable courage that one sees and admires... Gravitation is defied. The impossible is possible.' Circus personalities Terry Elflett and Keith Nichols have both lived in the village.

Terry Elflett

It is a feeling of defiance of the laws of nature that makes Circus folk a race apart. Although gathered from all races, I never felt a stranger among them. Their acceptance of me always seemed a miracle, as like fishing folk, they can be difficult to know intimately.

Terry played at hundreds of venues, including the Old Vic, the Victoria Palace, the Palladium, Churchill's Club, The Best Cellar, La Scala and Maxims. He rubbed shoulders such personalities as John F. Kennedy, Elizabeth Taylor and Richard Burton, Roger Moore, Christian Barnard, Nina Mouskouri, Grace Kelly, Prince Rainier, Rex Harrison, President Botha and Stefan Grapelli – his favourite.

Travel and showbusiness were in Terry's blood. When only 13 years old, he longed to be a muscle-man. He learned more about his body as he

Keith Nichols with his hand-turned roundabout at the Rider Haggard Festival, 1990.

practised and experimented. His hard work paid off, and eventually newspaper reports were written about him:

A man who can twitch his muscles in time to music has arrived in Port Elizabeth to star in the 1966 Olympic Circus, which opens on Tuesday. Terry Elflett, known as the Musical Muscle Man, from Britain, arrived with his wife and two children. He says his act was the only one of its kind in the world... Mr Elflett said that he could 'Turn his stomach inside out', showing the reverse side of the muscles. Doctors have told me that they did not know it was possible to move muscles to such an extent.

Terry perfected his act and travelled with companies and circuses all over the world, performing in Africa and Asia, the USA, Scandinavia, Europe (they stayed for three years in Paris) and sometimes in Britain. He also did a lot of charity work.

Terry was born in the Fens, where his father also achieved fame with his book *The Wild Goose Man*, by which name he was known. Terry said:

My father knew Prince Charles well, as he often accompanied the Prince of Wales on shooting trips on the vast Fen marshes. When he died, Prince Charles

attended his funeral. After that the place where he lived was renamed 'Royal Close'.

In 1990, Terry and wife Joyce commented on what their travels and career had given them:

Not riches in a material sense, although we have had the good times, but our riches are in the wealth of friends we have made, experiences we have known and the richness of understanding other peoples and cultures. Our children had formal education through postal courses, but they learned far more because of their lifestyle. Education is not learning A, B, C from a book. It is learning to respect and understand other people. It is knowing that home is where love is.

Terry died in the 1990s.

Keith Nichols

The village boasts its own showman, Keith Nichols. He was instrumental in the organisation of the HRH Festival and has written books about his early life and fairground experiences. Kipper Kate, children's page editor in the local magazine, said of him, 'If enthusiasm could be bottled and sold, that man would be a millionaire.'

Above: *The annual gang show, 2001.*

Dora and Ron Addison's wedding anniversary, 2002.   *Colleen and Ted Hall, September 2002.*

Chapter 14

Clubs, Organisations and Charities in Kessingland

There are many charities and charitable organisations in the village, relying on the never-failing support of residents. The churches, pubs and clubs have done an amazing job over the years in supporting deserving causes.

An example of this generosity of spirit is the example of a young boy who suffered head injuries in a road accident, came out of hospital and did a sponsored 'walk' when he could hardly toddle himself, for a fellow hospital patient. In addition, the Methodist Church held an annual sponsored walk for many years from Kessingland to Pakefield or Lowestoft (according to age and ability).

Kessingland is today a more affluent village, yet still spreads its wealth to the less fortunate. Most of the voluntary organisations, e.g. the Little Fishers pre-playschool group, MASK, the Friendship and Over 60s Club and the churches, all rely on public support for their own expenses as well raising money to support others.

Scouts, Brownies and Guides

Before and all through the Second World War, the Guides and Brownies were run in the Methodist Church by Queenie and Nancy Watson, who lived in Ferndale, in the High Street. The sisters were also Good Companions Club leaders, as well as youth leaders and Sunday-school teachers at the Methodist Church. The year 1997 saw the fiftieth anniversary of Kessingland Brownies and the organisation, along with the Scouts and Guides, has been involved in numerous charitable activities over the years.

Brown Owl Debra Ripper
(Taken from a 1997 interview)

When Debra was a girl she became a Brownie as soon as she was old enough. Much later, however, she got involved in the Brownies at Kessingland almost by accident as she accompanied her daughter Sarah to a meeting in 1996. The group needed help with the leadership and Debra stayed, later becoming Brown Owl when Jill Beadle retired due to ill-health, after giving over 30 years of voluntary service to Brownies and Guiding (although not all in Kessingland). Debra already had a busy life, with commitments to the Salvation Army at Lowestoft South as well as leading the Singing Company (children's choir), teaching a Sunday-school class and working on the Junior Soldier Award Scheme.

Debra, who in her role as Brown Owl is supported by two hard-working assistants, Sylvia Barnes and Nikki Welch, spoke of the changes in the Brownies over the last 50 years:

It's still young girls learning, playing and having fun together. The changes mostly are in the uniform, now much less formal and more 'pick'n'mix', although I would prefer them to be all alike. The promise is now worded differently; we promise to 'Love our God' rather than to 'do our duty to God'. There is a new Promise Badge...

On the Brownies' anniversary they were issued with a new flag, the money for which the Brownies raised themselves, with a 'sponsored spell'.

Kessingland Playgroup
(Taken from a 1991 interview)

Theresa Clark runs Kessingland Playgroup with her helpers, Stephanie Spendlove, Sue Alison and Judy Pinion. They all thoroughly enjoy the challenge of working towards a good programme of activities for the youngsters.

The Playgroup meets twice weekly and takes 20 children each morning, the maximum allowed for insurance purposes, and there is a waiting list of new members eager to attend. The sessions start with free play, followed by milk and biscuits. After that the creative work takes place, before the session ends with storytime and rhymes. Theresa and team have perfected the indoor activities during the winter months and relish the outdoor activities when summer comes. Undoubtedly, as they grow and develop wider skills and interests, the children will remember those earliest years of fun and creativity at the Playgroup.

Today the Minnows Playgroup, which grew out of the earlier group, is going strong.

Over 60s

At the other end of the age range, the village had for a long time an Over 60s Club, but when the Lloyds estate was built, bringing an influx of retired people from London, Hertfordshire and Essex, it was full. Due to fire regulations, no more could join.

Mr and Mrs Grice, members of the Methodist Church, saw the need for a second club. This was also to meet fortnightly but in the alternate week, so that any special events or fund-raising efforts did not clash. So began the Friendship Club, with the same interests and outings as the Over 60s. There has never been rivalry and today, with many of the Lloyds estate houses now occupied by younger people, there is not the same pressure and there are some who are happily members of both.

Dora and Ron Addison

To achieve 60 years of happy marriage is a great cause for celebration, and when Dora and Ron Addison made this milestone in 2002, they shared their happiness, plus cake and a drink, with the members of the Friendship Club. Ron is the club's chairman, in his second year of office (the former chairman being Peter Francis, and Ron's vice-chairman being Brin Walsh), and the couple have had happy times with the club during the many years that they have been members, since they first moved to Kessingland.

> There's a good team spirit in the Committee and everyone works hard. We have good meetings, fortnightly... lots of social events, outings, holidays, Christmas dinner, etc. We spent our golden wedding anniversary with the club, on a holiday to Bournemouth. Transport can be provided for any who find it impossible to get to the club under their own steam. We are affiliated to Age Concern.

Dora and Ron are passionately interested in the Friendship Club and its future. Ron said: 'One of our most treasured gifts from the wedding anniversary was the card signed by every member of the club.'

Colleen and Ted Hall

Ted has worked both in paid and voluntary jobs which have served the public, including a number of years chairing the Over 60s Club, after he did his 'apprenticeship' of seven years chairing the Beechams Staff Retirement Club in Lowestoft.

Colleen's parents lived in Kessingland and the couple came on frequent holidays to visit them, falling in love with the area and deciding to settle here. After they moved they joined Kessingland Over 60s Club, where Ted has put a vast amount of energy and hard work and a sense of fun into being a full member. He has served the committee as secretary, treasurer and chairman.

The couple still look forward to events and enjoy life to the full, especially on the various outings and holidays organised by the club.

Waveney Eldercare Centre

In 1989 the Waveney Eldercare Centre was officially opened in London Road by Mr Tom Chipperfield, chairman of Waveney District Council. The organi-

Waveney Eldercare stall at a fête, with then care centre manager Thelma Chevington, 1995.

Entertainment at the Waveney Eldercare day centre, 1990s.

Youngsters hand over a cheque for Waveney Eldercare day centre from a sponsored walk, 2000. Margaret London, manager, accepts it.

sation also had a charity shop at Kessingland Beach.

The founders of the centre, Liz and Arthur Edgeley and Pauline and Hugh Wilding, gathered a team together who could relieve relatives and stay up with sick folk through the night, or give carers an occasional day off. Arthur fund-raised with bingo sessions once a week at the Church Hall and with car boot sales on Royal Green at Lowestoft, while local doctors and nurses, home helps and carers were all eager to help. The result was a day centre, which started for three days a week in the Methodist Church and later moved to its own premises,

Waveney Eldercare Christmas party at the Church Hall in the 1990s.

Elizabeth Edgeley House in London Road, in the former London Road Stores. The service was extended to five days weekly and that year, Waveney Eldercare was awarded the Suffolk Village Ventures Competition Award for new voluntary projects. Volunteers still did the home caring, while others ran the day centre.

Margaret London worked as a volunteer at the centre, eventually becoming the last of the centre managers. She felt it was all worthwhile because the centre always had a cheerful atmosphere. Sadly it was closed in 2003. There is now much else in place, such as transport to hospitals, more care in the home and another day centre run by Social Services.

Charity At Home and Abroad

There are family or individual efforts as well. George Crudgington has walked hundreds of miles for charity, even from Land's End to John O'Groats, while John Westley made the *Guinness Book of Records* for walking around the coastline of Britain in 1990/91. Also, the Sewell family at The Knoll had a wonderful Open Garden day in 2005.

As well as fund-raising for various causes in and around the village, many residents are involved in helping in the wider world. There have been lorry loads of goods transported to those in need in other countries, while Sid Wigg and four other

members of Lowestoft Community Church went to Romania in 1993 to help rebuild an orphanage there. He remembers:

The roads were incredible. It was a miracle how our elderly church mini-bus ever kept going through the potholes plumbing was a nightmare. Old Romanian houses have reinforced ceilings, as it's an earthquake area, and you would have to drill through two courses of bricks to get through to the next floor with the pipes... we learned to sing 'Jesus is Lord' in Romanian.

We went to take X-ray and medical supplies to a hospital, then on to a Baptist project for street children, called 'Jesus, Hope for Romania'. Eating with the children soon showed that they were used to just scavenging scraps of food... Even the thirty living at the hostel we were helping to convert could not take in that there would be another meal. They grabbed any odd pieces of bread or extra apples to put in their pockets for later. It is estimated that there are over 200 street children in Timisoara, and it is hoped to eventually take 50. The city has a population of half a million, but the one badly equipped, primitive hospital serves those and a large neighbouring area. We were thankful not to need their services.

Sid's experience in Romania so affected him that when an appeal went out through the *That's Life* television programme for 250 volunteers to refurbish a children's hospital in St Petersburg, Sid put his name forward. He had always wanted to see Russia, but the drive through the city to and from the airport was the only sightseeing the group had time for. The trip lasted a week, but one whole day was spent unloading the 30-ton containers carrying the £300,000 worth of donated equipment, including 5,000 square metres of tiles, 70 toilets, 6,000 cans of Lucozade and coke. Taking out travelling time, that left just three and a half days to strip the hospital out, rewire, install new plumbing, redecorate, paint and tile. Six of the volunteers were catering staff who fed the army of workers at the hospital. Sid says there was a good team spirit and everyone worked long hours with little sleep. It was an amazing and thoroughly worthwhile project – what an achievement!

Mike Rolfe and Tearfund

Mike Rolfe, now retired, is a volunteer with the Christian relief and development agency, Tearfund – a charity that works among the world's poor in over 600 projects in 19 countries. During Mike's fortnight in India a few years ago he saw, firstly in Calcutta and then in Bombay, how Tearfund's partners are caring for slum children, pavement orphans and abandoned children, providing them with a loving, family environment with health care and education. Young men are rehabilitated from drug addiction and alcohol abuse and clinics are provided for young

*The Knoll open day,
July 2005, for the
Sandra Chapman Unit
at the James Paget
Hospital.*

mothers and people with HIV/AIDS. Mike says, 'I witnessed hell and experienced heaven.'

Action during the Kosovo crisis

During the Kosovo crisis of the 1990s, nobody in the village could fail to notice the activity in and around a certain house in the High Street. Tracy Simmonds decided she wanted to do something for the refugees, so a group of likeminded people, including Dick Baldwin from Southwold and Wendy Milton, wrote an advertisement requesting that items be dropped off at Tracy's home in the High Street. Others, including Vicky and Polly Rushmore from Aldeburgh, got involved; women provided knitted items, people turned out their cupboards and the manager of Iceland in Lowestoft, John Gilbert, provided food for the helpers at the sorting centre. The support grew as various donations arrived from all over Norfolk and Suffolk by van, car and even horse box.

All this material was taken to Kosovo, until the crisis was alleviated and eventually the families concerned had to call a halt to the piles of goods in their houses and gardens. The piles of black bags, spilling onto the pavement for yards in every direction, showed the caring nature of the village.

Charity Concerts and Socials

There are annual charity concerts for such good causes as the Ellie Savage Trust (for a disabled child) and memorial concerts for John Hutson, the local butcher who died of a heart attack in the prime of life, and for Terry Catchpole, brother of photographer Richard.

Coffee mornings have also been held to help raise funds for the Macmillan Nurse's Appeal. Events such as these are a great excuse for villagers to get together, enjoy lovely food and a cup of tea – all for a good cause.

Moonbeams Shine Again

In recent times the Kessingland and Pakefield Moonbeams have become leading lights when it comes to raising money for local charities. They have raised funds for such beneficiaries as the doctors' surgery, Peter West, Shane Anderson, the Minnows Nursery, the Scouts, Barry Exton, Markey and The Kessingland School Nursery.

However, the whole community benefits from such fund-raising events. Days such as the Kessingland and Pakefield Moonbeams' Charity Summer Fête (which took place in Sue and Colin Price's garden)

Tearfund representative Mike Rolfe and wife Eunice.

encourage unity and good will and anything that does that nowadays must be a bonus. This event had all the usual attractions: egg-and-spoon race, sack races, tug-o-war and pony rides, plus assorted side stalls and a 'bonny baby contest' (Valerie Ward being one such star of this latter event).

Sue and Colin, along with a committed team, work very hard to help raise money for charities, worldwide and locally. The K & P Moonbeams work tirelessly to promote the community spirit. They deserve all the praise they get and their efforts are appreciated.

The Knoll Open Day

When Jill and Fred Sewell at The Knoll opened their garden in July 2005 in aid of the Sandra Chapman Unit at the James Paget Hospital, they were hoping to raise £100. The end of the day found them counting the unbelievable sum of £1,000!

Credit is due to their large and hard-working extended family for pulling out all the stops. The sun shone, the home-made refreshments were delicious and everyone turned out to support them. The atmosphere was friendly, with lots of chat between old and new friends. For those who wanted it, there was even a secluded spot to be found in the beautiful garden where a cream tea could be enjoyed. The tearoom afforded shade and company and the fresh strawberries were also on sale to take away.

What a huge boost for cancer relief!

Ron Murdoch shows his marquetry pictures to the Waveney Eldercare day centre clients.

Les from Livingstone's Restaurant (centre, with shaved head) *raised money for the Waveney Eldercare day centre with a sponsored headshave in 2001.*

Chapter 15

Kessingland's Women's Institute

The first president, Miss Lizzie Swan, was a quiet but lovely lady, a life-long member of St Edmund's Church. She said, 'My brother carried me on his shoulders when I was three to Sunday School and I later taught the children, until I was about 80.' Born and brought up in the village, she had earned her living, never having married, as a beatster.

WI Presidents

Freda Nathan

In 1917 when the German gunboats were bombarding Lowestoft, Freda was born at Clyffeside, High Path, Kessingland Beach. Her father made his living from the sea, being a herring drifterman. After the war Freda spent a happy childhood with the beach as her constant playground, watching the boats coming in, the fish being sold, the shrimps being boiled on the beach in huge coppers, the nets being tanned or the porpoises moving along parallel to the shore. Each summer the rector would ask his parishioners who could put up summer visitors and Freda's mother would offer accommodation. Later she was to move to Blacksmith's Corner, where she kept a shop and, again, life here fascinated Freda, especially accompanying her father to the farm across the road to buy his 'bed' (a sack of hay) to take back to sea.

She was always involved in the Church, as a child attending the Chapel Sunday school, then going to St Edmund's.

After marrying Charles she moved to Surrey for four years, where the couple had two sons, Tim and John. Freda had four grandchildren and three great-grandchildren. A keen WI member, Freda had been both secretary and president. She

Margararet Parker cuts the cake on the 40th anniversary meeting, 1992.

helped to compile the book on Kessingland which was in the Heirlooms Exhibition in London. A keen local history student, she was involved with Kessingland's contribution to the WI book on Suffolk. She supported many charities and enjoyed her fund-raising activities. She made those delicious eclairs so many enjoyed at the WI's 75th birthday celebration, 'Tea at the Ritz'.

Margaret Parker

Margaret was the 14th president of Kessingland WI. She held this position during the early 1980s, at which time the organisation was celebrating its 40th anniversary (the first meeting, which welcomed 76 members, took place on 6 March 1952).

Margaret moved to Kessingland from London with her parents in 1966, when she was aged 15. Starting at Catchpole's Holiday Camp, formerly The Grange, home of Sir Henry Rider Haggard, she started a career in the holiday business which was to take her, when the camp closed in 1977, to Pontins, Pakefield, first for three years as a chalet maid, then as one of two accommodation supervisors, looking after 50 chalet ladies between them. One day, Margaret went with her sister-in-law to a WI meeting because she wanted to hear a talk by Chris Durdin of the RSPB, having enjoyed him on the radio. She joined the organisation the following month and became heavily involved in various activities, including serving as chairman of the East Point Group of five WIs.

In 2006 the WI is as popular as ever under the current president, Diana Harrold.

Inset: *The WI committee enjoy the 40th anniversary meal, 1992. Left to right, back row:* Karolyn Smithson, Miriam Murdoch, Jill Walker, Enid Reeves, Judy Lewson, Ingrid Utting; *front row:* Joyce Smith, Freda Nathan, Margararet Parker, Hilda Block.

Above: *As part of the 40th anniversary celebrations in 1992 Margararet Parker planted a Red Acer tree in Kessingland churchyard. Canon Leslie Harris looks on.*

THE EDGE OF KESSINGLAND CLIFF

HE NEW CLIFF KESSINGLAND

Top and above: *Sea Row, 1905.*

Chapter 16

Bizarre Happenings and Strange Beachcombings

Lilias Arkell-Smith, alias Col Barker

Lilias Arkell-Smith came to Kessingland in 1947 and lived here until she died in 1960. Kessingland people, however, knew her as Geoffrey Norton, who had a 'wife', Eva, who died in 1957. A few days after her funeral the village was besieged with reporters and the whole story came out once more of how she had masqueraded as a man, Col Barker, retired Army officer. She rests in a quiet spot in Kessingland churchyard, where she was interred after the funeral service conducted by Revd Tom Drury.

Lilias was born in Jersey in 1895. Her father, Thomas Barker, was a wealthy sportsman, who had longed for a son, but the child was tall and strong and as she grew up he soon taught her to box, play cricket and fence. She was also a superb horsewoman. She had one brother. After her father's death, her mother moved to London and the family lived in a large flat near Hyde Park. She was able to give the children a good education. Lilias, who was mostly called Val, was well read and well travelled.

Handsome and wealthy, she fell in love with a dashing young subaltern from Australia, Harold Arkell-Smith, and married him in 1918, but the marriage was only to last six months. Not long afterwards she met and fell in love with a second Australian, Pearce Crouch, with whom she lived for four years. Their partnership produced two children, a year apart, Tony and Betty. When her daughter was two months old she split up with Pearce and the baby was given up for adoption. From then on she lived only for her son, with her new identity as a man. She is quoted as saying:

I was raised as a boy and always thought boys had a jolly good time. The man I truly loved and should have married was taken prisoner early in the war. Now I'm fond of no one – I adore only my son.

She became Tony's 'father when he was still an infant and he never knew any different'.

For the next seven or eight years Lilias went to extraordinary lengths to live as Colonel Sir Leslie Ivor Victor Gauntlett Bligh Barker, DSO, masquerading as a war hero, with an impressive array of medals across her

chest. She smoked cigars, made a good figure in a dinner suit and generally enjoyed life amongst the rich and famous. Her valet, who took in shaving water every morning, never guessed his employer was a woman.

He was one of the most charming men one could ever meet and generous to a degree. He and Mrs Barker appeared to be an ideally happy married couple. They dined out most nights. A boy of about eight used to come for the school holidays. He called the major 'Daddy' and his wife, whom I understood to be the major's second wife, 'Auntie'. I often saw him with his face lathered after taking in the shaving water, as though he was just going to use the razor.

In 1923 Lilias had 'married' a chemist's daughter, Elfrida Howard. She never suspected the truth, even when he blamed his failure to consummate the marriage on his 'war wounds'. She said later that the Colonel courted her passionately as any young man would.

They first ran an antique shop, then a farm. They took an active part in village life, riding with the hunt and the Colonel playing cricket, even with his war wounds! As Mrs Pearce Crouch she had bred and showed dogs at Clymping, becoming well known in breeding and show circles. It was in this environment (much later) that she first began dressing as a man and even dared to appear at the Middlesex Hospital Dog Show in 1927 smoking a cigar, with her 'wife'. When prominent fellow exhibitors thought they recognised her, she remarked coldly that, 'You appear to have made a mistake.' After more of this, she and her 'wife' left early.

The marriage broke up three years later and the Colonel moved back to London, ran a restaurant and became an actor. Used to the best of everything, the Colonel soon ran up enormous debts and was arrested in 1929. That was the Colonel's undoing, since Lilias could not hide her gender in Brixton prison. She was transferred to Holloway and, although she had committed no illegal activity in posing as a man, she was tried for making a false entry in a marriage register in 1923. The Old Bailey drew crowds of sightseers, all hoping to catch a glimpse of her. She was in tears as she

Colonel Barker.

was sentenced to nine months in prison.

On her release things went from bad to worse. In spite of her outwardly suave appearance, she lost many jobs, still masquerading as a man, because she was recognised, due to the intense press coverage of her trial.

During the Second World War her son, Tony, joined the RAF, inspired, so he said, by his 'father's' heroic record in France. He first joined the Grenadier guards, but later transferred to the RAF. He was killed over France not long after. Lilias would always have his photo near her, and read and reread his letters. His death broke her up and she started to drink more heavily. Tony had married shortly before his death, but she did not attend the wedding. As Tony was so young at the time of the trial and subsequent incarceration, he believed Col Barker to be his 'Dear Pops' and the colonel could not risk another illegal entry in a marriage register.

Once at Kessingland in the 1950s, she looked like one of the most masculine people to be found and no-one guessed she was really a woman. She lived in the village as 'Geoffrey Norton', with a companion, 'Mrs Norton', in an old cottage, now demolished, not far from the King's Head, on the main road. They frequented the public house, where the regulars knew 'Mrs Norton' as 'Brandy Lil'.

Her sad story finished in Kessingland with her death in 1960. Having to be admitted to Lowestoft Hospital, on the men's ward, obviously the staff found out but, ill as she was, she refused to go onto the women's ward and they gave in, screened off her bed and let her die 'as a man', as she wished. There is still a fascination with her brave and daring attempt to avoid her deception being uncovered. The extraordinary steps to which she went, for reasons maybe only known to herself and her maker, are still of public interest.

The Body on the Beach

A few years back a man walking his dog on the beach one morning found a body that had been washed up. He alerted the police and it was later reported that a young woman had been murdered, her body encased in chains and weighted. Suicide was ruled out, since it would have been impossible for anyone to have chained and weighted himself or herself and then walked into the sea. The 'himself' or 'herself' proved relevant, since after a post mortem at the James Paget Hospital in Gorleston, where the body was taken, further reports stated that the 'young woman' was a man who had undergone a sex change.

The chains and weights were later traced to a firm further along the coast where, it was presumed, the body had been chained and weighted. The police traced the crime to the victim's former wife and her brother.

Flotsam and Jetsam

Truth is definitely stranger than fiction at times, but with the exception of the incident outlined above, an early morning walk along Kessingland Beach is a pleasant experience with only a bit of flotsam and jetsam to impede your progress. In former times, the sea has thrown up some welcome surprises, however, such as a bonanza of oranges washed ashore from a wrecked vessel. The oranges were more than welcome with villagers for whom imported fruit would have been a luxury, and they would have been gathered up eagerly, taken home and shared with relatives, friends and neighbours.

In more recent times a large cargo of wood went into the sea after a shipwreck and the beach was strewn literally as far as the eye could see with good-quality soaking-wet wood. Many a fence or new shed went up that year, as those in the know took cars, vans and even lorries to grab as much of the free and unexpected bounty as they could transport away. In a few hours the beach was clear. Maybe in these more affluent times people do not see the need to share, and it was definitely a case of 'first come, first served'.

Another recent phenomenon has been the appearance of seals basking on the shoreline. It has only been for a few years that these lovely creatures have been seen swimming off Kessingland Beach. One elderly seal, who was named 'Brutus' by the local press, was taken from Lowestoft Beach several times to a seal sanctuary further along the coast, but he always made his way 'home' and decided to do his sunbathing at Kessingland instead. Walkers were warned not to let their dogs attack the seal, who is apparently blind and deaf, but well enough to know where he wants to rest. Walkers respected his privacy, but his presence drew crowds to watch him or photograph him from a distance. Kessingland

Aged seal on Kessingland Beach, 2002.

Flooded wildlife and plants, 1993.

Sea Row destroyed in the 1930s by high tides.

The Wavecrest Café was almost destroyed in 1933.

The sea flooded in over the beach and road in 1993. Beach warden Roy Brown looks on.

Beach is much quieter than Lowestoft seafront and he is not in danger to himself or others. He still enjoys the beach in 2006.

The presence of the seals these past years has inspired Kessingland artist John Westley to sculpture seals for sale in the MASK shop. Evelyn Mathias had already designed a teacloth showing a fictional Kessingland seal called Stewy. Over the past few years hundreds of Stewy and Sally seals have been purchased and taken home to grace gardens or for indoor ornaments, as door stops or book ends. A *Stewy Seal* book was also written for children.

George Swan remembers when the village went nuts in the 1940s:

I recall when as a lad we had more nuts than we could eat. I can't say which year it was, I was aged about 12 or 14 when Kessingland Beach was strewn with nuts between Kessingland and Benacre. Every wave washed more ashore. They were all small hazelnuts.

Also washed up were small wooden objects, which you would describe as ashtrays. Each one had a tulip painted on it. I presume they came from a ship that was in trouble caused by rough seas.

Another time I remember bales of cotton being washed up, but the Kessingland beachmen claimed them as salvage and wouldn't let us boys anywhere near them.

In 1942, on Jan 30th, disaster struck the SS Royal Crown. *She was bombed off the coast and beached at Covehithe. Many of her crew were lost. One small boat overturned and a second one just disappeared. An all-night search was eventually called off. Fire broke out and an AFS (Auxiliary Fire Service) crew from Lowestoft attended. They converted a longshore boat into a fire float. While all this was happening, a German plane machine-gunned them.*

But it wasn't all doom and gloom as the Royal Crown *had tons of steam coal on board, which had to be unloaded before any attempt to refloat her could take place. In the next few weeks the people from Covehithe and neighbouring places took their cars, hand-carts, barrows, and even their prams to collect the coal.*

I was talking to one of the fireman the other day, who attended the scene. He recalled one of the part-time fire crew worked for Corona, the soft drinks company, and once or twice he turned up at the scene with his drinks lorry and several empty sacks, which were filled with coal and then distributed to the families of firemen in Lowestoft.

The SS Royal Crown *was patched up and refloated in the February of that year. She was repaired only to be lost later in the war. A lot of people were kept warm that winter with the coal from the ill-fated SS* Royal Crown.

The largest single object washed up at Kessingland must have been the whale that beached here around 1910. When Peter Cherry researched the subject in 1970, he had a letter from a Mrs Goreham of Norwich, who had seen it. Apparently a photograph was taken of the local publican either in or near the mouth of the whale. It is uncertain whether it was alive or dead when it was washed ashore, but once beached, it is difficult to refloat a whale. In the New Year of 2006, Londoners flocked in their thousands to see a whale which had taken a wrong turn and ended up in the Thames. Sadly, that did not survive either, even with so much expertise at hand. It is hardly any wonder that the Kessingland whale did not survive. Apparently a beached whale has to be propped up, kept on an even keel and continually kept wet by covering it with sacking and keeping it well sprayed with water.

Mrs Goreham told Peter, 'I saw it and I shall never forget it. It was huge and caused great excitement at the time. I walked the length of the whale, from its tail to its head.' She remembers seeing dogs biting pieces out of the carcass and was there when men came to cut it up – a huge job – before it decayed. Small boys were having the time of their lives climbing on the huge mammal's back.

Peter was unable to discover the actual size of the whale, or what type of whale it was, although apparently the bones were around the village for some time. Indeed, John (Si) Blowers remembers the jaw bones being brought to a piece of wasteland known as 'Charlie Harvey's', where the boys used to climb on them.

One thing that is certain to come ashore is water! Mostly the tide turns and all is well, but there have been times when too much water has inundated the village. In 1834 the Sea Row was washed away, while a century later the other end of the Row was demolished and the sea frequently washed into the floor of the Wavecrest Café. On one stormy night it almost destroyed it. Often the fishermen would race around the village, shouting to householders to get upstairs quickly, because the spring tides were so high. Flooding has been a great fear, either from the sea or the rivers. The floods of 1953 and in the 1960s caused the marshes to flood, and only a few years ago a new housing complex at Cooper's Drive was flooded badly, leaving many residents in despair.

Treasures of the Deep

Some things are trawled up and Kessingland fishermen have found all sorts of things in their nets, from mines left from the wars, bodies (one poor Admiral who was buried at sea came up again several times!), old oak lockers or plastic containers, bottles and other treasures. Some larger items can cause damage if hit by a boat and at times even bringing them back can be dangerous, especially in the case of an undetonated mine. The skipper has to decide whether it is best to risk lives bringing it ashore or leave it and maybe hit it in more tragic circumstances.

Spring tide, 1993.

Floods leave mud at Cooper's Drive.

Clearing up at Cooper's Drive, 2002.

The water came almost up to the café, again!

During the 1990s, while fishing about a mile and a half offshore, beyond the Newcombe Sands buoy, Cock Robin's nets got caught on some wreckage. This broke the 20 foot trawl beam in half, ruined two of his nets and, as the giant timbers surfaced, made a hole in the side of his boat. He remembered, 'It took three blokes to lift one of the timbers and two to lift the other. I took a mark of where the wreck was, to avoid coming across it again.' He had been fishing with Terry Wylie from Pakefield. John Goldsmith of the museum said the origin and date of the timbers were unknown. They have still not been identified in 2006

Kessingland fishermen who brave the North Sea face many dangers. They take their lives in their hands each trip and most have a healthy respect for the sea. Today, with modern boats and radar, flares, coastguards with powerful rescue boats and modern telecommunications, the risk is slighter, but the danger is always there. The raging sea has never been tamed. Such is the price of fish!

Top and above: *The Beach School, 1950s.*

Chapter 17

Education

The earliest education in the village would have been that given by the church in Sunday school and reading classes. There would also have been private schools, such as Miss Mitchell's school, where the more well-to-do children would be taught the three Rs, as well as finer skills such as embroidery for the young ladies. The VP Church of England Upper School in Church Road was for the older children, while the younger ones attended the Beach School until its closure in 1986, when a new school was built in Field Lane. To celebrate the opening, Great Yarmouth Potteries manufactured a limited edition mug which was given to all the children at the opening. Since this was the year that Haley's Comet was seen, that was also incorporated into the design.

There would have been adult education of a sort, too, with a reading-room at the beach end of the village. The late Peter Cherry has also written of times when fishermen, at home due to bad weather or poor fishing, would join the children in class to learn to read and write, since many who wanted a skipper's ticket would not have these skills to pass the necessary examination. Apparently this mixed-age schooling was not thought to be good for the children, since the fishermen went off to the King's Head in the lunch hour, or even smoked their pipes in school, setting a bad example! A century on, there were free computer classes in the village, with the oldest pupil being a nonagenarian!

Beach School group, c.1910.

Roy Brown, veteran parish councillor, loaned photographs of the Beach School, as his late wife Hazel taught there and played the piano for the children. It was built in the early part of the 1900s.

The school in Church Road, formerly Chapel Road, was called the Upper School.

The Schools of Kessingland

The Beach School had 100 pupils and only three teachers. Boys started school at four years old and eventually moved to the Upper School. Girls stayed at the Beach School until they were nine. In 1908 the

Last nativity play at the Beach School, 1986.

Upper School was extended. In 1975 it became a nursery/reception school until it closed in 1986, when the present school was built.

The Upper School was erected in 1869, with 210 children and seven classes, somewhat smaller than those at the Beach School. The head teacher lived at the School House at the back of the school, later to become the village library, now housed in the present school. Without good health care, many children died of diseases such as measles, scarlet fever, chicken pox and whooping cough.

The school had School Inspectors as well as attendance officers, who visited the homes of absent children to ask the reason behind a child's absence and make sure it was genuine. The rector would set a Scripture exam each Easter. Everyone had to put their hand up – the left hand if the answer was not known and the right if the child did know. The results were therefore hard to assess – obviously the teachers wanted good results so that the rector believed Christianity was being taught properly.

The subjects taught were reading, writing and arithmetic, as well as gardening for the boys and needlework for the girls, as these were the skills needed for their future lives.

The school would be visited by the school nurse, mainly to find and eliminate head lice, by the doctor for medical examinations and the dentist to help preserve young teeth.

The 11+ scholarship was taken. Before the war and the building of the Domestic Science block, pupils had to get to Pakefield – the girls for cookery and domestic science classes and the boys for woodwork. Children from neighbouring villages had to walk to Kessingland School and when Pakefield School was closed in wartime, the school was overflowing with extra pupils.

In the second half of the eighteenth century the Anglican Church endeavoured to make education available for all with their Voluntary School programme. Kessingland and Carlton had such schools. The first problem was finding the resources to build the school, but the second was finding adequately qualified staff. Teacher training was in its infancy, but the Church opened training colleges as early as 1825 at St John's, Battersea and St Mark's, Chelsea. A century later these schools were being pushed out, as State-funded schools were built, but country villages fared better at retaining them. In the church schools the rector was (and is at Kessingland now) chairman of the school governors (or managers, as they were called). He took an active part in religious instruction and checked the registers.

Church schools often found it convenient to appoint head teachers who were also organists. This ensured the church had an organist and choirmaster. Another bonus was that choirboys were loathe to miss services if it meant a ticking off at school the next morning. Church schools had special religious holidays, such as

Upper School group in 1920s.

Upper School group with teacher Mrs Solomon, 1957.

Ash Wednesday, Ascension Day, the Parish Treat day, the Sunday-school treat and the Church Fête. School attendance was low when it was the Co-op Society's treat or that of the Chapel Sunday school. Other children had to miss school in order to work (crow-scaring, beet-topping, fruit picking, going to sea with the fishing fleet or, for the girls, being needed at home when a new baby was born or the family was ill). Absences during the winter were often due to bad weather, chilblains or lack of footwear. Many schools, including Carlton Colville, ran a boot club.

Carlton School logs record punishments for such misdemeanors as truancy, smashing classroom windows (these had to be paid for), chattering in class, stealing peas from farmers' fields and smoking in the lavatories. This merited six strokes with the cane. Once, when there had been a church wedding, girls were caned for going to the churchyard to collect the small silver horseshoes from the scattered confetti, making them late back after lunch.

The timing of the summer holiday, a four-week break, was movable according to when the harvest took place. Weather played a more important part in gathering everything safely in, before the advent of combines and large machinery. The corn would often be wet and dry several times before deemed fit to harvest. Then the 'shooks' had to be stood up to dry before threshing. It could take weeks and children were used to take meals out to the men or chase rabbits out of the corn before it was cut.

Upper School group with teacher Mrs Dalton, 1960.

Upper School group with teacher Mrs Spall, 1960.

Two days were given for Christmas (Christmas Day and Boxing Day), the same for Easter (Good Friday and Easter Monday) and one for the August bank holiday. Religious festivals and royal occasions were celebrated. For example, there was a half-day sports event at Benacre Park and 24 May was Empire Day. The end of the Boer War in 1902 merited a whole week off 'at the express wish of the King'.

Most schools were heated by a large open coke-fired stove with a massive fire-guard, but the fortunate children at the front would nod off with the heat while the ones at the back of the class froze! All this is a far cry from our well-equipped, warm, light and airy Primary Schools in Kessingland and Carlton Colville today, but they are founded on the rural schools that managed, with slight resources, poorly paid teachers, voluntary helpers and over-worked clergy, to provide a basic education for our parents and grandparents.

Today the Beach School and the Upper School are private residences, whilst the Street School complex, with its large playground, has provided new homes in Sanctuary Close, as well as the conversion of the actual school building, the headmaster's house, that was once used as the public library. The old Domestic Science block is now a residential property.

Upper School group with Mrs Flo Catchpole, 1965.

Upper School group with teacher Mrs Spall, 1962.

Upper School group with teacher Mr Spall, c.1963.

Upper School group with teacher Miss Pleasance Harvey, c.1962.

New houses between the old Upper School and the head-master's house.

When the new estate was built in the 1970s, joining the two parts of the village geographically, most of the properties were bought by retired people from London, Herefordshire or Essex. This did not put a strain on school numbers, but 20 years on, as some of those homes were vacated and sold, younger families came in and the younger population expanded. Portacabin schoolrooms were added, temporarily.

Back to the Future
**(Taken from the *Kessingland Times*, 1991,
and based on an article in the
1897 church magazine)**

The Upper School experienced something close to

Top and above: *The Kessingland VC Primary School, 1986.*

Top and above: *Kessingland Primary School.*

overcrowding in the late 1800s/early 1890s as there were more children on the books than the school had proper accommodation for. A number of the classrooms were too full to be comfortable, healthy or efficient. There were two causes for this: there were more children at school, and children were not allowed to leave as early as they once did, many being kept at school even beyond the compulsory limit. As a result of all this, one of the managers suggested moving the old Beach School and re-erecting it on a site adjoining the Upper School in the headmaster's garden. This plan proved to be highly satisfactory – the infants were given excellent and ample accommodation all to themselves, which was better for them, and the elder children, as well as Standards I–VII, were all moved to larger rooms. By giving up his garden, Mr Storm gave space for a playground for the girls and infants. The boys used the old playground separately.

Although it may seem odd to us in 2006, apparently it was not uncommon for wooden buildings to be moved, mostly on rollers, with men or horses doing the pulling. Elderly residents can remember other instances, when traffic was so light that this could be more easily achieved. Today large caravans from the beach holiday village frequently stop the traffic when transported to and fro.

Kessingland Primary School
By former school secretary, Pat Fitzsimmons

The school was opened in 1986 to cater for the needs of an increasing population and it replaced two separate Victorian buildings. Further additions were

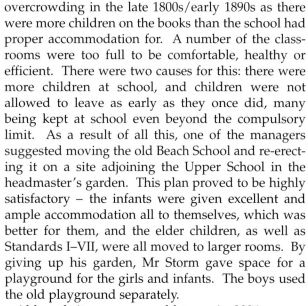

Field Lane Primary School assembly with headmaster Terry Wetherley, early 1990s.

made in 1995 so that the new building now contains carefully planned accommodation including a nursery unit with its own play area, ten classrooms, each of which is linked to a shared activity space, a library, a small group room, a music and drama studio and an ICT Suite (completed in 2003). A large central atrium provides a flexible space for a variety of creative activities/group work, etc. The school also has a hall, with large PE apparatus and stage lighting, a kitchen where school meals are prepared on site, a staff room and separate offices for the head teacher and secretary.

One of the last school sports days, in the 1990s.

The school site includes hard-surface play areas and a large playing-field with some seating and a wide range of shrubs and trees.

The school shares the site with the local Branch Library, which makes a large range of books easily accessible to the children, and full use of this facility is encouraged. The school aims to foster excellence through enjoyment, and give children super opportunities, challenges and support, as every child matters.

The Best Days of Your Life?
George Swan remembers his schooldays

I started school at the age of four, my mother taking me to meet Mr Caston, the schoolmaster. I was given a peg in the cloakroom and was told to go and play. My first teacher was Miss Winnie Brown, who played the harmonium and we used coloured chalks and a slate. My next teacher was Mrs Hazel Brown, in Standard II. In Standard III, I was taught by Miss Iris Catchpole, who later married Mr (Buddy) Larter, one of the teachers, who came to the village with the London evacuees. They attended Kessingland Upper School, as did several children from the outlying villages, such as Hulver, Henstead, Rushmere, Mutford, Carlton, Benacre and Gisleham.

If you lived, I think it was three miles from school, you were given a bike. Every morning you could buy a cup of malted milk for 1d. When I was 11, I was in Standard IV, my teacher being Mrs Annie Dunthorne, who was very strict. In this Class I sat an exam, but failed. It was a one-day exam, with the rest of the school having the day off. I also attended woodwork and cookery classes. Mr Kerrison was the woodwork teacher and Miss Maler took cookery. I was not very good at either. I made a five-legged stool, which was duly smashed in the vice, and my ginger pudding was poured down the sink!

I did some gardening, but most of the garden was taken for the air-raid shelters.

We played games and had PT (physical training) in the playground. We were all in teams and each given

a coloured band to wear, one of four colours, representing British admirals: Red for Haig, Yellow for Jellicoe, Blue for Beatty and Green for Albemarle. If you had a 'cossie' in the summer, a teacher would march you to the beach for a swim. Miss Pleasie Harvey taught Standard V. She was very nice, but strict. If you misbehaved she would smack your thighs, remembering all boys wore short trousers (long 'uns were not allowed!). By this time, we all carried our gas masks as we were at war.

Mr Godbold taught me in Standard VI. He died tragically. He used to play football for Kessingland United. Standard VII, the last class, was taught by Mr Griffiths, who married the village nurse. They later had a road named after them (Griffiths Close.) At 14 I left school, having spent all my schooldays at Kessingland Upper. I left on a Friday and started work on the farm on the Monday, all a long while ago.

I remember being in a school play with who is now Mrs Florence Catchpole, who lives in New Zealand. The play was called Cupid and the Ogre. *The extent of my acting was one line. I remember it now: 'He broke my stick, threw my basket in the river and threw me after it.'...*

Spring when I was a lad meant going out after teatime until it was dark. It also meant the beginning of the season for all the games to be played.

The boys would play the usual football and cricket, as well as marbles, hoops, go-carting and kite-flying... The main structure of a kite would be made from a briar cut from a hedge, covered with strong brown paper and stuck together with paste made of flour and water, the same paste that was used for hanging wallpaper when decorating. The tail was a length of tanned cotton, which was easy to come by if you knew one of the many beatsters, making and mending local fishing nets. We finished it off with screwed-up bits of newspaper tied to it. A kite made in this way would invariably last the whole season.

We also made our own pop-guns from a length of elder wood hollowed out, and a plunger to fit the hole. To get a better fit we would bang the plunger on the ground, forming a 'brush' on the end. The best ammu-

Games children used to play – sketches by Evelyn Mathias.

nition was chewed newspaper or a tight-fitting acorn. This would really pop and travel a long way when banged against a wall.

The whipping top was great fun. We would paint the top, which created a pretty pattern when it was spun. If the toe was lost or worn, we would take our tops to Eddy Catchpole, the shoemaker, for him to fix another one in the form of a hobnail.

The go-cart was much the same as those of today, only we had far more space to use them, as we had very few problems with traffic. One of the best places for go-carting was the Snab Hill.

Marbles was a great game and there were several ways of playing. The most popular one was to sit down, place a glass ally between your legs and the first boy to roll his marble and hit it took your place, after you had collected all the marbles that had missed. At the age of fourteen I left school, by which time I had accumulated literally hundreds of marbles. The week before I left school, I threw the lot into the boys' play-ground, which was only a few feet from my back yard. I often wish I had them now, as a keepsake...

My wife has reminded me of some of the games that the girls played: hopscotch, netball and rounders, but the most popular games were skipping variations and what was known as 'Up the Wall'.

When skipping, you could have a long rope with two people turning, where all the children could run in and out. If you were the one to stop the rope turning, then you had to take the place of one of those turning. The other way was as today, an individual length of rope. The best way of skipping was to include 'bumps' Bumps were when every time you came to a certain word in the rhyme you were singing, the rope was turned very fast. One of the best bumps was 'Salt, mustard, vinegar, ginger, pepper'. There were several rhymes to skip to, including:

Tiddlywinks the Barber,
Went to shave his father.
The razor slipped and cut his lip
Tiddlywinks the barber.

'Up the Wall'* was played with a ball, usually an old worn tennis or sponge ball. The object of the game was to start by bouncing the ball against the wall, then catching it, first with your right hand and then with your left. Next you passed the ball first under one leg, then the other, still catching it, then the most difficult move was to pass the ball first with one hand, then the other, behind your back, turning round at the same time. If the ball was dropped, you had to start again from the beginning.

I was thinking what the papers were like when I was growing up. My mother mostly bought the Daily Mirror, which printed cartoons six days a week... These included Jane with her little dachshund, Fritz. There was Belinda (Blue Eyes), Buck Ryan (whom every young lad wanted to be like when they grew up),

Garth the muscle man (whom everybody wanted as a friend), Captain Reilly Foul (a bit of a ladies' man), Ruggles (who didn't quite know where he wanted to go), Beelzebub was someone to feel sorry for and Popeye with his Olive would be good to have as a friend if you needed a helping hand. There was also Pip, Squeak and Wilfred. And later Andy and Florrie Capp – Andy was a beer drinking DIY disaster.

In another cartoon the same could be said of Useless Eustace. On Sundays, we never bought a paper, so most Sundays after dinner one of us children would go to our Aunt Aggie's to collect her papers after her family had finished reading them. These included the John Bull, the Everybody and the News of the World. We looked forward to seeing our aunt because as we were leaving she would give us a bag of sultana short cakes, and a bread pudding for our Sunday tea. These were baked in her oven in the wall. I can picture this oven now with its highly polished brass handles and hinges.

I recall the News of the World when it featured a fashion competition won by a Kessingland man and the prize was a lot of money in those days.

The war came along and about this time we acquired our first wireless. One of the things my father did was to cut a piece from the paper and stick it on the wire-less; it read 'We are anti Haw Haw here'. It was a reminder not to listen to the German propaganda broadcast by the British traitor who I believe once lived in Ipswich. His surname was Joyce.

I think it was about this time that cartoons finished in order to save paper to help the war effort. Most boys and girls bought comics with their pocket money. There were several different ones so you could swap them around. My favourite one was the Dandy which featured Desperate Dan, and his mother who would bake a cow pie. Another one I recall was Pansy Potter the Strong Man's daughter [featured in the Beano].

I still have a few of these comics which brought a lot of happiness to lots of children in not very happy circumstances. Nearly all newspapers, books, comics and sometimes parcels were brought to the village by the Eastern Counties buses and delivered to the shops, of which Johnny Dade's was one. The conductor stopped the bus outside the shop. Every bus had a conductor at this time.

I'm glad the council have introduced their recycling effort. Looking back we never wasted much paper as we always needed dry paper as the coal fire had to be lit every day either for keeping warm or for cooking and washing. We would take our newspapers to the fish and chip shop, also the greengrocer for wrapping our food in. I know it wouldn't be tolerated today.

Then there was the outside toilet with newspaper cut into squares and hung from a piece of binding twine and a nail knocked in the toilet door. There was much frantic looking through the pile by the light of a candle, torch or small oil-lamp, to find the continuation of the piece you had started to read. Murphy's Law decreed

Primary School children, teachers, governors and parents watch Bob Blizzard open new school equipment.

that it had always been used! This was before the luxury of soft toilet tissue.

Saturday night was Pinkun night when all the football results were printed and Sunday morning Albert Lee could be seen delivering his papers. This meant you could check your pools coupon hoping you wouldn't have to go to work on Monday morning. A few people in the village did win nice sums.

* Evelyn Mathias remembers a rhyme she sang to Up the Wall, which went something like this, 'Plainy, Clappy, Rolly, To backy, Left hand, Right hand, Through the window (under your knee) and back again (opposite). There was more to it, but memory fails her; maybe you can remember the rest of the words?

Kessingland School Puts Down Roots

During the 1980s, 39 children from Kessingland Primary School each planted a shrub and were featured on Anglia TV's local news. This was done as part of a project to regenerate Hart's Meadow on the High Street. New play equipment was erected and the grassed area has been transformed, with attractive shaped beds where the shrubs were positioned by the youngsters, with a little help from their teachers and Waveney Community Services Officer, Chris James. Leading up to the great day, they learned about caring for the environment, as well as how plants and shrubs grow. The shrubs were purchased with the money left over from that given by Persimmon Homes for the play area, and the site will be maintained by Waveney District Council.

The Friends of the School
Bob Blizzard MP opens new equipment, 2005

The Friends of Kessingland School raised half the finance for a new piece of playground equipment, a state-of-the-art slide, whilst Suffolk County Council's Locality fund supplied the other half. Bob Blizzard

stopped off on his election trail to open the new equipment and play with the children on it.

The Friends' fund-raising was supported and encouraged by the school staff, governors, parents and relatives, local businesses, the Parish Council and the children themselves. The events included last year's Summer Fayre, discos, jumble sales, Boogie Nights, charity concerts, etc.

After School Activities

These days Kessingland has a very popular and much-needed Out of School Club. It offers a vital service to families, as many mothers and fathers work full time.

But what did children of former times do when out of school? John (Si) Blowers sheds some light on this:

What I would like to write about is very much a diary of traditional activities boys and sometimes girls have done for centuries and basically haven't changed over the years. I will also add a lot of 'one off' things which I have personally been involved in but hasten to add that I think it would be wise not to include everything.

Many things were probably peculiar just to Kessingland due to the environment we lived in such as having access to the beach, the marshes and lanes, the harvest fields, etc. The River Hundred with its dykes and often flooded areas were fully utilised. There was generally a season for everything and I know many of the boys who read my writings will share in my memories and correct me if I am mistaken.

There was the 'Roaching' season starting in the late spring, this of course was fresh-water fishing with equipment of our own manufacture. Usually the rod was made from a bamboo selection from the water gardens of the farmhouse at the bottom end of Cooper's Lane. The remains of this can still just be seen. I feel that this residence must have been quite grand in its heyday to have water gardens. I think the Gouldby family once lived there and a good lookout for Mr Arthur Gouldby and his dogs had to be posted when cutting (I avoid the word 'stealing') bamboo canes.

Those with parents who could afford it had proper hooks, lines and floats but the less fortunate of us had to work to make do with a bent pin and a float made from an old bottle cork. Bait was supplied in the way of dough from mother, although one of the boys who worked at the local butcher's would bury some waste meat to obtain the resulting maggots. We did not, of course, believe in fishing licences or close seasons and our catch was usually brought home alive in buckets to stock local ponds, one being the bomb crater on Cooper's Meadow where Cooper's Drive is now located.

Tree climbing was popular – a test of nerves existed in that one had to be expert in 'crossing'. There used to be a line of large elm trees bordering Cooper's Meadow, starting behind what is now the MASK shop and ending behind where the fish and chip restaurant now stands. The test was to climb the first tree at one end and swing or jump from branch to branch without coming down, rather like Tarzan I think. This experience I am glad to say certainly gave me a head for heights and good nerves as I am still called upon to climb and saw off a branch or two of a high tree.

In those days a bike was something only owned by kids of well off families. Not to be left out, we made our own. These were called GRIDS, made up of frames, wheels, etc., usually found on a rubbish dump or pit. These machines could not be pedalled and were powered by a boy pushing usually downhill – no tyres or brakes and usually no rider at the bottom of Green Lane or 'JR's' Hill.

Other self-made transport was what might be called a box car, this consisted of a plank or duckboard taken from the wartime trenches equipped with a pair of pram wheels back and front with the front part designed to steer. Again, boy power was crucial – moving downhill. We used to travel far and wide, with the downhill ride compensating for the pulling uphill.

In the winter when the roads had snow on, the box cars were redesigned into sledges and again used on the limited hills. How we cursed when the roadman sanded the best sledge runs! I think it was a gentleman by the name of Jimmy Mattocks who did the roads. A good fall of snow and a long hard frost were most welcome, the snow giving us the obvious delights and the remote hope that drifts might not allow us to get to school, although I cannot recall any occasion when this happened. There was no such thing as closing the schools for a few inches of snow – absolutely unheard of. How things have changed when we hear of schools closing if the weather forecast is bad, even before the snow arrives!

In those days the only drainage of the marshes was by the gravity-fed sluice at Benacre which in times of thawing snow or heavy rains was nowhere near up to the job of stopping the marshes from flooding. These

were exciting times as after a very hard frost the ice on the marshes would bear our weight and we could walk from Cooper's Meadow to the River Hundred on ice.

When the thaw came it was always disappointing but we were compensated in that the flood water came right into Kessingland as far as The Knoll. This meant, with suitable marine transport, we could still go all the way to the sluice at Benacre by water. Rafts were constructed from old oil drums and planks: crude but adequate .

I can even remember my older brother Alan taking a wooden horse trough as a boat – but being totally unstable it wasn't long before he tipped over and got soaked. There was a safer way and that was to sort of 'borrow' canoes from the bottom of Albert Utting's garden, being next to the 'Little River' this being part of the River Hundred system.

As I have mentioned, many old fashioned games were played such as marbles, tops, hoops all in their proper season, hoops were old bicycle wheels tyres and tubeless.

A focal point of meeting was always outside Stanley ('Start') Roth's fish and chip shop (the 'chipper') and when I was quite young we used to torment Stan mercilessly. Just to give one example, Stan used to bring his bins of peeled potatoes down to the shop on a builder's hand cart and it was a regular thing for him, when he closed for the night to find the hand cart hoisted on a rope to the top of a tree at the back of the shop. Stan was a well liked and happy-go-lucky character and somehow I always thought he revelled in the tormenting.

One thing I must mention (and I am sure my compatriots will remember this) is when myself and John (Mike) Kemp and Ivan (Funk) Catchpole decided to build a boat – seagoing, of course. The frame was made of ex-Army duckboard and covered with material salvaged from the remains of a downed barrage balloon. This stuff was a thin rubbery material no more than about two or three millimetres thick but it seemed to be waterproof. The great day of the launch arrived and the sea was calm. The venue was the fishermen's gap and to a horrified audience of longshoremen we set off. Catastrophe struck however and we split the bottom skin on the stony beach and began to sink. Abandon ship was ordered immediately and we got back alright.

We now come to scrumping, again a virtual religion observed by boys. We had this activity down to a fine art. Things were quite easy during the war as many owners of the larger houses that had orchards had been evacuated to supposedly safe areas and most of these had been taken over to billet soldiers; these new occupants weren't bothered about scrumpers so times were good. After the war we had to get a bit smarter when the houses became occupied by their rightful owners. One place was to target church and Bethel goers and we struck on Sunday afternoons and evenings when certain orchard owners were attending divine services.

Adult education classes with Bob Blizzard, MP (front left), 2002.

The oldest computer student, nonagenarian Mr Scollard.

These included the rector, a Mr Bob Catchpole, Miss Mitchell the church organist and Mr Hunter, a Bethel regular.

Not only apples and pears were taken but strawberries, gooseberries ('goosegogs') and red and black currants. I and another boy (who would well remember this) crawled under Mr 'Hundred' Catchpole's strawberry net and were so intent on eating that we only saw Hundred coming at the last minute. In a dash for freedom we both got tangled in the net and only escaped because he wasn't too fast on his feet.

Sometimes allotments and vegetable gardens were raided for carrot, turnip, swedes and peas. These were taken to make stews. A fire was made and an old saucepan produced from home was our cooking pot. Vegetables thrown with an OXO or something were added. When ready, baked potatoes were then recovered from the fire ashes and the meal commenced. We also extinguished our fire after the meal by a method which I cannot mention.

We hear or read a lot these days about boys being bored and relying on computers, PlayStations, TV and the like. We got our enjoyment from creating our own activities and not relying on others to provide these.

Let me give you an example. We did not have the

luxury of the council providing playing-fields with proper goal posts, etc. What did we do? We made them. We were lucky in having Cooper's Meadow to play on, I never did know who owned it but generations of boys used it. Having got our pitch, nothing like full size but adequate, we were fortunate in finding an old trawl net washed up on the beach. There was enough to make up two goal nets. The remains of the steel pipe traps were visited and the necessary posts and cross bar were found and installed, and the nets fitted. The pitch was marked out with sand off the beach and this completed the job.

Many games of the Beach versus the Street were played and despite an inherent hostility between the two populations it all usually went well.

We also played against schoolboys staying at the Fellowship camp and this was the only time in my footballing career that I was sent off by the referee for arguing with him. I think he was a somewhat over-zealous schoolmaster.

It would be a shame if all these memories are lost and we must remember that many of us are all getting on a bit. All of you who read this and have other stories do please contact somebody, before, dare I say it, it is too late.

I would just like to say at this point that though we did our share of tormenting people with our tricks to my knowledge we never actually hurt anybody or caused serious damage by wanton vandalism and we had total respect for the police, especially PC Bruce.

I do however confess to being solely responsible for one or two incidents. I will mention one now. This involved the overhead power cables in Belvedere Drive which resulted in most of the Beach village being blacked out on a Saturday evening. I suppose I was about 14 years old...

The future looks bright, with a new library being built on land to the back of the school, meaning extra room for the pupils. And it is doubtful whether today's pupils will have cycles made up of scrap! Health and safety regulations would rule out a lot of John's boyhood activities.

Millennium Celebrations

The new millennium was also celebrated with a presentation mug to the children and teachers. At the first school assembly of 2000, when two youngsters also celebrated a birthday, head teacher Mrs Sheila Keegan thanked Karolyn Smithson and Joie Lloyd, who had led the fund-raising for needed equipment, through such events as school discos and the Summer Fayre. Items provided included cassette recorders and headphones, a CD player and world globes. Soft play equipment in the hall and a climbing frame were also purchased, as well as the money reserved over five years for the millennium presentation.

Chapter 18

Sport

Sports day and fête at the Old Rectory Meadow, 1920s.

Lots of sports abound in Kessingland, from pigeon fancying to indoor bowls, football to darts. Whatever the age or talents, there has always been something for everyone.

The Working Men's Club has been the base for some of these activities, whilst others make use of the playing-field in Frances Road, off Field Lane, provided, with the Community Centre, by public subscription in the 1970s.

Lyndajane Hood, wife of local plumber and current chairman, Richard, has researched the history of the Working Men's Club. Known as the Reading Room or the Kessingland Village Hall, the Kessingland United Working Men's Club was registered on 12 May 1921. The club was overseen by a large group consisting of nine trustees and various executives, as well as a committee. Open only to Kessingland men, this establishment was frequented and supported by the local gentry who, in the main, were boat owners and local businessmen. The objectives of the club laid down in the rule book stated that:

This club is established for the purpose of providing working men the means of social interaction, mutual

helpfulness, mental and moral improvement and rational recreation.

Membership fees were set at one guinea per year (£1.05 in modern money) and therefore it is doubtful that many working men could actually afford to join.

However, in 1926 Henry Smith was awarded life membership by the committee in recognition of his outstanding bravery. On 31 October of that year the SD *Sarepta* was four miles off Corton lightship when, in heavy, squally weather, one of the crew, A. Marjoram, was thrown overboard by a sudden lurch of the vessel and was soon 300 yards astern. The *Sarepta* was brought back and a lifebuoy was thrown but Marjoram was sinking. Henry Smith, at great personal danger, gallantly jumped overboard and rescued the unconscious man. He successfully applied artificial respiration, thereby saving his colleague's life. Henry Smith was awarded the Stanhope gold medal for bravest deed of the year and his photograph and story can be seen at the Bethel in Kessingland.

Currently there are five members who hold lifetime membership, each having given long service to the club either as members of staff or members of the committee.

Kessingland Village Hall, as it was known, was the hub of the community and hosted many events such as the annual village fête. This included a fruit and vegetable show and a bonny baby competition. In 1945 John Weavers was voted bonniest baby, followed by brother Paul some time later. John's success was reported in the *Lowestoft Journal* and this issue is available for viewing at the Heritage Centre in Lowestoft.

The club boasted three tennis-courts and two bowling-greens. Sadly, the tennis-courts were turned into car parks and one of the bowling-greens gave way to the new extension in 1970. This work was funded from money gratefully loaned by Adnams Brewery. The remaining bowling-green, which was on land donated by local farmer Percy Mobbs in 1947, is today the pride of Kessingland and is renowned throughout the bowling community as one of the very best, as are the bowls team, who have held both county and national titles.

Dominoes, Darts and Dancing

In 1952 Roy Brown and John Saywack approached the committee and suggested that a bar be installed, as well as a fruit machine, to boost membership. The once quiet card-and-domino playing gentlemen's club soon became a thriving business. To some much had been lost by these changes, but to many a great deal had been gained. So began the era of whist drives, Saturday night dances and bingo sessions. For one shilling (5p) you could dance the night away to Freddie Wigg and his three-piece band.

The bar was staffed voluntarily for a number of years but as the membership increased so too did the workload and therefore the decision was taken to employ paid staff.

The Kessingland Boxing Club was founded in 1963 by Colin Brown and David Edmunds. Twice weekly they roped off a ring in the main hall for practise sessions, preparing for boxing tournaments which often took them to London. The team won several Area Championships before disbanding in 1970.

The original Reading Room is now known as the Pigeon Room. This room hosts the weekly meetings of the Kessingland Flying Club. Founded in 1973 by John Sherwood and Ronnie Rouse, the club is justifiably proud of the fact that it has some of the top flyers in East Anglia.

There has undoubtedly been much more to the club's history than this potted history can portray. What began as a gentlemen's club in a tin hut has gone on to be so much more. Many community groups now use the club's facilities for their regular meetings, thereby ensuring that the spirit of Kessingland Village Hall lives on.

At the time of writing, Kessingland United Working Men's Club, established in 1921, boasts a membership of 1,650 and growing. The longest-serving member, for an incredible 70 years, is Roy Brown (recently awarded an MBE for his services to the community of Suffolk). Those wishing to join the club, perhaps even to challenge his record, can do so by being nominated by an existing member. There is also presently an amnesty for lapsed members. Fees are £10.00, with a reduced rate for senior citizens and £2.00 for junior membership.

The club is managed by trustees and committee members, led by the club president, who is nominated and voted for by members on a yearly basis. Any member can join the committee after six months. This is voluntary but is recognised by the club with the awarding of a certificate of merit, such as was presented to Cora Sherwood for ten years' service. Its function is to represent members' opinions and should anyone wish for their views to be discussed they should write to club secretary, John Weavers.

The club offers financial support to various charities when approached via the committee. Monies donated are raised from the sale of raffle tickets. There are also many individual fund-raising functions held on the premises, such as the annual concert in aid of Quidenham Children's Hospice, arranged and orchestrated by Lynn Bullard.

Musical entertainers at the club in recent years have included 'Rollercoaster', 'Rhythm and Greens', Johnny Cleveland, Dave Fontana, 'Budgie Coleman & Mustard' and 'Me-an-'im' to name but a few.

Many community groups use the facilities for their meetings, including the Women's Institute, Waveney Crossroads and the Wrentham Town Band.

The Jugganauts football teams also use the club as a base. Established in 1968 by John Hunn, there are two teams. Sponsored by Richard Pont of Kessingland Service Station, the teams have become well known for their support of the Kessingland Funday and the now-infamous match between themselves and the PT Mums.

The club has two pool teams and six darts teams. The men's darts A team, established for over 50 years, has won numerous trophies. There is also a B team and C team.

The ladies A team, established for over 20 years, has won trophies including the Captain's Cup and the Chairladies Cup. There is also a B team.

Twice-weekly bingo sessions complete the list of events held at the club as it continues in its quest to be the hub of village life.

Football: A Way of Life
(Taken from 1998 interview with Trevor Edwards)

For one Kessingland man at least, football is a way of life. His garage door is painted in his team's colours, much to the amusement of some of his

Football team, 1946–47.

neighbours, and his house is named 'Selhurst'.

Trevor Edwards came to the village from South London in 1989, bringing his allegiance to Crystal Palace with him. He had attended football matches at this local club since boyhood. Feeling rather isolated in East Anglia, football-wise, yet realising that there must be Palace fans around, he formed the Eastern Eagles Supporters Club, which has now grown to over 100, many in the Lowestoft area. It is his full-time hobby, along with his voluntary work scouting for Palace.

He arranges coaches to Crystal Palace matches and runs stalls at charity events for Palace. Although Trevor only played football at school level, the club was pleased to welcome him as a talent scout. Trevor spends most weekends watching local games, looking out for promising young stars in the 12–16 age bracket. At least two of his protégés have been taken by the club and others sent for trials. Obviously one big ambition of Trevor's is to have one of his lads make the club's First Team.

Songwriting is another of Trevor's talents. He wrote 'We all follow the Palace', which sold over 700 copies and was then incorporated into a Crystal Palace CD of football songs.

Trevor also produced a local Palace fanzine until lack of time forced him to stop, when he began scouting. He is also involved in the other kind of Scouting in the village.

Squash Club and Beauty Room

For a number of years Stella and Mike Goodall ran Kessingland's Beauty Room and Squash Club. Mike continued to play squash competitively, was secretary of the Waveney Squash Leagues for many years, and encouraged and promoted the sport. He was also a dedicated coach for junior players. Indeed, some of his youngsters have become superb players, in the first Norfolk County League Team.

As well as the beauty room, Stella wrote a monthly health and beauty article for the *Kessingland Times*.

Kessingland Squash Club is now owned and managed by David Waters.

Kessingland Squash Club.

133

Martial Arts in Kessingland
(Taken from interviews with Keith Plummer, and Reg and Chris Penson)

When, as a child, Keith Plummer complained of being bored, his parents helped him find something that was fun, where he could make friends and have something to aim for. He eventually found the Kuk Sool Won School. This is a Korean ancient art that mainly focuses on self-defence and self-preservation. It teaches how to deal with aggression constructively and is all about your attitude to your opponent. It also emphasises relaxation and controlled breathing. All of these aspects contribute to a healthier lifestyle.

Keith has achieved his black belt and in competitions has won several medals, most of them gold, in UK championships.

Reg Penson has also gained achievements in martial arts. Having given up smoking and wishing to avoid putting on weight as a consequence (a common problem for those giving up) he went along, with his eldest son, to Kung Fu classes in Lowestoft. After five years' training with Mr J.D. Johnson, in 1987 he started the Kessingland Gung Fu Club, which has never looked back. Chris explained: 'Society teaches that people should always want to win, but life is not like that. We need to be taught how to lose as well... and survive.'

Running and Jumping

Showjumping is another popular sport – probably made more so by television coverage of national events. Kessingland has its own local champion, Trina Goddard, who lives just out of the village in Gisleham.

Then there is athletics. As a lad, Glen Thurgood was known as 'the running paper boy', because not only was he delivering papers, he was also training for his next big event. Aged 16 he was described as a hopeful for the Olympics, having won competitions and taken part in a variety of national events.

He was a bit of an all-rounder, playing in at least a couple of football teams, he also played the piano and flute. His younger brother, Darren, was similarly talented – a keen sportsman and a drummer!

In 2006 Glen is a trainee canoe instructor, following in his Dad's footsteps (or should it be oar sweeps!) You may see him riding the surf waves at the beach.

Boxing

Kate Mickel's father, Jim Reynolds, was self-made 'Rock King of Cambridge' and was a friend of the Docwra Rock family of Great Yarmouth. He took his sweets and rock stall all over the area, especially to Newmarket Races and local gymkhanas, where Kate met her husband, Mick.

They were both born and bred in Cambridge, Mick in 1912 and Kate two years later, and from 12 to 14 years of age Mick worked in Captain Tebb's stables, grooming, exercising, cleaning out and bedding down, and learning to ride and enter events. Being only four stone in weight, he was an ideal rider and, on leaving school, went to be an apprentice jockey in Newmarket with Basil Jarvis, who had around 90 horses in training. Because of his previous experience, Mick was exercising race horses only one week later.

Again because of his weight, he was encouraged to enter local boxing tournaments, and won a gold medal in the Stable Lads Boxing Championship in London for the best performance. He rode at Newmarket and Great Yarmouth, meeting many famous jockeys, trainers and racing personalities. Gradually, Mick's weight increased so, after four years, he left his job, joining the Cambs Amateur Boxing Club and returning to Captain Tebb's stables. Since he was undefeated time after time, promoters came after him and persuaded him to turn professional.

Two years after Mick had met and danced with Kate at the evening dance after the gymkhana (with her father's approval, of course), they were married. In March 1992 the couple went to Portugal for three weeks to celebrate their diamond wedding anniversary and came back to great excitement and wonderful surprises. A family party had been planned by their son, Roy, who helps daughter Alison and other members of the family to run Ashley Cafe. One of their many cards was from the Queen.

Mick has fought all over London, mostly undefeated. He has a photograph of himself and Lowestoft boxer Seaman Jim Lawlor with Henry Cooper when he opened Building Scene's Warehouse in Commercial Road, Lowestoft, in 1984.

On retirement they decided that Cambridge was too busy for them so when son Roy took Field Lane fish and chip shop some years back, they moved here – and immediately loved it. Now, with most of the family living only doors away from them, they are content.

As Kipling said, 'when you can meet disaster and success head-on and treat them both the same', to misquote, you are ready to take up a sport.

Chapter 19

Kessingland's Artists and Writers

In exhibitions of arts and crafts, one village treasure never fails to impress. It is a sampler, owned by Joe Utting's family and stitched by nine-year-old Letticia Catchpole in 1828. It incorporates all the stitches that little girls were supposed to learn in order to run a future household – either their own, or as servants in bigger houses. It is an enlightening insight into the life of a child in that era, and Letticia probably spent many dull days or evenings sewing by oil or candle-light. The sampler is framed and 'signed' with her name and the date at the bottom. It is a rare work of art and Joe is justly proud of it.

Another old piece of real craftsmanship is owned by Roy Brown. He has a carving, done by a fisherman ancestor, which hangs above his lounge fireplace. The Lord's Prayer has been painstakingly and beautifully 'engraved' in a piece of wood, making a natural frame around the lettering. In the days before libraries, radio or television were available, it is surprising what treasures were created to pass the time and relieve the boredom.

The MASK committee at the exhibition, 1990. Left to right, back row: Roy Brown, Maureen Long, Gill and Michael Knights; front row: Eve Haddock, Joy Smith, Jean Purkis and Alan Waller.

More recently, there was an art group in the village that put on an annual Art Show, organised by Mrs Iris Martin each year. Her husband made the stands which displayed the local paintings from a wide range of artists. Beginning in the Church Hall, the Art Show was moved to the Methodist Church in the 1980s. It finally had to close, just before the Rider Haggard Festival year, when it was suggested that a two-day Art Show could be tried, at the Bethel Hall, incorporated into the exhibition which had already started there. Local artists were informed and it was a great success. Some asked if they could leave their work for the rest of the season, after which many asked, 'See you next year?' This was the start of the seasonal shows from Easter until the end of September, which continued until it was no longer possible to use the Bethel Hall. The following year a ten-day Exhibition and Art Show was held in the Church Hall, after which MASK had the offer of renting the Knights Holiday Shop from Michael Knights. Here arts and crafts and local books have been exhibited and sold for the past 12 years, the proceeds going towards a longed-for museum or heritage centre for the village.

Sampler worked by Letticia Catchpole, aged 9 years, 1828.

Mother Hubbard's Cupboard, the MASK shop, 1995.

Maureen Long inside the MASK shop, 1998.

A Wealth of Talent

Artists include Evelyn Mathias, a volunteer at the MASK shop, who paints fairies, local beach scenes, does silhouettes and also sketches of people, children or animals from photographs. This service is extremely popular with locals and summer visitors alike. She has had her paintings made into greetings cards by Clover Cards, which sell well in the shop.

She is also a published writer, with children's stories on cassette and in books. She does all the artwork for the local magazine and is always ready to try her hand at designing other items for seasonal sale in the shop, having produced designs for Kessingland tea towels, coasters, bookmarks, pictures and the like.

Jackie Gardiner paints evocative pictures, as well as keeping the shop supplied with an infinite variety of canal art. Dawn and John Day both paint and produce collages, greetings cards and other crafts.

Geoffrey Mallett has exhibited his pictures and others have sold woodwork and wood-turning products. The late Miriam Murdock painted pictures and glassware, whilst her husband has exhibited his marquetry. Eve Haddock painted pictures and also drew the popular Kessingland map, which helps visitors to negotiate the twists and turns of the central estate.

Two members of the original Kessingland Art Group were Isobel and Trixie Brock – wives of the Brock brothers. Isobel loved to paint flowers, especially as she was a keen gardener. Trixie produced exquisite silk embroidered pictures of old-fashioned scenes, such as baking day, wash day, and the like. She also painted pictures for framing, decorated stones from the beach and once made a beautiful doll's house.

Personality Profile:
Lanyu and Douglas Kemp
(Taken from a 2006 interview)

Many village people will have spent a lot of time in the home of Lanyu and Douglas Kemp, though maybe not in its present form. Not so many years ago, their imposing house on the corner of Sanctuary Close, near the Methodist Church, was the old Woodwork and Domestic Science building belonging to Kessingland Upper School. Before Gisleham School was built, when Kessingland pupils stayed at the Upper School until their leaving age, this building furnished many of the practical skills of woodwork, housekeeping and cooking, later to be used in village industry, homes and kitchens, as well as in the kitchens of local holiday camps. Today, this spacious and functional home retains many of the solid features of the old building, noticeably the lovely old wooden floors, now sanded and polished, still as strong and firm as when they were installed.

Even in the conversion and new ownership, there was a strong link with the past. Douglas Kemp may not have been born and raised in Kessingland, but he comes from solid Kessingland stock. There have been Kemps here since around 1830, when they 'emigrated' from Somerleyton. 'My uncle, Ben Kemp, helped build this and his mark was found on the roof rafters. Our family have been farmers, fishermen and builders in the village for generations.'

Fred Kemp joined the Navy and left the village and his son, Douglas, was born in London. As with most Naval families, they moved around quite a lot. Fred retired back to the area, but Douglas went into computer consultancy work and this took him abroad; it was in Lucerne that he met Lanyu.

Lanyu was born and brought up in China, but after university, where she studied electronics, she took a job as a University Professor of Electronics in Hamburg, Germany. She was desperately homesick for the first week, but doing a job she loved and had studied intensely soon absorbed her. Next she took on a post at the European Research Centre in Geneva, Switzerland. She met Douglas and they fell in love and married there.

Douglas and Lanyu visited Fred in Kessingland and bought the empty school building in 1992. They spent the next two and a half years renovating it. Still living and working in Switzerland, Douglas came over once a month to check on the progress of builders, plumbers, electricians and other workmen who were transforming the building. For the next few years the couple spent Christmas and summer holidays in Kessingland; they eventually moved here in 1996.

As a student, Lanyu had loved art and once won a prize in her home town for a watercolour painting. On retirement, she took up painting again, and it took her only 12 months to paint enough pictures to exhibit in Lowestoft Library, where she sold most of her paintings in the week. One picture shows a Lowestoft fishing scene of yesteryear, tying in again with Douglas's family. His grandfather was 'Turkey' Kemp, so called because of his red face, a result of having had rheumatic fever as a child. 'Turkey' skippered three boats out of Lowestoft. (The book by Peter Cherry, *The Richest Village in England*, features the story of Turkey and the boats.)

The couple love living in Kessingland, enjoying their home, neighbours and friends. It seems that history is repeating itself in the Kemp family, with their fishing and building heritage being preserved.

Personality Profile: Michael Vincent
(Taken from a 1990 interview)

Famous for his large gouache paintings, Michael Vincent, an artist of international repute, lived here for some time, celebrating the Suffolk landscape through his art. In 1990 he said: 'My paintings depict the countryside and coast between Lowestoft and Aldeburgh, with a focal point being Kessingland, Covehithe and Benacre.'

His paintings present the changing face of rural Suffolk to the world at large, with such names as 'Landscape with Wild Flowers, Kessingland', 'Summer Heather and Birches on Westleton Heath', 'A Suffolk Garden in the Spring', 'Winter Bracken on the Cliffs at Benacre', 'The Moon rising over the Sea at Pakefield' and 'Autumn Sun over Benacre Lake'.

For me landscape painting has always been a love affair with nature. Paintings without passion are dead. Fuse this passion with a technical skill and a painting is born.

As a child I spent hours exploring the quiet beauty of a landscape swept by ever-changing skies and bathed in a magical light. Suffolk has produced many noted painters and when I returned to live by the coast, the magic was heightened. The countryside retains its quiet and dignified beauty with the sea just beyond the fields, adding so much more. Painting the landscape here, embraced by a purity of light or shrouded in soft-coloured mists, is a challenge, but today there is an added urgency, a disturbing undercurrent dominating my work. Countryside which for generations has provided succour to man and inspiration to Art, is in mortal danger. The increasing threat from development and pollution can no longer be ignored by the landscape painter. Friends tell me that my work could become a 'monument to Suffolk' as already paintings which I have done of parts of Benacre and Covehithe are of areas which no longer exist. The threat from flooding is frightening and not much seems to be happening to conserve what is left. You cannot paint and stay

Ken Smith, artist and radio ham, June 1993.

Ken Smith with some of his paintings and certificates, 1993.

uninvolved. When I exhibit away from home, people cannot believe the beauty that is Suffolk.

Looking at Michael's 'Landscape with nuclear glow. Sizewell, Suffolk', his concern that a nuclear accident could totally wipe out his beloved landscape is clear to see. However, most of his paintings bring to life small corners of the area, such as wild flowers behind the water-tower, close to his home. Working with oils or gouache, his flowers are so lifelike that they invite you to reach out and gather them. His three-dimensional approach, oozing that vitality and truth which he seeks from working out on site, gives his work a remarkable quality.

Personality Profile: Ken Smith
(Taken from a 1993 interview)

The late Ken Smith retired to the village after a full working life. He lived in a former coastguard cottage in Kessingland and was an amateur radio 'ham', artist, draughtsman and newly discovered poet. He had a busy life and had strong memories of the Second World War:

I remember having to go directly to areas being blitzed. Bristol particularly was a dreadful experience. My car was hemmed in a queue of Green Goddesses but I eventually got there to inspect the aftermath and report on rebuilding plans...

When there was time, you had to try and 'switch off' from the horrors of war. I continued to paint and draw, but when I tried pastels in 1953, I found my true artistic medium and never wanted to use water-colours or oils again...

Ken exhibited at several London galleries and his work sold well.

Ken also remembered the First World War, when he was 8–12 years old. His most vivid memories were of queuing up for meat for his mum, also of the German Taubes and Zeppelins crashing all around.

His parents were strict church folk. However, it stood him in good stead, and his strong faith carried him through all life's ups and downs, giving him that confidence to start a new life after his wife's death. He joined Kessingland's Methodist Church, where his talents were put to use illustrating the children's work in the morning all-age worship sessions.

Personality Profile: Tommy Cornelius
(Taken from a 1992 interview)

Born Cornelius Kontides, son of a sea captain, Tommy's mother gave birth to him in Catherine Dock in 1917 (Greek captains were allowed to have their wives with them), thereby giving him British nationality. Tommy was equally at home in Greece or here, but lived for most of his life in France, holding the French 'Carte de Residence'. His was inextricably bound up with all three countries, although he lived in many more.

His father worked here, then fought for England in the war and was killed. His mother remained in the East End, where the young Cornelius Kontides had been to school. 'Once you've lived and been educated in the East End, you're a Cockney all your life, wherever you go,' he laughed.

After his mother died (during the war years) he decided to go to Greece and find his family:

I felt at home in Greece, in fact I call three countries home. I've always been able to work and make a living for myself anywhere, then the wanderlust would take me to far-off places again. I keep up with my family, natural and 'adopted', because I write a lot of letters. Wherever I go my typewriter goes too. I've written poems and stories all over the world, as well as painted pictures. Art is my greatest love.

Tommy (he changed his name legally to Thomas Cornelius when he went to work, as his mates called him everything from Corny to Concertina!) had the walls of his retirement home hung with his pictures; he painted from imagination or memory. Cats, birds in the Japanese style, dogs, English or faraway scenes, all feature in his work. Whatever he did, he did it prolifically. Hundreds of paintings have been given to family and friends, sold or raffled for charity, as well as the model boats, dolls' houses, etc., which he loved to make. He said:

Anyone can have a fuller life. But not everyone stretches their minds enough. They're satisfied with too little. Most of us never realise our full potential, what our brains are capable of. I don't think anyone is ever too old to achieve new things.

Personality Profile: Hugh Wilding
(Taken from a 1994 article)

The late Hugh Wilding was a man of many parts – Chairman of Waveney Eldercare, a Deacon at London Road Baptist Church, a prolific artist and a good friend to many.

Born in South West London, Hugh grew up in New Maiden, Surrey, with his sister Peggy. Interested in drawing and design, he became an architect, and joined his uncle's firm. There he worked with a young secretary called Pauline, later to become his wife. When war became imminent and private architecture virtually ceased, he joined the Ministry of Works, later to be called the Department of the Environment. During the war Hugh served in the Royal Engineers, principally in Gibraltar. After the war the DoE seconded him to the Palace of Westminster, during the rebuilding of the House of Commons.

When the couple retired and came to live in Kessingland, they were no strangers to the village, since Pauline's sister, Phyllis, was already happily settled here. Hugh soon became involved at the Baptist Church, while Pauline attended St Edmund's. There she worked closely with Liz Stephens, later Liz Edgeley, whose vision it was to see a hospice in Kessingland; they worked and fund-raised to set up Waveney Eldercare. Hugh and Pauline were founder members of the organisation and when the need was seen for a luncheon club, leading on to a day centre, they did much of the administrative work, whilst Liz and her husband attended to the training, interviewing and fund-raising. Hugh's architectural experience was a great help in the planning. After Liz's sudden death Hugh became more involved in the centre, later becoming chairman. His kind and gentle personality went a long way to putting elderly people at their ease.

Hugh was an exhibitor in art shows, his striking colours and deft strokes bringing to life scenes from holidays abroad or landscapes captured at home. This was an interest which he shared with Pauline and during the summer months they tried to go out painting once a fortnight, working with pastels outside, then copying their pictures during the winter months in oils.

Personality Profile: Evelyn Mathias
(Taken from a 1996 interview)

Her childhood, some of the happiest years of her life, were spent six months of the year in London and six months in Lincolnshire, until she was nine. This was because her father was a butler and her mother a cook to a Lincolnshire family in Belgravia.

Evelyn became a nanny in Bournemouth and was

Evelyn Mathias with the teacloth she designed for Kessingland MASK shop, Mother Hubbard's Cupboard.

an emergency 'Mother's help' in 1970, when she wrote bedtime stories, some since published, to enthral her charges. She has also been a shop assistant and, when living in Alton, Hampshire, she exhibited and sold her work at the local Art Society exhibitions.

Evelyn received a copy of the *Kessingland Times* through her door and wrote to the editor to ask if there were any local writing or art groups. A small group of people, including Chris Wright-Murray, were trying to start a creative writing group. As soon as the editor knew Evelyn could sketch she was roped in for Cuthbert Capers! Evelyn admits, 'Since then I've been hooked on him and his friends!' The Cuthbert stories are educative, informative and are used to warn of dangers at the seaside.

Today she never has a moment to herself. She has her sketches, silhouettes, paintings and locally inspired notelets on sale in the MASK shop. She has exhibited in Gallery 61 in Church Road and has

teamed up with the editor Maureen Long to produce a book of poems and nostalgic sketches of children of yesteryear, called *Far Horizons*.

Personality Profile: Len Burrell
(Taken from a 1991 interview)

With friend David Jervis, Len Burrell formed a Waveney branch of the British Model Soldier Society, and has held exhibitions of their work. They have even been featured on Radio Suffolk, in a bid to get the branch advertised and to encourage new members. The society organises competitive shows that attract international exhibits. Len has entered his models against the best, and has many certificates and trophies to prove it.

Len was a founder member of the first Lowestoft modelling club in 1972, mainly to encourage his rather shy, eldest son in the hobby, but confesses that as a very young child he was always whittling at bits of scrap wood, creating primitive boats and aeroplanes. His son's interest flagged after a couple of years, but Len has been hooked ever since, and now builds highly detailed military models from all periods of history. Modellers tend to specialise in one particular period and Len finds the First World War the most fascinating. Research to achieve the highest degree of accuracy led him to collecting books of that period, since it was often quicker than spending hours in reference libraries and museums. His landing now groans under the weight of his collection of First World War volumes and (as long as you don't tell his wife) he will welcome any further additions to his collection when you are cleaning out the attic or 'pruning' the bookshelves. He remembered:

As a child I was helped and encouraged by a neighbour, a retired Thames lighterman and bargemaker. I also did carpentry and joinery at school, and during my National Service in the RAF shared a room with a chap called the Hon. James Symes, who spent his spare time tying fishing flies, and constructing very detailed model cars from balsa wood, wire and various other surplus scrap materials.

Creating things was in his blood; his mother was the artist who painted the Black and White Whisky dog adverts, and his father was a director of the Burrell Steam Engine Company.

After demob, and being an architect by trade and a qualified member of the Institute of Building, Len went into civil engineering, working in turn for both G. Percy Trentham Ltd, and W. & C. French Ltd. With them his projects included helping to build much of the Ford Motor Company's offices and factories at Halewood, near Liverpool, at Dagenham and at Warley, near Brentwood. Eventually, he went back into architecture, starting on his own as an architectural consultant in 1976.

Len wrote two books, one on making sea-fishing tackle, and another on sea fishing, both published by Pelham Press in the 1970s.

Having built up many years of expertise in modelling, especially in sculpturing miniature figures from clay-like materials, Len wrote another book about it, which he decided to publish and print himself. He bought a computer, taught himself to master it, and used it and a copier to publish his book in two parts. With a little help from a local printer with the binding, the book has helped would-be miniature sculptors all over the world.

Len's view on hobbies is:

When you spend a great deal of time pursuing a hobby, you often find easier ways of doing things, and make new, or alter existing bits of commercially available equipment. This is knowledge that should never be lost, but passed on to others, and if you can make a few bob doing it, so well and good!

My greatest interest in modelling, is the sculpturing of 1/12th scale military figures. They are about seven inches high and are made from an epoxy resin putty on a wire frame. In order to save time, I have now made a kind of skeleton pin man, and used it to make a mould from which I cast as many basic figures as required. All that is needed then is to animate the basic figure and build up the particular uniform.

As well as the large-scale models, Len makes scenic, smaller, 54mm scale models. One, entitled 'Yuletide Blessings', shows the way light industrial railways were used to transport food and ammunition over the morass of mud in France during the First World War. The model is set at Christmas 1916, and even includes a local padre blessing the soldiers. Len's father was badly wounded during this war, and often told the story of seeing Allied troops playing football with the Germans in 'No man's land'. They were back trying to kill each other the next day!

Louisa Briggs, a lady from Columbia, who married a local man, produces striking jewellery in the Colombian style.

Mother and Daughter Partnership: Susan Quinlivan and Margaret Stone
(Taken from a 1995 interview)

Mother and daughter Margaret Stone and Susan Quinlivan spend their lives surrounded by tutus; Margaret makes them and Susan sells them, in their shop, Veriannes Dancewear, in London Road South, Lowestoft, near the corner of Carlton Road. They opened there in May 1987.

Both Susan and Margaret live in Kessingland. When she is not at her sewing machine, Margaret enjoys keeping fit. She has been attending classes regularly for 20 years, and has recently taken up tap-dancing

lessons too, not bad for a 'great gran'. Another hobby is gardening and her attractive garden with pond shows her and her husband's industry there.

Susan relaxes with ballet classes at the Rainbow Academy at Sunway House, the former Bally Shoe factory, in Raglan Street.

Personality Profiles: Ruby and Dennis Richardson
(Taken from a 1994 interview)

Dennis was 71 when he bought a bright red tandem, on which he and Ruby, six years younger, rode about the village.

Since their retirement they have owned a caravanette which has taken them all over the country, exploring new areas and revisiting some of the places where Dennis stayed as a professional musician. On the tandem they explore closer to home, often cycling 40 miles a day. They did 1,000 miles in the first two months!

Dancing is another way of keeping fit and has featured a lot in Dennis's career, as he has played at hotels, holiday camps, concerts and with dance halls as well as doing classical work. Firstly a bass player, as well as being proficient on the violin, the cello has been his third instrument and the best-loved one. He remarked: 'There is more variety on a cello and you never stop learning and stretching yourself to cope with the scope of its potential.'

In 1952, playing at the Royal Hotel, Lowestoft, Dennis was able to explore Suffolk some more after he got a taste for the beautiful countryside before D-Day when his regiment trained at Rendlesham and Peasenhall in 1943. He played extensively in Lowestoft, with a few seasons at the Golden Sands Holiday Camp.

Meanwhile, Ruby worked at Morton's canning factory, now closed, which she described as having a lovely family atmosphere, from 1944 to 1952, then left to have her family. She went back 14 years later, first part time, then full time, until she was made redundant in 1987. In between her stints at Morton's, she did casual work at Pontins and fruit-picking at Grove Farm.

A long time after each of them had been deserted by their first partners, Ruby and Dennis met at a Friendship Club in Lowestoft. However, they were friends for seven years before marrying, since their children were teenagers. When their offspring were all settled, the couple married. Between them they have five sons, five daughters-in-law and nine grandchildren to keep them busy.

Ruby is an avid member of the WI and was a member of the award-winning darts team (with a medal to prove it). She also loves working at her tapestry, having won a first and second prize for two framed examples in her home.

Dennis described the joy of tandem-cycling as

'pulling together and sharing the work, the power and the energy'.

Personality Profile: Janet Hawkes
(Taken from a 2000 interview)

A resident who also lives with her work is Janet Hawkes of Ivy House, High Street, where she has a gallery. She explains:

Most of the textile side of my work is self-taught, by experimenting to see what works best. I have also been on occasional workshops. We moved to Kessingland and when the twins, Michael and Andrew, began playgroup and Rachel was at school, I took up this hobby again and dabbled in embroidery. One day I wandered into the gallery on the Green at Walberswick and booked a week for the next year for an exhibition. Everyone thought I was mad, because at that stage I had only done one picture!... It was harder than even I had imagined and meant a steep learning curve and working late into the night, but I did it and it was a wonderful sense of achievement, especially when I sold about 25 of my 30 creations that week. Obviously that spurred me on to book for the following year.

After four successful years and lots of contacts and new friends made, came the disappointing news that the gallery was to be closed. As a result, Janet set about designing an addition to their house for use as a studio.

The sea and her art could be 'in the genes', as her grandfather's cousin was the late Harry Hudson Rodmell, famous for his marine and shipping posters. Janet has a book of some of them.

Not content to sit back, she made a millennium promise to herself to conquer computing, so is now producing her necessary promotional material herself.

The Heriz-Smith Family

In the early 1900s, the talented Heriz-Smith family lived at Fourwinds in Holly Grange Road, near the beach. The family enjoyed the countryside and beach in the summer as well as reading, painting, music and embroidery for the girls. All well educated, they produced a remarkable set of magazines, entitled *The Noonstar*, with poems, stories, sketches, paintings, jottings and the like. By kind permission of descendants Revd Tim and Marion Hollis, they were loaned to the Rider Haggard Exhibition in the Festival year of 1990. They are a unique record of the social life and times of that era. The covers were made of green cloth, embroidered with the title and other emblems. The eldest daughter, Sybil, was a talented actress, the son, Denzil, was killed during the First World War and his younger sister, Gillian, became the flower lady mentioned in Chapter 20.

Personality Profile: Rosa Wake
(Taken from a 2001 interview)

After a lifetime of putting her thoughts on paper, Rosa Wake did not tackle a novel until well into her retirement. After that she never stopped weaving her tales of murder, mystery, mayhem, romance, misunderstandings and happy endings.

Many Kessingland people first met Rosa when, after her retirement and move here, she produced a Passion Play during Lent in the 1970s. Those who took part found she was thorough, sincere, full of fun, yet able to obtain just what she wanted from her cast. This was no doubt due to her training and experience as a teacher of English, history and drama. She soon had much of the village involved. She remembered:

We [Rosa and her sister] stayed in a chalet in Green Lane when these bungalows were being built. I had fallen in love with East Anglian wide skies while on a course at Cambridge University and knew I would like to retire here. We bought the bungalow and have never regretted it.

As she became more housebound, writing became her means of enjoying life through the lives of her characters, along with her other relaxing hobby of listening to classical music.

She had gained a BA Honours degree in English and taught in Birmingham, where she helped to found the Birmingham Children's Theatre. She was a member of the staff at the first experimental County College in Bilston, Staffordshire, where young adults went for day release from local factories. She later became principal lecturer and head of English at the teacher training college in Dudley. As well as her job, she found time to produce plays and operas, from classical to contemporary.

Rosa died in 2004 when in her nineties, having published eight or ten novels in the last decade of her life.

Personality Profile: John Westley

John Westley is probably the most famous fund-raiser in the village. He made the *Guinness Book of Records* by doing a sponsored walk, in 1990/91, all around the coasts of the British Isles for Multiple Sclerosis, after his mother contracted the disease. He stopped to swim across the largest lake in each country, and to climb the highest peaks in each of England (Scafell), Scotland (Ben Nevis), Ireland (Slieve Donard), Eire (Carrantuohill) and Wales (Snowdon). From the copious diary notes he made each night, he wrote *The Road Below*, the story of his marathon effort, published in 1993. A significant amount of the royalties generated from the book were donated to the MS Society.

It is gratifying to note that after seeing all the coast of the British Isles, he chose Kessingland in which to

Keith Nichols, showman and writer.

live with his parents in their retirement. He also makes sculptures and necklaces for the shop.

When I first knew that my mum had MS I was so angry, I didn't know what to do. I soon realised though that I could do nothing about it but to try and help the victims, so the idea of the walk and book came... meeting such a lot of wonderful people and their generosity in terms of donations and hospitality opened my eyes to what a lovely world it is...

As well as working for the Royal Mail, devising board games, writing articles and short stories, poetry, stage musicals, TV plays and genealogical research, John continued to fund-raise, with the ultimate aim of eradicating MS.

More Authors

Gillian Bligh, who came to the village with the family when she was two years old, is married to Michael Knights of Knights Holiday Homes. She has had two novels published – set in the eighteenth and nineteenth centuries, *The Cornelians* and *The Stick Man.* Her third, in the writing, is eagerly awaited.

Steven End wrote a book on Ipswich Town Football club, of which he is a fan. Keith Nichols has written a book on the life of a fairground showman, entitled *They Seek Him Here, They Seek Him There,* as well as writing booklets on *Kessingland Ghosts* and his own early life.

David Porter MP went to Bidnall's Printers to see the production of the Kessingland Times, *1995. He is seen here with typesetters Pam and Mrs Bidnall.*

Peter Cherry was one of the most prolific writers in the area and his work has been cited throughout this publication. His contribution to local history studies and his writing are greatly missed.

The Kessingland and Broadland Times

Keith, along with Evelyn Mathias, John Westley and others, write a column in the *Kessingland and Broadland Times,* the local magazine. This was started by Michael Knights in 1989, with Maureen Long as

The pages are made into plates for printing.

The first pages off the press, with George Bidnall and his son Jim.

The collating and packing department with Carol.

editor. Three years later it was taken over by Maureen and was a monthly for the first 14 years. It is now produced every two months. It is a community magazine, supported by loyal local advertisers and contributors from a wide range of interests, including, gardening, pets, wildlife, local history, sport, health and beauty, news from local Over 60s and Friendship Clubs as well as voluntary and youth organisations.

A Parish Council newsletter is inserted with extra local news, views and reports. Eric, Maureen's husband, delivers the magazine each issue, with the help of a few local volunteers. It is also distributed in nearby Carlton Colville, resuming the tradition of the past when the parish magazine was produced by the two churches. The magazine is now printed by Rondor Printing Co. of Lowestoft.

Kessingland Writers have produced annual booklets or calendars containing members' work. An annual memorial trophy is awarded. Robert Church is a published writer of books on famous trials, including that of Jack the Ripper. A former police officer, he was invited to speak at a meeting, came once to see what it was like and stayed on as a member, bringing his invaluable experience to the group.

Chris Barker from Black Street, although officially in Gisleham, an appendage to Kessingland, has written booklets on the history of the street, as well as articles and short stories for various magazines.

With a thriving Writers' Group and the local magazine on which to cut one's scribbling teeth, the hope is that many more will be tempted to jot down their memories and ideas for the pleasure of future generations.

Country corner at top of Catchpole's Close, 2005.

The Avenue, 1905.

Chapter 20

Kessingland's Flora and Fauna

Wildlife in the village ranges from the field mouse to the lion, the 'Lupinland' rabbit colony to the giraffes and rare breeds at the Suffolk Wildlife Park. Just about every wild animal that is normally found in the British Isles, either wild or in a zoo, inhabits our village.

Personality Profile: Richard Straton
(Taken from a 1990 interview)

A Scot by birth and son of a consultant anaesthetist, Richard ('Dick') Straton was educated at The Edinburgh Academy (following in the steps of such illustrious students as Sir Walter Scott, Sir Robert Louis Stephenson and Magnus Magnusson). It was while at school that Richard developed his keen interest in agriculture and wildlife, particularly bird-watching, and he was appointed a warden of the Royal Parks of Edinburgh. School was followed by agricultural college, but before settling down to a career in farming Richard joined the staff of the Royal Society for the Protection of Birds and was a warden at such reserves as Ramsey Island (Dyfed), Leighton Moss (Lancashire) and Havergate Island (Suffolk).

After a variety of jobs, Richard came to work at the 'The Suffolk Wildlife & Country Park' (as it was then known) during its first season and, after spending time at Bristol Zoo, returned to join the permanent staff for several years

Rob and Catherine, his uncle and aunt, and their family had moved to the village during the 1960s. They lived first at The Beeches in the High Street and latterly in White's Lane before returning to Scotland after taking an active part in village life over many years.

Although he loves all animals, Richard likes water-fowl best of all and he assisted Dr Arthur Anderson-Brown in his research for his world-renowned book on incubation while at the park. Furthering his now chosen career in wild animal husbandry, he left in 1976 to become head keeper of a park at Cricket St Thomas in Somerset. He also appeared as an extra in the *To The Manor Born* TV series, later moving to Hampshire as assistant curator at Marwell Zoological Park.

Possessing a rich practical and theoretical knowledge, Richard has been greatly involved with consultancy and advisory work. One of the initial members, he was chairman of the Association of British Wild Animal Keepers for ten years (now an honorary life member) – the only professional association for wild animal keepers in this country. During this period Richard successfully negotiated with other major zoological and wildlife organisations. Other involvements at this time included advisory committees in connection with government wildlife and wild animal husbandry legislation (some held at the Houses of Parliament).

Following the implementation of the Zoo Licensing Act in 1984, Richard was appointed an Inspector of Zoos on behalf of Her Majesty's Government.

After many years of employment in zoos, Richard became an independent consultant and was the chief consultant to the European Survey of Zoological Collections, commissioned by the European Community to establish the numbers and status of wild animal collections open to the public within the member states. He quickly realised that Great Britain has the most extensive legislation in respect to zoos.

Now settled in Kessingland, Richard is recognised as a leading specialist in the area of public safety matters in zoos, travelling to places as far apart as Cornwall, Wales and Scotland to advise zoos and District Council authorities, and many others on such matters. In addition he does computer work and office administration.

Richard's hobbies include bird-watching and photography. He has also been chronicling on film the erosion of the coastline at Benacre and Covehithe.

Nature Lovers

Since the first few issues, Colin Jacobs has written a column in each copy of the local magazine on watching out for wildlife, which includes fauna and flora as well as bird-watching. He is a member of the Suffolk Wildlife Trust and is often to be seen leading a party of wildlife enthusiasts on a walk on a Saturday to observe the prolific wildlife of the village.

There have been sightings of the dusky warbler and other rare species, so cameras and tripods have emerged from vehicles on the overflowing beach car park, with a steady stream of enthusiasts heading for a good hideout to observe and photograph the unique visitors.

Evelyn Mathias has photographed many of the plants on the beach, which she weaves into her evocative local paintings.

Ornithologists and botanists find the area fascinating and the more plants that flourish to bind the sand together, the more the beach is conserved for future generations of human, plant and animal life.

Kessingland in Bloom

During the earlier part of the last century, 'Kessingland in bloom' would have referred mostly to the wild flowers in the woods. Most houses had long gardens, but these were used for vegetables and the inevitable chickens at the bottom. The only formal gardens would be those of the larger houses, which would employ a gardener and which had more unusual plants and garden furniture in the form of statues, seats and urns. For most of the village, however, there was only a glimpse of such wonders through the hedge.

Older residents remember the excitement with which children tripped to the woods at snowdrop and bluebell time, to bring their mothers and grandmothers fresh flowers, which would be lovingly cherished. One lady said: 'We used to go and gather armfuls of bluebells and take them to relatives, neighbours and friends. We loved it.'

Many little girls, some as young as 12, went into service. Those from the village would be able to visit their homes occasionally or see their families at church, but some had to go to work in Lowestoft establishments. However, for those from neighbouring villages who worked in Kessingland, the one Sunday in the year when they would see their mothers, was Mothering Sunday, when everyone would go from St Edmund's congregation to St Margaret's Church, Lowestoft, which was the mother church. On the way, since they had to walk, they would gather wild flowers for their mums. If they worked in a generous household, sometimes the cook would slip a little simnel cake into their bags for their families. They would have to work on Christmas Day, so Mothering Sunday became the highlight of the year and those wild violets were picked with love and care.

The Heriz-Smith family of Fourwinds, Holly Grange Road, will be remembered for many things, as outlined in the chapter on Kessingland writers and artists. The younger daughter, Gillian, is remembered as 'the flower lady'. She grew masses of wild flowers, as well as cultivated ones. Early each Friday she would be on the bus into Lowestoft with her baskets crammed full of blooms, which she would sell to flower shops in the town. She was a shy and gentle woman, but because she talked to people on the bus and mixed in the village, she was well loved and well respected.

Some of the beautiful paintings of flowers in *The Noonstar* show the Heriz-Smith family's love of nature and their acute observation of plant life (see photograph page 71).

At the time of the construction of the Lloyds estate (early 1970s), one resident, Mrs Harold, a domestic science teacher, remarked:

I've just walked through that new estate and it's disgraceful! They only have tiny gardens, but they are all grass and flowers. Not one thing is being produced on that large area, which was farm land, feeding the village. Whatever are we coming to?

To a generation who had gone through a world war and had had to make use of every inch of available earth as part of the appeal to Dig for Victory, this was fair comment.

Today, Kessingland in Bloom means other things. In recent years The Knoll gardens have won awards in the Lowestoft in Bloom annual competition, as have the gardens at Livingstone's.

One result of a Parish Plan Action Group was the formation of a Gardeners' Club in 2005, which has been hugely successful. There are many beautiful gardens now in the village and in 2006 an Open Gardens Day is planned by the Club, something that resident landscape gardener Keith Nichols has wanted to see for many a long year.

With the large number of current TV programmes about gardening and landscaping, a deluge of gardening books in print, and the variety of outlets in Kessingland where plants are sold (including the MASK shop and outside people's own houses) the Gardeners' Club is thriving.

As the old Chinese proverb so wisely says: 'If you have two loaves, sell one and buy a lily.'

Chapter 21

The Parish Council

It seems Parish Councils began with the Local Government Act of 1894, but before then the Parochial Church Council seems to have run village affairs, maybe under the name of Parish Council. Gerald Brown did some research into the family of 'Blind Horace'.

It appears that Horace was the son of Shadrach Newson, who died in 1864 and was clerk to the Parish Council for 38 years. He was born in 1793 and given that he would have been an adult before being clerk, it appears that Kessingland was run by such a body in the early 1800s. Before that, it seems that the overseers of the poor were responsible for any social services to be had. Kessingland's overseers' accounts were twice dramatically saved from burning.

Records in Kessingland are pretty limited but we know that the parish councillors are volunteers who give their time and energy to making decisions for the parish. The longest serving member today is Roy Brown, now a nonagenarian, who has done much to promote the community spirit and to try to stop unnecessary building, although walking around the village today it would appear that every empty space has a house being built on it.

With much new government legislation and regulations, it is perhaps a more complicated job than before, with a lot of paperwork. In 2002 a Parish Plan was introduced, with many other volunteers as well as councillors meeting regularly to discuss ways of improving village amenities. In 2004 the Plan was published and has been implemented where possible. Proposals for improvements were in the realms of education, employment, information and communication, leisure, housing, policing, health, transport, emergency services, public conveniences, local government and leadership – in fact most areas that involve the Parish Council.

There are regular reports of meetings in the local press. Nobody need feel that they do not know what is going on – and there is a lot going on! A debt of gratitude is due to the councillors.

Personality Profile: Trish Hazell
(Taken from a 2003 interview)

Trish Hazell was clerk to Kessingland Parish Council for 22 years until she retired in January 2002. She took on the job whilst still a young married woman, looking for a little extra 'pin money', but even when finances improved and her workload became much greater, she still kept on with the post through which

Trish Hazell, former parish clerk.

she had come to know and love the village and its many characters.

Kessingland is unusual because it could so easily become a suburb or dumping ground for Lowestoft, which we have had to fight in the past, but it is unique in that it still has its own strong community spirit and rich characters. Parish Council meetings have been at times stormy, turbulent, enjoyable, exciting, but never dull. In the past 22 years I have seen a lot of village history made, sad things happening like businesses forced to close, many controversial projects and lots of new councillors coming and going.

Born in Leicestershire, Trish came from a talented family. Her mother was a journalist, her father a musician who was always busy in community affairs. It was he who persuaded her that she could manage the job, even though she had no previous experience of working in local government. She went ahead, secure in the knowledge that he would always be there with help and advice.

In 1975 she became secretary to the promotions officer for Walt Disney Travel Company, London, doing administration and promotional work for Walt

Disney World, Florida, and Disneyland, California. Two years later she was a placement officer for the International Voluntary Service, back in Leicester, placing volunteers in work camps both here in the UK and abroad.

Trish moved to our area in 1977, becoming secretary to the chief engineer in the East Anglian Water Company in Lowestoft. It was whilst working there in 1981 that she took on her second part-time job of clerk to Kessingland Parish Council.

Starting in 1992 she spent a further two years as office manager for a diamond drilling company, which led to her setting up, with her husband, their own firm, Contract Diamond Drilling Ltd. She became a director, responsible for all the financial affairs of the firm, handling the secretarial work. This was all in addition to bringing up two sons and three step-daughters.

Kessingland has appointed a new clerk, Lesley Beevor another young mum, who will hopefully find the job as interesting and rewarding as Trish did. She remembered:

The first big project I was involved with was building the Community Centre. Since then there has been debate, argument and controversy over such things as further development in the village, the gypsy camp, the toxic waste pit, vandalism, the traffic congestion at the beach end of the village, road calming in Field Lane and lots, lots more. After taking the minutes in shorthand and then trying to write it all up coherently, it has been challenging to say the least. When issues get heated, everyone talks at once and it takes some doing. I reckon I could do it for Parliament after all this practice...

Trish maintained her links with Kessingland by staying on as secretary of the Help-in-Need Trust.

Personality Profile: Jean Purkis
(Taken from a 1991 interview)

When Jean's husband, Arthur John, was offered a new job as lecturer in Business Studies at Lowestoft College, she was thrilled, remembering childhood

Seaside Award, 1993.

Parish details and advertisement board at the beach.

Parish councillors with the new board.

holidays at Hopton with her family. Jean was longing to renew her acquaintance with sandy beaches, exciting cliffs and the varying moods of the sea, but when they first moved to Kessingland in 1978, Jean suddenly had new worrying situations with which to cope. The upheaval of moving had caused her rheumatoid arthritis to accelerate and almost cripple her. Relegated to a wheelchair, trying to unpack and sort out her new home, she was suddenly forced to spend her first 11 weeks in East Anglia in St Michael's Hospital, Aylsham.

Returning home on Christmas Eve, she then had to face nine months of twice-weekly physiotherapy. Very gradually, with her dogged determination, Jean fought her way out of the wheelchair and onto elbow crutches.

Many people in Kessingland first knew Jean as the arthritic lady who rode a tricycle around the village, her answer to no longer being able to ride her two-wheeler cycle. The exercise and determination helped her mobility and soon many more began to know her as a founder member of the local DIAL branch and the chairman of Kessingland Parish Council.

Born in Highgate, London, Jean learned about the

The Starfish Award, presented for Kessingland's clean beach.

Ices all round – Primary School children celebrate another clean beach award, 2004.

Seaside Award, 1998.

city and its people by touring the capital on foot with her grandfather, a Scot who felt that bus fares were a waste of money. Jean is proud of her grandfather, who was first an undertaker, then a carpenter on Clydeside, working on both the *Queen Mary* and the *Queen Elizabeth*. These contacts took him to Buckingham Palace as foreman carpenter when he helped repair the famous Chair in Westminster Abbey, ready for the Queen's coronation, after it had been vandalised during the attempt to remove the Stone of Scone from beneath its seat.

In spite of Jean's interest in history and people, she hated school, but realises now that it was because of her teachers' inability to understand her slight dyslexia. In her schooldays, however, it had not been recognised and many otherwise bright children were also labelled 'dunces'.

Later, after marriage and the birth of her only son, Jean returned to commerce, but this time in insurance, running Edward Lumley's administration department. However, Arthur John's job kept him on the move and they next went to Leicester. Here Jean became a registrar of births, marriages and deaths.

In spite of spending the next two years in rural Yorkshire, where it snowed during both winters, and despite her bad start in Suffolk, she eventually managed to get by without too much use of the wheelchair.

Although she sadly lost her husband, Jean now lives a full life with a variety of hobbies and charitable activities and is still fighting that arthritis.

Personality Profile: Judy Lawson
(Taken from a 1998 interview)

Judy Lawson first came to Kessingland on holiday from Wymondham in Norfolk in 1938, when she was three months old. She attended Wymondham Primary School, then East Dereham High School, until she was 13 when, to her great delight, she came to live in this area. She attended Sir John Leman School in Beccles, where 'I learned more about the facts of life in three days than I had in all my first 13 years!'

Nine months later the family moved to Lowestoft, but Judy continued attending school in Beccles. She became a member of the Lowestoft Athletic Club, and went on to represent Suffolk in the All England School Sports.

I was an only child and I adored my father, but when my mother remarried I gained an ideal stepfather in Harry... I first met him in the shop he kept near the Triangle in Lowestoft... I went to Harry's to buy my mum a bunch of flowers. He chatted with me and I went home to tell my mum about this lovely man. She eventually married him and I don't know to this day whether or not she

Councillors with the Seaside Award, 1998.

knew him first – I asked them straight out on their silver wedding anniversary, but they still weren't telling.

I spent a lot of my time cycling to Kessingland, wandering on the beach and growing more attached to the village, but at last I had to wrench myself away, when I left school and went to Teacher Training College at East Hampstead Park. It's a crematorium now!

After training Judy moved to Birmingham to work in a secondary school, but in 1988 she finally achieved her ambition – she came to live in Kessingland. She joined the WI and became secretary and met her new husband at Kessingland Working Men's Club. She has worked as a receptionist at Pontins.

She got involved in the Parish Council and eventually became chairman. After Judy was invited to become a councillor, she was put on Amenities:

One of the jobs associated with this was putting the lights on the Christmas trees which we erect every year at Field Lane corner and at the beach end of the village. Each morning I have to go and replace the bulbs that are stolen or broken.

Judy loves Kessingland and its history, although she has changed a bit of it; she changed the name of her house after hundreds of years of it being known as something else!

Joe Utting, the previous chairman, had a long spell on the Parish Council. With so many people moving into the village on their retirement and having the time and willingness to serve on the Parish Council, the local knowledge of Joe's that Judy soon recognised is invaluable in keeping village affairs running smoothly. In the early days, when often no plans or maps were made of where pipes, ditches, footpaths and the like were situated, a practical man like Joe was often the only source of information. He certainly deserves recognition for the tremendous experience he brought to Parish Council affairs, as did Roy Brown, the other veteran, with often difficult and unwelcome decisions to be made in the interests of the community. Today Liam Martin is chairman.

All Parish Council members, mentioned or not mentioned here, deserve praise for the many hours of thankless dedication that their roles require.

Sluice Cottage with the River Hundred, 1905.

Children in Church Road, 1905.

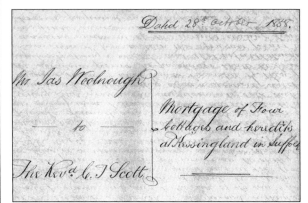

Beach Road, 1907.

Above: *Post Office deeds and receipts for stamp duty paid on the property.*

Sailor's Home, 1905.

The Beach Post Office just before its closure in 2004.

Sailor's Home, 1950s. Note the motor bike and sidecar.

Chapter 22

Then and Now

Kessingland has changed rather a lot over the years – although it is possible to go around the village with some of Ford Jenkins's old photographs from 1907 and recognise chimney-pots, dormer windows and even the houses themselves.

Modernisation meant that when piped water was laid on, many old wells became almost redundant, used only for watering gardens, animals or in emergencies. The water-tower was built during the Second World War. In the 1990s, when work was being done there, photographer Tony Ackers went up in the crane platform to record photographs, showing the top of the tower, the nearby allotments and the houses in White's Lane.

Ashley Nursery, once a successful business and much missed today, was not only a comprehensive garden centre, it had an extensive tropical fish section, a café, a remaindered book section, toys, Christmas lights, Santa's grotto in season, a florist's,

The demolition of Ashley Nursery, February 2006.

Only the original house is left at Ashley Nursery.

The demolition of Kessingland Car Centre; only the sign remains, 2002.

The water-tower was renovated in the 1990s, when Tony Ackers took these photos from above, showing the Mardles Allotments and opposite, the Market Place.

The Archway, built on the Car Centre site, 2003.

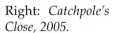

Left: *Lincoln Court, built on the old school playing-field, 1980s.*

Right: *Catchpole's Close, 2005.*

Fisherman's Way, 1993.

Ancient and modern, where Church Road bends at the bottom of White's Lane, 2005.

and units for letting outside, which included a garden shed or conservatory and double glazing facility. As this is being written, the bulldozers have moved in, but by the time this book is read, it will be just another housing development, if all goes to plan.

The former school playing-field at the top of Field Lane was developed in the 1980s, when the new school was built. It became a sheltered-housing estate, Lincoln Court, much needed by older residents, and is a close and harmonious community.

An extensive new housing complex sprang up opposite Kessingland Service Station, next to the new play area, on the rest of the old Hart's Meadow. Because the new lighting there outshone the old village street lighting, it soon became known as 'Satellite City'.

Kessingland Car Centre, formerly Pifco's, mentioned in the chapter on travel, did not sell petrol as before, but became a thriving car sales business until owner Richard sold it for building land. Today it is a little development in the High Street known as 'The Archway'.

Catchpole's Close, once open meadows used by Miss Mary Clarke of Dambrook House to graze her rescued donkeys and eastern goats, was developed when Mary died and the house was sold. New houses in Church Road were built on the front of the site, with the Close at the back.

The corner of Church Road has been developed, but opposite, in Cooper's Lane, it is still possible to walk into open countryside. The bottom of the village was developed in the 1980s, east of Wash Lane, with Fisherman's Way, Manor Walk, Glebe Road East and Turrell Drive built, as well as Damerson Went, Kipling Close and Strowger's Way

springing up each side of Rider Haggard Lane.

In the Beach village, Cooper's Drive is a new development on the Green where formerly 'Stutt's' wooden fish shop and a community room (also wooden) formerly stood. It housed a clinic during and after the war, where mothers could have their babies weighed and vaccinated and obtain dried milk and orange juice on certain days, when the district nurse or doctor would attend.

Green Lane, with cottages at the Church Road end, had houses to the left but now bungalows are springing up on the right-hand side, before the holiday chalet sites are reached. In Coastguard Lane, off Green Lane, the former Ocean View caravan site has been replaced by brick-built holiday chalets of the same name.

The former wartime prefabs in Wash Lane and Hall Road have been replaced either by council bungalows or by private housing. The prefabs were built between the existing Field Lane council-houses and Hall Road and were a boon to families resettling after the Second World War.

Kessingland is a mixture of old and new, ancient and modern, and although some infilling has not been as expertly planned as it should have been, the overall impression is of an attractive place where many people have settled in retirement, adding to the richness of talent, experience and community spirit which was always evident in the village. It is definitely a community, and not a suburb of the next town, as some villages have sadly become. It has everything: beach, wildlife, countryside, amenities and clubs, pubs, churches and friendly people. What more could anyone ask?

Opposite Church Road is the quiet Cooper's Lane, 2005.

Cliffs and beach, showing brick Ocean View Chalets in place of caravan site in front of D'Arcy's House.

New homes at Badger's Holt, built on the site of the old Four Dwellers during the 1990s, seen here in 2005.

Hall Road, where new bungalows have replaced old wartime prefabs.

Generations of Kessingland Folk

It is fascinating to note that through the generations certain family names have been tied closely to the community – and continue to be so even in 2006. The list below – be no means exhaustive – includes just a few names of folk who have contributed to the vibrant life of the community in the past, and features many who contribute still, and no doubt will continue to do so in the future.

Abel	Brown	Dav(e)y	Gouldby	Julings	Murray	Rogers	Swan
Adams	Bruce	Davi(e)s	Green	Keable	Muskett	Rolph	Thacker
Allen	Bunn	Dennington	Griffiths	Kemp	Muttitt	Roth	Thorpe
Austin	Bullock	Dent	Guthrie	Kerr	Nathan	Satchell	Thurston
Bagot	Burch	Doddington	Guymer	King	Newson	Saywack	Todd
Baggott	Button	Dowding	Haddock	Kittle	Nichols	Sanders	Turrell
Bailey	Calver	Durrant	Haggard	Knight(s)	O'Brien	Saunders	Utting
Barker	Cantor	Ellender	Hall	Knightley	Oddy	Scott	Utton
Batchelor	Carter	Ellis	Hammond	Knivett	Parker	Self	Wade
Beamish	Catchpole	Eyre	Hart	Lawson	Partridge	Sewell	Wall
Bell	Cherry	Fox	Harvey	Layton	Patel	Shipley	Walsh
Bennett	Cheyne	Fo(y)ster	Hickleton	Lincoln	Peak	Sims	Ward
Betts	Chipperfield	Francis	Hollis	Locke	Peck	Smith	Warner
Bird	Clark(e)	Fulcher	Honeywood	Long	Perrèdes	Spall	Watson
Bligh	Clifford	Gage	Horn	Lyne	Prentice	Spillings	Weavers
Block	Coleman	Gardiner	Hunn	Mallett	Podd	Sterry	Welch
Blowers	Collyer	Garrod	Hunter	Marjoram	Pont	Steward	Westley
Bond	Cook(e)	Gillings	Hutson	Martin	Raven	Storm	White
Briggs	Cooper	Giltroy	James	Mason	Read	Strowger	Wigg
Brock	Coote	Good(e)	Jillings	Moyse	Reader	Studd	Woodgate
Broom	Dann	Gooch	Johnson	Mudd	Robinson	Summons	Wright

Coronation day, 2 June 1953. Ferndale House in the High Street, home of a Barclay's Bank branch, trimmed up in the pouring rain.

Village party to celebrate the golden jubilee, June 2002.

George Swan's collection of commemorative mugs.

George with his collection, 2002.

Bethany Parsons with a mug showing her winning design, 2002.

Chapter 23

Special Occasions

Special occasions in Kessingland have always been celebrated in much the same way, despite the passage of time.

There are records of mugs being awarded to the children of the village to commemorate the coronation of King George V and Queen Mary. Mugs were also presented for subsequent coronations, even for Edward VIII, who later abdicated. George Swan has a wonderful collection of all kinds of celebration mugs. He explains:

The jubilee year gave me the chance to add to my collection of royal memorabilia. I have a large selection, mostly of mugs. The earliest is a Charles II dated 1646. I am not sure if this is genuine or a copy.

Other mugs include Edward VII 1901, Edward VIII, who was never crowned, George V, George VI, and of course the present-day royal family.

I have a nice mug of Prince Charles at his Investiture at Caernarvon Castle on 1 July 1969.

I also have mugs reminding me of the time the Queen and Prince Philip visited this area. There are the weddings of the other princes and princesses and their children as they came along. I have other mugs of the Queen Mother's birthdays and two commemorating the visit of the Pope to this country and another of the sad death of Louis, Earl Mountbatten, on 27 August 1979.

Apart from the royal connections, I have mugs celebrating the Armistice of the First World War, 11 November 1918...

What I like about my hobby is you don't have to wait long before you can add to your collection. There is a set of Lifeboat Tankards, with all the names of the coxwains and their history, made by Great Yarmouth Pottery, also some local characters, not forgetting the set about Kessingland village which I acquired through the Kessingland and Broadland Times *for the millennium.*

Kessingland Jubilee Celebrations, 2002

The rain held off, even permitting the sun to shine in intervals and a wonderful party was enjoyed. The afternoon kicked off with a fancy-dress competition, the overall winner being Sir James Markey of Church Road, a young and handsome knight.

A good deal of organisation and hard work went into the day, as there was plenty of food, ice-creams for all, a raffle, a bouncy castle, a children's disco and other entertainment.

The MASK shop on jubilee day, 2002.

All the children received a golden jubilee mug with a picture of the Queen on one side and the winning design by nine-year-old schoolgirl Bethany Parsons on the other. The design, which features a drawing of the Queen against a backdrop of the beach and a Viking ship (the school logo), has a real feel for Kessingland and as Bethany has only been living in the village for about a year, the design was a true success. As part of her prize, Bethany visited the Norwich China Factory and, while inundated with orders for the jubilee celebrations, the staff showed her round and presented her with the first mug of the special limited edition. The Parsons then placed an order for a further 20 mugs for friends and family.

The Methodist 'Wednesday Club' wrote a letter and drew pictures for the Queen, to congratulate her on her golden jubilee. They were thrilled during jubilee week to receive a thank-you letter from Her Majesty.

After the jubilee party at the Community Centre, young Billy Clarke asked if he could have one of each of the red, white and blue left-over balloons. He then tied them together, wrote his name and address on a card, attached them, and let them off into the stiff breeze. A week later Billy was surprised and delighted to hear that they had reached London, although not quite the Queen's backyard.

This is amazing, considering that there was also a news item that some helium balloons specifically released at a jubilee party down south, actually turned up in a hedge on the Sandringham estate. They must have passed each other on the way!

Having Fun

Street or beach parties with fancy dress have been a feature of past celebrations. Several streets had individual parties to celebrate the marriage of Prince Charles in 1982. Closing streets to traffic is getting more difficult, but beach barbecues are popular, with the hard-working councillors doing the catering.

Bonfires for the 50th anniversary of VE Day and VJ Day were also appreciated. Whether it is a Sunday-school treat, Harvest Supper, local or national occasion, Kessingland has always celebrated in style.

The early-twenty-first century has seen a lot of celebrations in quick succession, with the millennium, the Queen Mother's 100th birthday, the jubilee, then 50 years since the coronation. Many china cabinets like George Swan's display the set of various Kessingland celebratory mugs. It is good to look back, even as the village looks forward to many more community events.

On the dawn of the new millennium, the lights of anglers along the shore were much in evidence, but they were enhanced by the lights of the millennium candles in their little jars, distributed from the churches. One little toddler, taken down to the beach just before the sun came up to join his grandparents under their fishing umbrella, showed great excitement, holding his own little light as the sun rose on the most easterly village in the country, and the beginning of a new year, a new century and a new millennium. Memories of special occasions such as this are never forgotten.

Kessingland, Suffolk

'It's so peaceful here!' visitors say:
A peace that stormy undertones of history,
unfathomable depths of mystery
would deny.
Children shriek and paddle, build castles in the
sand where elephants once fed, their ancient habitat
buried deep in the trunks of the sea's bed.
Silted marshes, a Wildlife Park, cover the harbour
into which Roman galleons proudly sailed and
Vikings used to over-winter.
Modern-brick holiday chalets
desecrate the ground
where Kipling stayed with Haggard
among the marram grass he planted.
Seed sent from the land of Cetowayo, grew
to protect his cliff-edge home.
Sir Rider, knighted not for literary wit
but for clothing England's shifting sands
with solid roots,
for vision and reform to Penal Laws.
Tiny, tidy gardens, Lego-land dwellings
slice up the land on which he 'grew'
The Gardener's Year, romantic fiction and
'the best asparagus' for miles around.
Kites rise and fall above the Beach where
Captain Sanders tried to reach the skies, with
early aviation skill, crashing against the
Lifeboat Shed for good, or ill.
Now powerful engines, high-tech teams
rescue the perishing from wintry swells,
off the coast where salvage boats
sacrificed men's lives for gain.
The A12 bypasses the ancient Coaching Inn
on the old tolled turnpike road to London.
Here locals formed the Suffolk Humane

Society, forerunner of the RNLI,
to save men rather than their sinking 'loot'.
Glass cabinets in neat bungalows show medals
won against the raging sea, often posthumously.
Barney Smith, Gaffer Strowger, George Knights,
John Davie, to name but a few, threw caution
to the raging gale, set sail, to save
their fellows or to share their fate.

Coffee mornings, sales of work, respectability,
cloak gossip of bygone days: incest, illegitimacy,
even a military man, who was a
member of the gentler sex!
Small terraces with roof-light windows stand
where first cinematograph images
flickered into youthful minds:
The Kinnodrome projected fantasy.
'The Adventures of Elmo the Mighty'
now juggle for pre-eminence in octogenarian
heads, full of Star Wars or the TV soaps.
Sunday market, sport, fêtes and rallies,
rally the faithful to worship.
Their day will pass.
The Church stands solid,
towering above these lesser shrines:
St Edmund, saint and martyr,
Nuns of St Clare,
Nonconformist social witness and Bethel,
nurturing seafarers' simple faith,
all interwoven in the village peace,
surpassing knowledge of its tense present
and the rich heritage that's past.
'It's so peaceful here!'
(above the turbulence of humankind).

M.L., 2002

Subscribers

Esme Vera Adams

Leslie J. Allen, Kessingland, Suffolk

Ray and Gale Allen, Kessingland

Melanie J. Anderson BSc,
Kessingland, Suffolk

Colin Atkins, Lowestoft, Suffolk

Anne August, Kessingland, Suffolk

Miss L-J. Bagot, Kessingland

Violet E. Bakewell

Ann Baldwin (née Stringer)

Mary Barber (née Stringer)

Miss Tessa P., Mr William C., and
Miss J. Beamish, Kessingland,
Suffolk

Henry and Barbara Bennett, Riseley,
Berkshire

Gillian Bennett, Kessingland School

Marie and Don Bennett,
Kessingland, Suffolk

Roger and Joan Benton,
Kessingland, Suffolk

Vera and Brian Biggs, Kessingland,
Suffolk

Reverend John Blacker

John Blowers, formerly of
Kessingland, Suffolk

Molly and Dennis Blowers, Carlton
Colville, Suffolk

Norman and Tina Blowers,
Kessingland, Suffolk

Irene J. Branson (née Shipley),
Lowestoft, Suffolk

Alan G. Britton, Kessingland,
Suffolk

Mr James J. Brock, Kessingland

G. Brooks, Wrentham, Beccles,
Suffolk

Mrs Daphne Brown, Kessingland,
Suffolk

Millie Bruce, Kessingland, Suffolk

Robert Bruce, Swanland, East
Yorkshire

Mrs Mollie Bryant, Pakefield,
Suffolk

Mark, Frances and Amy Bullard,
Kessingland

Maurice G. Bunn, Kessingland,
Suffolk

Patricia and Peter Burch,
Kessingland, Suffolk

Jayne Burrell, Carlton Colville,
Suffolk

Phylis Button

Tracy M. Byrne, Kessingland, Suffolk

Caron and Kenny Cantor,
Kessingland, Suffolk

Mr Carl Capps, Kessingland, Suffolk

Miss L.D. Catchpole, Kessingland

Mr and Mrs Richard Catchpole,
Kessingland, Suffolk

David R. Charlesworth, Kessingland

Karen and Ernie Childs, Great
Yarmouth Potteries

Alan Clarke, Kessingland

Mrs Norma Cole, Beccles

Diane Coleman, London Road,
Kessingland

Malcolm D. Coleman, Birdland,
Kessingland

Mr A. Collins, Kessingland

Christine Cook, Geneva Cottages,
Kessingland

Gladis Cook, Geneva Cottages,
Kessingland

Michael S. Cook, Geneva Cottages,
Kessingland

Tina Cooper (née Spillings), formerly
Kessingland/now Beccles

Colin D. Cornwell, Wenhaston,
Suffolk

Mick and Brenda Critoph,
Kessingland, Suffolk

Mrs Helen Cushion, Kessingland,
Suffolk

Sarah M. Dale, Kessingland, Suffolk

Leslie Daplyn, Kessingland

Daisy M. Day, Kessingland,
Lowestoft

Dr Tom Doy, ex Kessingland boy

Colin Durrant, Tewkesbury,
Gloucestershire

Edna M. Durrant, Suffolk

Stephanie A. Durrant, Kessingland,
Suffolk

Joan M. Ellis, Kessingland, Suffolk

Elizabeth Evan, Boston, Lincolnshire

Mrs Jonquil F. and Mr Rodney G.
Everett

Angie and Gary Fickling, Copper
Coin, Kessingland

Mr and Mrs D. Flynn, Kessingland,
Suffolk

Mark Forwood, Kessingland

Mr Nigel Fox

Russell Gage (in memory of)

Mr M. Gale

Mr and Mrs K. Gardiner

T.R. and W.E. Gillings, Kessingland,
Suffolk

Noel W. Gladwell and Dorothy J.
Barber (née Summons),
Kessingland, Suffolk

Eric (Happy) and Sylvia Gooch,
Kessingland, Suffolk

Joan and Cliff Gorton, Kessingland,
Suffolk

Alison M. Gostlow, Adelaide,
Australia

Mr and Mrs M. Guymer,
Kessingland, Suffolk

Evelyn M. Haddock, Kessingland,
Suffolk

Mr W. Hancock, Kessingland

Carol and Peter Hendra,
Kessingland

Mrs Betty Highland, Aberdeen,
Scotland

Dale Henry Hood, Kessingland

Les and Ann Horne, Kessingland,
Suffolk

William J. Huckle

Derek C. Hunn, Kessingland,
Suffolk

Mr Michael J. Hunter, Kessingland,
Suffolk

The Hunter family, who lived at
Laurel Farm

John and June Hutson

David C. Ife, Kessingland, Suffolk

Colin A. Jacobs, Lowestoft, Suffolk

Colin F. Jacob, Kessingland, Suffolk

David C. Jacobs, Kessingland,
Suffolk

Leslie H. and Kathleen Jacobs (in
memory of), Kessingland

Kevin Jeckells, Gorleston, Norfolk

Valerie Jenkins (Lyne Family, Denes
Holiday Camp), Aberystwyth,
Wales

George D. Jesson, Kessingland,
Suffolk

Jennifer and Peter Jones, Barrington,
Cambridgeshire

Ivan Julings, Kessingland, Suffolk

Kelly/Noble/Usher, Kessingland

Kate Kemp

Reggie Kent, Kessingland

The Kirkpatrick Family, Oaklands
Terrace, Kessingland

Gillian and Michael Knights, Lowestoft
Roger H. Knights, Kessingland
Mandy and Harvey Knock, Kessingland, Suffolk
M. Laughton, Kessingland, Suffolk
The Livermore Family, The Old Surgery, Kessingland
David and Tina Long, Kessingland, Suffolk
Ken and Judy Long, Oulton Broad, Lowestoft, Suffolk
Maureen and Eric Long, Kessingland, Suffolk
David Marjoram, Kessingland, Suffolk
John Baker Marjoram, Colorado Springs, Colorado, USA
Mrs Joan E. Marshall (née Hart), Kessingland, Suffolk
Liam Martin, Kessingland, Suffolk
Evelyn Mathias, Kessingland, Suffolk
Mrs Evelyn J. McBride (née Foyster), Kessingland
Jonathan and Marianna Meen, Kessingland, Suffolk
Paul and Vera Meen, Kessingland, Suffolk
Mr George and Alice Montague
Kathleen Muttit, Kessingland, Suffolk
Deborah and Keith Nichols, Kessingland, Suffolk
H., E., and J. Page, Kessingland
Margaret and Michael J. Parker, Kessingland, Suffolk
William M. Parker, Kessingland, Suffolk
S.J. Partridge, Kessingland
John, Terry, Sam and Ruth Payne, Gisleham
Maureen M. Peak, Kessingland, Suffolk
Wink Pearson, Wood Farm, Mutford
Andrew and Sarah Pedder, Kessingland
Derek and Freda Pedder, Kessingland
Hilary Penstone, Kessingland, Suffolk
Mr K. Perry, Green Lane, Kessingland (River Inspector)
Mrs M.L. Pinkney, Kessingland
Michael John Podd, Kessingland, Suffolk

Patricia M. Qualters, Kessingland
John Rapley, formerly of Attleborough, Norfolk
Dan and Jane Read, Kessingland
Mr and Mrs D. Read, Kessingland
Chris and Caroline Read, Kessingland, Suffolk
Mrs Irene Reekie, Kessingland, Suffolk
Brian and Jean Reeve, Kessingland, Suffolk
Ruby and Dennis Richardson, Kessingland, Suffolk
Mrs B. Ripley, Kessingland, Suffolk
Eric Sturdee Rouse, born 1914, Kessingland
Terence S. Rouse, White's Lane, Kessingland
Trevor and Christine Rouse, Kessingland, Suffolk
Pauline and Robert Shipley, Kessingland, Suffolk
Mr and Mrs P. Simmons
Shane and Tony Smith, Kessingland, Suffolk
Joy Smith (née Hambling)
Stanley Soloman, Kessingland, Suffolk
Ann Spillings, formerly Kessingland/now Lowestoft
Elizabeth A. Spillings, Kessingland
John and Linda Spillings, Kessingland, Suffolk
P.J. and L.A. Spillings, Henstead, Suffolk
Pamela Mary Stanley
Mr and Mrs Stibbon, Belvedere Drive, Kessingland
Caz and Steve Summers, Kessingland
George and Pam Swan, Lowestoft
R.W. and P.R. Sweetman, Kessingland, Suffolk
Amber Jean Symonds
D. Tarry
Kevin Thacker, Kessingland
Kathleen Thompson, Laxfield Way, Lowestoft
Ivy A. Tibbenham
Pamela Todd, Kessingland, Suffolk
Kathleen Tomlin, Kessingland, Suffolk
S. Tomlin, Kessingland, Suffolk
Paul Toplis, Kessingland, Suffolk

Frances and Patrick Townsend, Kessingland, Suffolk
Nicky and Brian Townsend, Kessingland, Suffolk
Mr A.A. Turrell, Kessingland
Brian S. Turrell, Beccles, Suffolk
Mr and Mrs D.J. Turrell, Kessingland
George R. Utting, born Kessingland 1923
Ingrid C.D. Utting, Kessingland, Suffolk
Mark P. Utting, Cambridge
Paul Utting, Kessingland, Suffolk
Robert E. Utting, Kessingland, Suffolk
M. and F. Vaisey, Kessingland, Suffolk
Julie Vassar and Sue Morgan, Kessingland Estate Agents
Alexander and Penny Walker,
John F.W. Walling, Newton Abbot, Devon
Mrs Lanyu Wang-Kemp, Kessingland, Suffolk
Maureen and Terry Ward, Kessingland, Suffolk
Rose and Graham Waumsley, Wolverton, Milton Keynes, Buckinghamshire
Jean F. Waylen, Kessingland, Suffolk
John Westley, Kessingland, Suffolk
Phillip Whatling, Wrentham, Suffolk
Benjamin N. Wigg, Louth, Lincolnshire
Keith Wigg, Lowestoft, Suffolk
S. and A. Wigg, Kessingland
Molly Wilds, Orchard End, Cotterer, Hertfordshire
Margaret and Gordon Wilkins, Havant, Hampshire
Sheila Wilmot (née Smith), Kessingland fishing family
John and Sheila Woodcock, Kessingland, Suffolk
Den, Ruth, Thomas and Joshua Woodhead, The Old Bakehouse, Kessingland
M.K. Woodrow, Kessingland
Graham Wright, Kessingland, Suffolk
Mrs Joy (cake lady) and Mr Bruce Wright

There are now almost 160 titles in the Community History Series.

For a full listing of these and other Halsgrove publications, please visit www.halsgrove.co.uk or telephone 01884 243 242.